Stuart Davis

Documentary Monographs
in Modern Art
general editor: Paul Cummings

Stuart Davis

edited by
Diane Kelder

Praeger Publishers *New York · Washington · London*

Frontispiece: Stuart Davis in his studio, *ca.* 1958. Photograph courtesy of Mrs. Stuart Davis.

PRAEGER PUBLISHERS

111 Fourth Avenue, New York, N.Y. 10003, U.S.A.
5, Cromwell Place, London SW7 2JL, England

Published in the United States of America in 1971
by Praeger Publishers, Inc.

© 1971 by Praeger Publishers, Inc.

Library of Congress Catalog Card Number: 70–122089

Printed in the United States of America

contents

I CHRONOLOGY, AUTOBIOGRAPHY (1945)

II EXCERPTS FROM THE NOTEBOOKS OF STUART DAVIS, WITH DIAGRAMS AND SKETCHES

III MURALS

IV SPECIFIC PAINTINGS—MEANING AND METHOD

V THE PLACE OF ABSTRACT PAINTING IN AMERICA

VI THE ARTIST, GOVERNMENT, AND SOCIETY

VII WRITINGS ON OTHER ARTISTS

VIII WRITING AND CRITICISM ABOUT STUART DAVIS

list of illustrations

preface

> *Again let it be reiterated that painting is an art of color and that means that a finished work will appeal to the spectator by the coordination of colored shapes placed in logical order on the canvas.*
>
> From the *Notebooks,* December 30, 1922

Whether reminiscing about youthful experiences in the studio of Robert Henri, spelling out the functions of drawing and color, or arguing with a critic about the aesthetic isolationism of American art, Stuart Davis was consistently direct and forceful; his style left no room for equivocation, compromise, or preciosity. Davis spent many years of his life teaching, and a good deal of his writing has a pedagogical or didactic ring to it, concerned as it is with posing problems, analyzing them, and searching for valid solutions. The previously unpublished Notebooks especially reveal a constant process of questioning and testing that complements the artist's periodic reassessment of theories in his painting.

Although Davis wrote extensively on a variety of subjects (indeed, the selections in this volume represent only a part of his output, which includes some 20,000 pages given to the Fogg Museum of Harvard University by his widow), significant recurrent themes in his Notebooks, essays, letters, and lectures are the assertion of his Americanism and an unshakeable belief in the future of modernism in this country. Certainly, his faith has been justified, for American painting of the last twenty-five years has finally engaged those issues he proclaimed in his own art and writings, calling attention to a native pragmatism in the process.

In editing this collection, I have tried to organize the writings under topic headings that accurately reflect their general content. A good deal of this was, of course, indicated by the very titles of some essays, but it was not always evident in the more spontaneous prose of the Notebooks and Daybooks. Discussions of a formal or technical problem would often stimulate thoughts of a more philosophically or politically speculative nature, as Davis restlessly surveyed the state of contemporary painting in a complex and changing society.

This book would not have been realized without the advice and guidance of the artist's widow, Roselle Davis. She allowed me to use the Notebooks, sketches, scrapbooks, letters, manuscripts, and photographs that constitute it, and she kindly consented to the photographing of important works of art in her collection. Unless otherwise noted, all unpublished material included here is printed with her permission. In addition, she provided that rare combination of intimate knowledge and genuine insight that make the writer's task considerably easier.

I should also like to cite for their cooperation and assistance the Archives of American Art, the numerous individuals and institutions who granted permission to reprint articles and other writings in this book, and those museums and collectors who allowed me to reproduce their paintings.

At every step of the book's development, Paul Cummings, the editor of the series, gave me the benefit of his vast knowledge of American art sources, and John Hochmann and Nancy Reynolds of Praeger Publishers helped clear away some of the technical obstacles that can temporarily detour the progress of a manuscript. I reserve special thanks for my editor, Ellyn Childs, who has worked diligently and congenially with me in seeing the book through its final and crucial stages.

Diane Kelder
May 7, 1971

Introduction *Diane Kelder*

> *The two dominant forces in my early art education were the teachings of Robert Henri whose school I attended and the Armory Show of modern European art in 1913. These influences were foremost in forming my ideas and taste about what a modern picture should be. Both were revolutionary in character, and stood in direct opposition to traditional and academic concepts of art.*[1]

The impressive *oeuvre* of Stuart Davis, spanning more than fifty years of creativity, testifies to the remarkable clarity and consistency of the artist's grasp of "what a modern picture should be." In the face of strong challenges by critics who sought to undermine what they regarded as foreign influences in his work—influences outside of the limited mainstream of American art—Davis repeatedly asserted his firm conviction that the "picture is an independent object with a reality of its own."[2] For most of his life, Davis's role was that of a loner, an outsider, rejecting the regionalism and provincialism of most American painting in the 1930's and 1940's and withstanding the strong current of Abstract Expressionism in the 1950's. Never a follower, he preferred to think for himself and thus attempted to establish and clarify a set of aesthetic and ethical principles by which he could live. In his writings, as in his paintings, the testing, refining, and reiteration of those principles provide a glimpse of the painter's temperament. Tough-minded, seeking for reason and order, yet fascinated with the spontaneous and evanescent, Davis combined the openness of the liberal with the methodology of the strict disciplinarian.

Unlike most American painters, Davis was born into a household where art was part of daily experience. Both his parents were practicing artists, and his father, art editor of the *Philadelphia Press,* employed some of the most controversial painters of the day—such disciples of Robert Henri as William Glackens, George Luks, Everett Shinn, and John Sloan, who were later to constitute half of a celebrated group labeled "The Eight." Davis was fifteen years old when Henri decided to open an art school in New York City. Davis's father, then working for the *Newark Evening News,* permitted him to leave high school and join Henri's classes in 1910.

In describing his experiences as a student of Henri, Davis provided an objective though generally enthusiastic evaluation of the methods that educated a group of artists who influenced the direction of American painting for a generation. The Henri approach, according to Davis, "stressed the student's fundamental right to freedom of expression. It encouraged experimentation and taught the student to look for subject matter and inspiration in the world about him. It rejected conventional artistic ideas of the 'beautiful' and held that any subject matter, even that commonly regarded as ugly, was fit material for the artist."[3] Davis later acknowledged the importance of this aspect of Henri's teaching, which "placed the origins of art in life" instead of in academic formulas or in the artistic studio composition.

The emphasis on unrestricted subject matter and on the individual's response to it led to the development of a socially oriented art. Davis, like the other Henri students, tramped the streets of Chinatown and the Bowery and frequented Negro saloons, where he became a devotee of jazz, the new music that had come out of the South and Midwest. The drawings, paintings, and other works that resulted from these encounters with the raucous and frequently desperate life of the city poor provoked strong and hostile criticism, primarily because of their thematic content. The Eight, subsequently termed the Ash Can School, were regarded as revolutionaries. Their attack on the inherited academicism of American painting was two-pronged: In championing new, "vulgar" subjects they effectively challenged the hierarchic structure that sanctioned certain types of painting while consigning others to an inferior status; in attacking the antiquated rules that dominated such institutions as the Pennsylvania Academy of the Fine Arts and the National Academy of Design, they encouraged closer examination of the materials and techniques of painting itself.

For several years, Davis was content to explore the urban realism that was encouraged by Henri. Davis's ability to portray "life in the raw" earned him the respect of John Sloan, who was then art editor of *The Masses,* a radical, socialist-oriented magazine for which Davis produced cartoons and even a cover, in 1913. Although Davis was associated with the magazine for about three years and was obviously sympathetic to its avowed ideological purpose, he resigned from its staff in 1916 when the editor-in-chief attempted to censor the work of *The Masses'* contributors so that it might reflect more forcefully the political and social philosophy that motivated the publication. Davis was incensed that the "artist's freedom of expression" could be abrogated so arbitrarily in the name of political or social expediency. Despite a genuine social commitment, Davis steadfastly maintained that artistic integrity and the cause of "pure art" must always take precedence over political considerations. The character of painting, as he saw it, was antithetical to utilitarianism of any kind. Davis persisted in this attitude throughout his life. In the 1930's, the devastating effects of the Depression stimulated the social and political awareness of artists, prompting them to organize a union and then a Congress, of which Davis was later

National Executive Secretary. Initially optimistic about the cultural role the Congress might perform, Davis subsequently broke with its board when the members actively promoted political causes that compromised the stated cultural aims of the organization.

In reminiscences about the Henri school and the sense of freedom and vitality generated by its founder, Davis perceptively criticized his teacher for unduly stressing subject matter. He recognized that the freedom that resulted from the repudiation of academic conservatism contained the seeds of compositional anarchy. He observed that the encouragement of students to rely "on the vitality of the subject matter . . . prevented an objective appraisal of the dynamics of the actual color-space relations on the canvas,"[4] and acknowledged that he was made aware of this through the progressive European works in the Armory Show.

The International Exhibition of Modern Art that was housed in the Sixty-ninth Infantry Armory in New York City opened in February, 1913. Organized by artists rather than by academicians or dealers, the exhibition declared the organizers' intention of familiarizing their colleagues and the general public with the work of European modernists. At the opening, a spokesman for the organizers declared that "American artists—young American artists that is—do not dread and have no need to dread, the ideas or culture of Europe."[5] The native distrust of foreign culture was not easily overcome, however, and when the exhibition traveled to Chicago, students from the Art Institute burned a Matisse in effigy. Of the foreign artists included in the Armory Show, those whose work Davis found particularly appealing were Gauguin, Van Gogh, and Matisse. Davis, who exhibited five watercolors, recalled his excitement at seeing the Europeans' "broad generalization of form and non-imitative use of color" and in perceiving the presence of "an objective order which . . . was lacking in my own work."[6]

In resolving to become a modern artist, Davis set out to educate himself anew. The summers of 1914, 1915, and 1916 found him working in Provincetown and Gloucester, Massachusetts. In Provincetown, he met Charles Demuth, another Pennsylvania-born artist who had lived and worked in Paris during the first decade of the century when the Fauvist and Cubist styles were formulated, and who provided the kind of companionship and intellectual stimulation that the young painter required. The pictures Davis produced over the three summers afford a glimpse of his budding modernism. Some of the loosely organized and thickly painted canvases possess an intensity of color that reflects Davis's interest in Van Gogh and the Fauves, while the remarkable abstract composition of *The President* (1917), with its fragmented space and flat areas of color, suggests the influence of Cubism. Although a work like *Multiple Views* (1918) scarcely aims at the systematic analysis of Cubist painting, it contains the seeds of Davis's mature style in its insistence on the creation of a new reality established through the assertion of the painting's inherent two-dimensionality.

For a number of years, Davis had made his paintings on the spot as he traveled with easel, paints, and canvases in search of subjects. Around 1918, he discarded these cumbersome materials in favor of a sketchbook and pen or pencil, instituting a practice he was to follow for the rest of his life. His numerous notebooks are filled with drawings —drawings that later served as the point of departure for studio pictures. These multipurpose sketches were synthesized, in the artist's words, "into a single focus." The very process of relating the individual spatial character of the drawings to the whole picture helped Davis to form "an objective attitude toward size and shape relations," and the notes and extended observations that frequently accompany the drawings illuminate his growing formal consciousness and provide an impressive record of one of the steadiest artistic developments in the history of modern art. Having formulated certain aesthetic principles as a young painter, he continually subjected them to tests of a reflective and practical nature. In his writing, as in the paintings, Davis often returned to an idea or a problem several times in order to clarify it.

It has been suggested[7] that the artist's interest in words may have been stimulated in part by his father's journalistic career. Even before he started doing collages, Davis had painted his first "mural" utilizing words, in a candy store owned by a friend in Newark, New Jersey. In high-spirited, free-flowing letters, it proclaimed the joys of Banana Royal, Orangeade, and Nut Sundaes. The mural is marked by a rather unorthodox handling of the letter/space sequences, with words overlapping or canceling one another out, and a strong use of color. Davis first made collages similar to those invented by the Cubists and later, in the early 1920's he also evolved a type in which the conventional collage elements—labels, wrappers, or wallpaper—were simulated rather than real. In these imitation collages, such as *Lucky Strike* (1921) and *Sweet Caporal* (1922), he introduced words or word fragments. In initially stressing the application of scraps of paper to the surface of the canvas, Davis was tacitly acknowledging its two-dimensionality. Moreover, this process of recognition coincided with his developing awareness of the importance of size-shape relationships and what he later referred to as the concept of "color-space."

By 1922, the artist had completely rejected the notion of the primacy of subject matter for an emphasis on formal analysis. It mattered little if "The subject matter of a work of art [was] of the most trivial nature or . . . of the highest moral and social significance . . . in either case it was of secondary importance."[8] He had begun to see "all expression in terms of color. The word COLOR, includes AREA, PLANAL, BALANCE, TEXTURE. A work is built by the super-imposing of color planes."[9]

During 1924 and 1925, Davis painted a group of pictures that reflected the principles clearly enunciated in his writings: "a generalization of form in which the subject was conceived as a series of planes and the planes as geometrical shapes—a valid view of the structure of any subject—these geometrical planes were arranged in direct relationship to the canvas as a flat surface."[10] In *Odol* (1924), the forms are drastically simplified and the surface of the canvas is affirmed by the overlapping though transparent planes. Representational elements are retained but reduced in an effort to establish the more fundamental nature of the object's structure. Davis's notebooks of 1926 contain a number of drawings of fragmented New York street views, in which the artist is still attempting to convey essential structural relations. Often a small diagram accompanies a crayon drawing, providing a type of visual shorthand to illustrate what the artist called its "construction planes."

In notebooks dating from 1922 and 1923, Davis had posed questions about the nature and procedures of painting. By 1927, he had formulated a number of answers to the written queries, and he decided to test these in several paintings. In a conversation with James Johnson Sweeney, he described the manner in which he set up an eggbeater in his studio, subsequently nailing it to a table and painting it repeatedly for one year. He remarked that these pictures were called

> . . . Eggbeater, number, such and such, because it was from the egg-beater that the pictures took their impulse . . . Their subject is an invented series of planes which was interesting to the artist. . . . They were a bit on the severe side, but the ideas involved in their construction have continued to serve me. . . . I got away from naturalistic forms. I invented the geometrical elements. Gradually through this concentration I focused on the logical elements. They became the foremost interest. . . . My aim was not to establish a self-sufficient system to take the place of the immediate and accidental, but to . . . strip a subject down to the real physical source of its stimulus . . . So you may say that everything I have done since has been based on that eggbeater idea . . .[11]

The *Eggbeater* series represents Davis's first truly abstract painting. It was followed by similar "stripped down" analyses of matches and percolators, in which he further reiterated his developing concept of "space-color logic," a concept he repeatedly addressed in notebook observations of the early 1930's arguing that color is space, line is direction, and plane is both color and form. The eggbeaters, matches, and percolators constitute what Davis called "formula pictures." "The formula [could] only be arrived at through wholesale observation of Nature and intellectual selection of the common denominator of varieties . . . which can be rationalized and used over and over again with success. . . ."[12]

The purchase of several paintings in 1928 made it possible for Davis to make a trip to Paris. He remained in that city for nearly a year, executing a considerable number of paintings that seem less radical than the *Eggbeater* series. In such streetscapes as *Place Pasdeloup* and *Place des Vosges* (1928), he summons up all the picturesque charm of Paris—her color and the architectural flourishes of cafés, hotels, and monuments. Yet he scrupulously respects the flatness of the canvas and directs the viewer's attention to its surface by stressing the color and texture of paint. The surface is alternately smooth and rough, and the use of the palette knife results in a granular texture, unrelated to the forms perceived, while frequently abrupt color transitions make it impossible to interpret space in any traditional fashion.

Davis responded to Paris on a personal basis as well: "I liked Paris the minute I got there. Everything was human-sized. The pressure of American anti-art was removed. You could starve to death quicker there but you had the illusion that the artist was a human being and not just a bum."[13] Yet despite his enthusiasm for the city's atmosphere, which he found "conducive to the kind of contemplation essential to art," he returned to the United States because of his need for "the impersonal dynamics of New York City." He painted a group of pictures entitled *New York–Paris* (1931) that amusingly project his visual and cultural dislocation, combining characteristic symbols or signs of the two cities with occasional souvenirs of Gloucester, Massachusetts, where he continued to do much painting and writing during the summers.

In the notebooks of 1931 through 1933, Davis devotes considerable energy to the problem of drawing. He writes about the need to see beyond the superficial optical sensation and states unequivocally that the artist's "subject is not that which we see in front of us but a limited and arbitrary analysis in two dimensions."[14] The *New York–Paris* canvases reflect Davis's growing concern with the function of line, a concern also evident in a number of paintings employing harbor motifs, executed between 1931 and 1935, in which the role of color is minimized.

At the same time, Davis experimented with a curious type of composition utilizing dual or disparate views that challenge the eye to order the shifting planar fragments and prefigure such later canvases of a more emphatically bilingual character as *Deuce* (1954) and *Pochade* (1958).

If the 1930's were artistically fruitful years, they were also marked by Davis's most sustained political activity. When the federal government attempted to solve some of the economic problems caused by the Depression by organizing a Federal Art Project to employ artists in the creation of public works, Davis was one of the first to enroll. He hoped that the project not only might aid artists materially but might enable them to speak to a larger audience and thus eliminate the dictatorship of taste in art by an "economically enfranchised class." Active in the Artists' Union and the Artists' Committee of Action from their inception, he was an editor and frequent contributor to the Union's lively publication, *Art Front,* advocating such institutions as a municipal art gallery and center administered by artists, to provide "a cultural impetus . . . in the community which [would] make possible a powerful art expression, having its roots in the masses of the American people."[15] Davis participated in the organization of the politically and socially oriented American Artists' Congress, which held a large and impressive meeting in 1936 when Davis was its National Executive Secretary. More than four hundred "academicians and modernists, purists and social realists, were brought together on a platform in defense of their common interests."[16] Papers, including Davis's own vigorous and controversial answer to the question "Why an Artists' Congress?" were read and discussed. Sensitive as he was to the social and political concerns that motivated many artists in the Congress, he nevertheless refused to allow utilitarian considerations to play a major role in the creative process. Writing in 1941, Davis described what he called "genuine art" in painting as

> . . . the language of color-space, or form and color. Paintings are not preserved because of the message they convey. The form and content of this message is a unit. The form is always . . . of a certain kind of space, and of objects that have reference to objective reality. It is not an "abstract" form, because it is always interpreted by those who understand in terms of their own optical and motor experience. This is equally true, whether the subject of the picture is an assemblage of human figures associated with an epic myth, a group of kitchen vegetables, or a set of geometric relations, commonly called "abstract" or "non-objective" art. All of these subjects have meaning on many different levels of human action, which represent different human needs outside art. But the need of the artist is to assimilate his subject on the level of its dimensionality in color-space.[17]

During the 1930's, Davis undertook four murals, exploring a medium that permitted a new expansiveness and at the same time suited his persistent emphasis on the common or unifying background. He addressed himself to his new task with characteristic thoroughness. As part of his preparation for the Hall of Communications mural at the 1939 New York World's Fair, he listed the varied sources that contributed to its theme, the history of communications, and later extended his initial informational and procedural observations into a fairly lengthy discourse on the nature of mural painting and its possible aesthetic and social relevance. In the mural, long since destroyed, of which a preparatory scale drawing and Davis's notes constitute an important record, color was kept to a minimum. The artist originally intended to have luminous paint applied to the black surface, but the plan had to be abandoned for economic and practical reasons. The limitation of color minimized the surface tensions that exist in so many of Davis's works, while the swinging calligraphic white lines effectively constituted an informed, monumental graffito.

In both the World's Fair mural and a work painted the same year for Studio B, WNYC (Municipal Broadcasting System), Davis consciously drew the viewer's eye along the surface of the entire wall, anticipating some of his crowded canvases of the early 1940's—*Report from Rockport* (1940), *Ursine Park* (1942)—and the later, denser *Mellow Pad* (1945–51).

Davis's return to mural painting after some fifteen years was carefully considered. In *Allée* (1955), a mural in the student dining room designed by Eero Saarinen for Drake University, Des Moines, Iowa, the four-color, geometric abstraction possesses an almost classic balance. The black-and-white scale drawing for the tripartite composition reflects the tightness of the basically vertical-horizontal composition and realizes Davis's intention of demonstrating his "theory of the Whole as a Sequence of Pieces." The pronounced severity of the Drake mural undoubtedly was influenced to some degree by the spare functionalism of Saarinen's structure, with its shiny black floor, white ceiling, and reflecting glass walls, but there is no question that the work was conceived during a period of considerable self-examination and self-criticism.

Cubism, especially Synthetic Cubism, continued to serve as a stimulus for compositions in the 1940's. Comparison of *Report from Rockport* and *The Mellow Pad* reveals that the two paintings are based on different organizational principles. The earlier work is more spatially fragmented; sections advance and retreat in accordance with color intensity, and the general feeling is one of a series of intervals. In the later, more geometric picture, the sharp contours of animated shapes fairly jump on the surface, inviting comparison with the syncopations of the jazz idiom the artist so intensely admired.

In the 1950's, Davis turned to the re-examination of earlier formal statements. In *Tournos* (1954), he utilized motifs that first appear in a line drawing from one of the 1932 notebooks, expanded subsequently into an oil painting, *Shapes of Landscape Space* (1939). In *Tournos*, Davis purged the few vestiges of spatial reference that marked the

1939 composition. In so doing, he demonstrated that while his aesthetic was open to periodic scrutiny and revision, its theoretical foundation was sound enough to survive the test of time.

The Paris Bit (1959), which Davis once called his favorite painting, is a complex visual reminiscence of some of the streetscapes Davis had painted thirty years earlier. The words "Belle France" and "Eau" and the number "28" are combined with the words "any" and "pad," which had been used in canvases of the 1940's and 1950's, to suggest a continuum of interest and inspiration. As in the majority of Davis's works, drawing on canvas was the first major step in the creative process. After he was satisfied that the "all-over configuration . . . reached a degree of complexity and completeness satisfactory to the impulse that initiated it,"[18] Davis added color. While in many ways one of the most intricate of the artist's later works, *The Paris Bit,* by virtue of the drastic restriction of color areas to red, black, blue, and white manages at the same time to project that classic simplicity toward which the artist aspired throughout much of his life.

In reviewing a large retrospective exhibition at the Walker Art Center in Minneapolis (1957), one writer observed[19] that Davis's work had "a distinctly argumentative character." Certainly Davis never evaded an issue, aesthetically speaking or otherwise. He had little patience with hesitation or imprecision, and this is communicated in his writings as well as his paintings. He believed that everything that could be seen could be measured; that every visual experience could be translated into a logical formula.

Throughout his life, Davis stubbornly resisted being classified as an "abstract" artist. Although he championed modernism for over fifty years and was one of the few informed voices in America during the long period of aesthetic isolationism that marked the 1930's and the years of World War II, Davis always maintained he was a realist.

> I regret that I have long been "type-cast" as "Abstract" because my interest in Abstractions is practically zero. Real Abstract art exists only in Academic painting, or in the minds of Art critics, historians and iconographers. My work is a statement of constant intuitive purpose understood as an Objective Form, consisting of the Relations between simultaneous Percepts of a Subject and Color-Space logic. There is no consideration ulterior to that purpose. As such, allowing for personal preferences of Subject and a New York visual dialect, it is like any Art in which the sense of universality is realized as the concretely topical.[20]

Davis was always a painter of the American experience. His personal style was forged between two world wars, and although he acknowledged a debt to some European modernists, he fashioned a testily independent art that eschewed the intellectual elegance of Cubism in favor of the bold, brash language of popular Americana. Claiming that his paintings always had their impulse in the contemporary environment, Davis once listed some of the things that had stimulated him:

American wood and iron work of the past; Civil War and skyscraper architecture; the brilliant colors on gasoline stations, chain-store fronts, and taxicabs; the music of Bach; synthetic chemistry; the poetry of Rimbaud; fast travel by train, auto, and aeroplane which brought new and multiple perspectives; electric signs; the landscape and boats of Gloucester, Mass.; 5 & 10 cent store kitchen utensils; movies and radio; Earl Hines hot piano and Negro jazz music in general, etc. In one way or another the quality of these things plays a role in determining the character of my paintings. Not in the sense of describing them in graphic images, but by predetermining an analogous dynamics in the design, which becomes a new part of the American environment. Paris School, Abstraction, Escapism? Nope, just Color-Space compositions celebrating the resolution in art of stresses set up by some aspects of the American scene.[21]

Davis's work has often been compared with jazz, the form of music he spent much of his time assimilating. He once remarked that jazz was the first native expression of modernism and likened the excitement he had felt at seeing Matisse paintings in the Armory Show to that he received when listening to piano players in the Negro saloons he frequented as a Henri student. In speaking of his mural for Studio B, WNYC, Davis had asserted that "the tonal intervals of music have their counterpart in painting in intervals of tone, color, contrast, size and direction."[22] Carrying his analogy to the dynamics of music even further, Davis described his *Hot Still Scape for Six Colors* (1940) as ". . . 'Hot' because of its dynamic mood, as opposed to a serene or pastoral mood. Six colors, white, yellow, blue, orange, red, and black were used as the materials of expression. They are used as the instruments in a musical composition might be, where the tone-color variety results from the simultaneous juxtaposition of different instrument groups."[23]

In an article written in 1957, Davis spoke, as he had on numerous other occasions, of the place of modern painting in American life. His observations are marked by a customary wry humor:

Its continuing appeal . . . since the Armory Show of 1913 is due, I believe, to American dynamics, even though the best Reporters were Europeans operating in terms of European Identifications. Fortunately, we have our own share of Aces today. In his Professional Capacity the Modern Artist regards the subject of Subjective Feelings as a casualty and never confuses them with the Splendor of the Continuity of Process, the Event itself. I see the Paintings as being made by Competent Workmen outside the Self—not as a signed convulsion communicating an Enormous Capacity for Frustration with the Outside. I am aware that a number of excellent Artists today might seem to fall into the latter category and would regard my remark as offensive. But Offense is no part of my intention which is entirely one of Notation. I believe that there is a vast Audience which, like myself, is more interested in the Scenery than the Familiar Furnished Room of their own Short-Circuited Emotional Wiring.

I think that if the Contemporary Artist, with a reasonable amount of Taste for the Excitement and Impact of contemporary Culture in the sense I have indicated, will make his report to the very Hip People—then both Art and Culture will do all right.[24]

Stuart Davis was certainly the "Cool Spectator" of his generation, though not from any want of passion or commitment. At certain times, his art projects a New England spareness, and yet there is also an expansiveness that is indeed New York inflected. Despite periodic variations in style, his work reflects an abiding interest in translating the dazzling ephemera of our existence into a meaningful, permanent statement. This is its amazing strength: the ability to confront chaos and create stability without sacrificing energy.

Notes to Introduction

1. "How to Construct a Modern Easel Picture," a lecture delivered by Stuart Davis at the New School for Social Research, December 17, 1941.
2. *Ibid.*
3. *Ibid.*
4. Quoted in *Stuart Davis* (New York: American Artists' Group, 1945), unpaginated.
5. Quoted in Milton Brown, *The Story of the Armory Show* (New York: Joseph H. Hirshhorn Foundation, 1963), p. 63.
6. Davis, *op. cit.*
7. E. C. Goossen, *Stuart Davis* (New York: Braziller, 1959), p. 17.
8. Stuart Davis, *Notebooks, 1922.*
9. *Ibid.*
10. Quoted in James Johnson Sweeney, *Stuart Davis* (New York: Museum of Modern Art, 1945), p. 17.
11. *Ibid.,* pp. 16–17.
12. Stuart Davis, *Notebooks, 1932.*
13. Quoted in Frederick S. Wight, "Stuart Davis," *Art Digest,* XXVII (May 15, 1953), 23.
14. *Notebooks, 1932.*
15. *Art Front,* No. 1 (November, 1934), 2.
16. Stuart Davis's Introduction to the publication issued by the *First American Artists' Congress,* New York, 1936.
17. Stuart Davis, unpublished essay, "Modern Art and Freedom of Expression," June, 1941.
18. Stuart Davis's statement on *The Paris Bit,* quoted in Lloyd Goodrich, "Rebirth of a National Collection," *Art in America,* LIII, No. 3 (June, 1965), 89.
19. Elaine de Kooning, "Stuart Davis: True to Life," *Art News,* LVI, No. 2 (April, 1957), 42.
20. Artist's statement in *40 American Painters 1940–1950,* catalogue of an exhibition at the University Gallery, University of Minnesota, Minneapolis, 1951, pp. 18–19.
21. Stuart Davis, "The Cube Root," *Art News,* XLI, No. 1 (February, 1943), 34.

22. Stuart Davis, *Notes* on WNYC mural, March 23, 1939.

23. Stuart Davis, "Hot Still-Scape for Six Colors–7th Avenue Style," *Parnassus,* XII, No. 8 (December, 1940), 6.

24. Stuart Davis, "The Place of Painting in Contemporary Culture," *Art News,* LVI, No. 3 (June, 1957), 17.

Stuart Davis

chronology, autobiography (1945)

Chronology

1894   Born in Philadelphia, December 7, to Edward Wyatt Davis, art director of the *Philadelphia Press,* and Helen S. Davis, sculptress.

1901   Family moves to East Orange, New Jersey.

1908–10   Attends East Orange High School.

1910–13   Leaves high school to study with painter Robert Henri in New York. Beginning of association with John Sloan, Glenn O. Coleman, H. C. Glintenkamp. First exhibition with Independents.

1913   Does covers and illustrations for *The Masses,* cartoons for *Harper's Weekly,* and a story for *Harper's Bazaar.* Davis leaves Henri; shows five watercolors in Armory Show. Sets up studio in Manhattan.

1915   Spends first of many summers in Gloucester, Massachusetts.

1916   Resigns from *The Masses* after argument about editorial policy. Exhibits with Independents.

1917   First one-man show at Sheridan Square Gallery, New York.

1918   Service in World War I as map-maker in Army Intelligence Department. Trip to Havana, Cuba, to recover from influenza. One-man show at Ardsley Gallery, Brooklyn.

1923   Spends summer in New Mexico.

1925   One-man show at The Newark Museum.

1927   Edith Halpert becomes his dealer. First of eleven one-man shows at The Downtown Gallery, New York. Begins *Eggbeater* series.

1928   Juliana Force of Whitney Studio Club purchases two of his paintings, enabling him to leave for Paris.

1929   Returns to New York in August. One-man show at the Whitney Studio Galleries, New York.

1930   One-man shows at The Downtown Gallery and Crillon Galleries, Philadelphia.

1931–32   Teaches at Art Students League, New York.

1932   Paints mural for Men's Lounge, Radio City Music Hall, New York. Contributes to mural exhibition at The Museum of Modern Art, New York. One-man show at The Downtown Gallery.

1933   Member of Federal Art Project, later incorporated into Works Progress Administration (WPA).

1933–39	Member of Artists' Union and, later, Artists' Congress, of which he becomes national secretary in 1936.
1934	One-man show at The Downtown Gallery.
1935	Editor of *Art Front,* publication of Artists' Union.
1938	Becomes national chairman of Artists' Congress. WPA mural, *Swing Landscape,* is completed at Indiana University, Bloomington. Marries Roselle Springer.
1939	Executes mural for Hall of Communications at New York World's Fair (destroyed). WPA sponsors mural for Studio B of radio station WNYC, Municipal Broadcasting Corporation.
1940	Resigns from Artists' Congress
1940–50	Teaches at New School for Social Research, New York.
1941	Retrospective exhibition with Marsden Hartley at Cincinnati Modern Art Society and Indiana University.
1943	One-man show at The Downtown Gallery.
1945	Retrospective exhibition at The Museum of Modern Art. Winner of J. Henry Schiedt Memorial Prize at 140th Annual Exhibition of Pennsylvania Academy of the Fine Arts, Philadelphia.
1946	One-man show at The Downtown Gallery. One-man show at The Baltimore Museum of Art. Represented in American painting exhibition at Tate Gallery, London.
1948	Winner of the Norman Wait Harris Bronze Medal and Prize at 59th American Water Color and Drawing Exhibition of The Art Institute of Chicago.
1950	Winner of the John Barton Payne Medal and Purchase Prize of the Virginia Museum of Arts, Richmond.
1951	Visiting Instructor of Art, Yale University. Represented in first Bienal, São Paulo, Brazil. Winner of Ada S. Garrett Prize at 60th Annual American Painting and Sculpture Exhibition of The Art Institute of Chicago.
1952	One-man show at American Pavilion, XXVI Biennale, Venice, Italy. One-man show at The Downtown Gallery. Winner of a John Simon Guggenheim Memorial Foundation fellowship. Birth of only child, George Earl.
1954	One-man show at The Downtown Gallery.
1955	Executes mural, *Alleé,* for Drake University, Des Moines, Iowa.
1956	One-man show at The Downtown Gallery. Represented in

the XXVII Biennale, Venice, Italy. Elected a member of the National Institute of Arts and Letters.

1957 Retrospective exhibition at the Walker Art Center, Minneapolis (jointly sponsored by Des Moines Art Center, San Francisco Museum of Art, and Whitney Museum of American Art, New York). Executes mural, *Composition Concrete,* for H. J. Heinz Research Center, Pittsburgh.

1958 Represented in Primera Bienal Interamericana, Mexico. Winner of the Solomon R. Guggenheim Museum International Award.

1959 Represented in American National Exhibition, Moscow, U.S.S.R.

1960 One-man show at The Downtown Gallery. Winner of the Guggenheim International Award for second time.

1962 One-man show at The Downtown Gallery. Winner of the Fine Arts Gold Medal of the American Institute of Architects.

1963 Group show at The Downtown Gallery.

1964 Winner of Joseph E. Temple Gold Medal of the Pennsylvania Academy of the Fine Arts. Winner of the Mr. and Mrs. Frank G. Logan Medal and Prize of The Art Institute of Chicago. Dies June 24, New York. U.S. Post Office Department issues the Fine Arts Commemorative postage stamp designed by Davis, on December 2.

1965 Memorial exhibition organized by National Collection of Fine Arts, Smithsonian Institution, Washington, D.C., travels to The Art Institute of Chicago, Whitney Museum of American Art, Art Galleries of University of California, Los Angeles.

Autobiography* *Stuart Davis*

In writing autobiographical sketches it is not unusual for artists to dwell on the obstacles they have had to overcome before gaining opportunity to study. But I am deprived of this satisfaction because I had none.

* Stuart Davis's writings throughout this book have been slightly edited.—*Ed.*
From *Stuart Davis* (New York: American Artists' Group, 1945). Reprinted by courtesy of Mrs. Stuart Davis.

The reason for this is simple. My mother, Helen Stuart Foulke, and father, Edward W. Davis, were artists, who met as students at the Pennsylvania Academy of [the] Fine Arts in Philadelphia. At the time I was born my father was Art Editor of the *Philadelphia Press,* a leading newspaper. Among the artists working in his department were John Sloan, George Luks, William Glackens, and Everett Shinn. These, along with Robert Henri, were later to form the backbone of the famous group called, "The Eight." Robert Henri had studied earlier at the Academy and had the means to continue his studies in Europe without interruption. On his return to Philadelphia he became, in a sense, the art mentor of these artists, whose painting ambitions had been partly curtailed by the need to do newspaper illustration and comic strips for a living. Because of the continuing association of my parents with these artists it was natural that my desire to study art was encouraged.

Subsequently they all moved to New York City, where Henri opened his own school in 1909. My father was then art editor and cartoonist of the *Newark Evening News,* and later held the same capacity on *Judge* and *Leslie's Weekly* in New York City. We lived in East Orange, New Jersey, and after a year in high school I was permitted to join Henri's classes in 1910. For the novitiate, acceptance on an equal footing with the other members involved the purchase of a large quantity of beer. Subtlety played no part in bringing this intramural statute to his attention. In my own case, the athletic George Bellows was called in from an adjoining studio to insure speedy acceptance of the proposal. Following successful passage of this test I formed a close friendship with Glenn O. Coleman, another member of the class, which lasted until his death in 1932. He was one of America's most gifted artists, whose work has yet to receive the high place it deserves among his contemporaries.

The Henri School was regarded as radical and revolutionary in its methods, and it was. All the usual art school routine was repudiated. Individuality of expression was the keynote, and Henri's broad point of view in his criticisms was very effective in evoking it. Art was not a matter of rules and techniques, or the search for an absolute ideal of beauty. It was the expression of ideas and emotions about the life of the time. We drew and painted from the nude model. The idea was to avoid mere factual statement and find ways to get down some of the qualities of memory and imagination involved in the perception of it. We were encouraged to make sketches of everyday life in the streets, the theater, the restaurant, and everywhere else. These were transformed into paintings in the school studios. On Saturday mornings they were all hung on the wall at the Composition Class. Henri talked about

I. *Sweet Caporal,* 1922. Oil and watercolor, 20″ x 18½″.
Collection of Mrs. Stuart Davis.

II. Untitled *(Odol),* 1924. Oil, 24″ x 18″.
Collection of Mrs. Stuart Davis.

III. Sketch from the Notebooks of Stuart Davis, 1926.
Collection of Mrs. Stuart Davis.

IV. *Place Pasdeloup,* 1928. Oil, 36¼" x 28¾". Collection of Whitney Museum of American Art, New York.

V. *Windshield Mirror,* 1932. Gouache, 15⅛″ x 25″. The Philadelphia Museum of Art.

VI. *Bass Rocks, Number 1,* 1939. Oil, 33″ x 43″. The Roland P. Murdock Collection, Wichita Art Museum, Wichita, Kansas.

VII. *Ultramarine*, 1943. Oil, 20″ x 40″. Courtesy of the Pennsylvania Academy of the Fine Arts, Philadelphia.

VIII. *Deuce,* 1954. Oil, 26″ x 42″. San Francisco Museum of Art.

IX. (opposite) *Something on the Eight Ball,* 1954. Oil, 66″ x 53″. Philadelphia Museum of Art.

X. Last painting, 1964 (unfinished). Tempera with tape guidelines, 54¾″ x 41¼″.
Collection of Mrs. Stuart Davis.

them, about music, literature, and life in general, in a very stimulating manner, and his lectures constituted a liberal education.

Paint was all over the place, and the student's smocks were heavily armored with it. Enthusiasm for running around and drawing things in the raw ran high. In pursuance of this compulsion, Coleman, Henry Glintenkamp, and myself toured extensively in the metropolitan environs. Chinatown; the Bowery; the burlesque shows; the Brooklyn Bridge; McSorley's Saloon on East 7th Street; the Music Halls of Hoboken; the Negro Saloons; riding on the canal boats under the Public Market, and lengthy discussions with Gar Sparks, talented artist-proprietor of a candy store, the latter all in Newark, New Jersey. Coleman and I were particularly hep to the jive, for that period, and spent much time listening to the Negro piano players in Newark dives. About the only thing then available on phonograph records was the Anvil Chorus. Our musical souls craved something a bit more on the solid side and it was necessary to go to the source to dig it. These saloons catered to the poorest Negroes, and outside of beer, a favorite drink was a glass of gin with a cherry in it which sold for five cents. The pianists were unpaid, playing for love of art alone. In one place the piano was covered on top and sides with barbed wire to discourage lounging and leaning on it, and give the performer more scope while at work. But the big point with us was that in all of these places you could hear the blues, or tin-pan alley tune turned into real music, for the cost of a five cent beer.

It seems fantastic to think that today I can sit in my centrally-located and centrally-heated studio and hear this kind of music without taking a bus to Newark or Harlem. It is only necessary to lean slightly to the right and turn the radio dial, at the right time and place. Or if it isn't the right time you lean slightly to the left and turn on the phonograph to hear Wesley Wallace's "Train 29." If some question as to personnel on an obscure recording arises it is only necessary to take a few steps forward and call up Ralph Berton. The crisis is immediately resolved by an automatic and correct answer. I am forced to admit however that there are still occasions when it is necessary to leave the premises to satisfy the desire to hear creative music. But even here a great improvement has been made. My wife Roselle and I merely go out the front door and bear to the left. After a healthy hike of two blocks we dive into a joint where the great Earl Hines is sadistically murdering a helpless piano. On other occasions the sorties call for sterner resolve, running up to distances as high as six blocks. But the Spartan effort is always well repaid by the musicianship of such men as James P. Johnson, Pete Johnson, Vic Dickerson, Max Kaminsky, Frankie Newton, and a great many others. At one time or another, in darker mood, I have questioned the possibility of cultural advance in the United

States, but on the evidence here presented I guess I must have been wrong.

In this early period of riding, walking, and gadding about all over the place, it seems that a great many drawings and paintings were made. I have no idea what became of most of them, but their existence is indicated by some contemporary comment which I quote. "Davis is absolutely without method. He is tied down to no defined rhetoric, to no rhetoric at all. He has ideas to express, and puts them forth with a wild and impetuous eagerness that causes him to soar to glorious heights or else to fall to the ground, an incoherent and inexplicable mass. His work is never mediocre. It is bad or good." Guy Pène du Bois, *N.Y. American,* October 31, 1910. I had a cover of two girls' heads on *The Masses,* for June, 1913. Franklin P. Adams wrote in the *N.Y. Evening Mail* that it was "the best magazine cover of the year." Of an exhibit at the MacDowell Club in 1913, Henry McBride in the *N.Y. Sun* wrote, "Upon the day of the press review half a dozen young men sat upon the MacDowell Club cushions, and we presumed they were of the artists. They seemed so stern and so angry. We supposed they were too cross to dream. They deal in facts exclusively, like the Americans that they are, but there is one of them that shows a disposition to distort the facts with malice aforethought. We refer to the wicked Stuart Davis. We think he has great 'talent.' Two of the studies give you the baffling sense that they are screening something awful. His third 'study' is an innocent arrangement of the flow of a tide creek over the sands, but even in it there are two kinds of water, pale blue and pitch black." Of another exhibition in 1914, Charles Caffin says in the *N.Y. American,* "Stuart Davis is one of Robert Henri's pupils, and in a 'Portrait' he reflects his master's cleverness of technique, and also the latter's tendency to use it for purposes of little or no significance. Does Davis really believe that art is only or even mostly a monkey shine of technique?"

These few comments selected from a great many indicate that a difficulty often complained about by artists, lack of opportunity to exhibit, was never a factor in my case. I was rushed into print a few months after I started to study.

Whatever the Henri School may have lacked in systematic discipline was more than made up for by other positive contributions. It took art off the academic pedestal and, by affirming its origin in the life of the day, developed a critical sense toward social values in the student. If there may have been a tendency toward anarchistic individualism, any preconceived ideas about racial, national, or class superiorities, could not thrive in its atmosphere. By developing the student's confidence in his own perceptions, it gave his work a freshness and personality that was lacking in the student work of other schools. But the emphasis on "anti-artistic" subject matter, which was implicit in the whole Henri idea, tended to give subject matter, as such, a more important place than it deserves in art. In repudiating academic rules for picture structure, new ones suitable to the new purpose were insufficiently established. The borderline between descriptive and illustrative painting, and art as an autonomous sensate object, was never clarified. Because of this, reliance on the vitality of the subject matter to carry the interest prevented an objective appraisal of the dynamics of the actual color-space relations on the canvas. I became vaguely aware of this on seeing the work at the Armory Show.

The International Exhibition of Modern Art was held in the huge Armory of the Sixty-ninth Infantry, New York City, in February, 1913. Hence its popular title, the Armory Show. It was organized exclusively by artists, and its purpose was clearly set forth in the foreword to the catalogue as follows, "The American artists exhibiting here consider the exhibition as of equal importance for themselves as for the public. The less they find their work showing signs of the developments indicated in the Europeans, the more reason they will have to consider whether or not painters and sculptors here have fallen behind, through escaping the incidence through distance, and for other reasons, of the forces that have manifested themselves on the other side of the Atlantic. Art is a sign of life. And to be afraid of life is to be afraid of truth, and to be a champion of superstition. This exhibition is an indication that the Association of American Painters and Sculptors is against cowardice even when it takes the form of amiable self-satisfaction."

The exhibition was a complete panorama of the progressive developments in European art for three quarters of a century up to the year 1913. There was a large American section as well, in which I was represented by five water colors. It is difficult today to visualize the impact on the imagination of this gigantic exhibition, because at that time only isolated examples of the modern movement had been seen in New York. Here indeed was verification of the anti-Academy position of the Henri School, with developments in undreamed of directions. Its challenge to all accepted standards caused a reaction among artists and students that was either violently pro or con. In Chicago, where it was later shown at the Art Institute, students burned a Matisse painting in effigy. I was enormously excited by the show, and responded particularly to Gauguin, Van Gogh, and Matisse, because broad generalization of form and the non-imitative use of color were already practices within my own experience. I also sensed an objective order in these works which I felt was lacking in my own. It gave me the same kind of excitement I got from the numerical precisions of the Negro piano players in the Negro saloons, and I resolved that I would quite definitely have to become a "modern" artist.

Around this time, my ability to draw life in the raw, as far as it went, made me a candidate to join the staff of *The Masses,* a radical magazine. John Sloan was art editor and held my work, along with that of Coleman, Glintenkamp, and Maurice Becker, another Henri student, in esteem. We drew cartoons and pictures having either remote or direct sociological reference, and a number of the things we did were pretty good. The magazine was really alive. This episode lasted from 1912 to 1916, when something happened. In the beginning the magazine was edited by the entire staff of artists and writers at meetings where each had equal vote. The available material was presented, discussed, and a majority vote was taken. But as time passed, Max Eastman, editor-in-chief, began to develop the idea that a more conventional editorial procedure was mandatory. Pictures and articles must be edited at his discretion. Prominent among those on his side were John Reed and Art Young. This threatened invasion of the artist's freedom of expression caused great indignation among us. Sides were drawn, proxies were feverishly garnered from share holders, and a meeting was held. Lovable Art Young spoke scathingly of our "arty" ideas. He said, "They want to run pictures of ash cans and girls hitching up their skirts in Horatio Street—regardless of ideas—and without title." Finally a vote was taken and Max snowed us under with proxies. John Sloan and the rest of us resigned. Apparently the battle between "pure art" and an "art of ideas" is not merely a contemporary manifestation.

Through the publication of my work in *The Masses* I received an offer in 1913 to make a full-page drawing a week for *Harper's Weekly,* then being revived by Norman Hapgood. With this steady employment I set sail for Provincetown, Mass. Whatever the merit of these drawings, they fitted in with the "liberal" kick on which the magazine was oriented. Provincetown was a new experience for me, and made me a continuing addict of the New England coast. On arrival I hired a room and a dory. My desire was to get into this boat and row around a lot all over the place. I did, and at nightfall tied it up close to a piling where it floated on the same level with a wharf next to my room. Unfamiliar with the local habit of the sea, I was amazed next morning to find it hanging perpendicularly from its mooring. The water had disappeared, a large expanse of sand flats had taken its place. Ten foot tides were out of my experience, but adjacent townsmen thought the incident very funny. At that time, Provincetown still retained a considerable vestige of its sea-faring past. On clear days the air and water had a brilliance of light greater than I had ever seen, and while this tended to destroy local color, it stimulated the desire to invent high intensity color-intervals. The presence of artists and writers, not too many, added intellectual stimulus to the natural charm of the place. I met Charles Demuth, and his superior knowledge of what it was all about was a great help to me. I returned again the following year and left in the Fall with considerable reluctance.

The next year I went to Gloucester, Mass., on the enthusiastic recommendation of John Sloan. That was the place I had been looking for. It had the brilliant light of Provincetown, but with the important additions of topographical severity and the architectural beauties of the Gloucester schooner. The schooner is a very necessary element in coherent thinking about art. I do not refer to its own beauty of form, but to the fact that its masts define the often empty sky expanse. They function as a color-space coordinate between earth and sky. They make it possible for the novice landscape painter to evade the dangers of taking off into the void as soon as his eye hits the horizon. From the masts of schooners the artist eventually learns to invent his own coordinates when for some unavoidable reason, they are not present. Another very important thing about the town at that time was that the pre-fabricated Main Street had not yet made its appearance. Also the fact that automobiles were very few and their numerous attendant evils were temporarily avoided. When I made my initial entrance into this port at 18 miles per hour, in a classy second-hand roadster with two flat tires, I was ambushed by a cop on horseback. He chased me into a garage uncoiling a lasso as he got up momentum. I gained sanctuary however and the matter was amicably settled. I would not want my reference to the evils of the automobile as being indicative of opposition to mechanized progress. I have even drawn and painted automobiles on occasion, and for several years introduced filling station gas pumps into my landscapes. This compulsion was abruptly terminated when their designers went sur-realist and produced things which were far beyond my capacity to draw.

I went to Gloucester every year, with few exceptions, until 1934, and often stayed late into the fall. I wandered over the rocks, moors, and docks, with a sketching easel, large canvases, and a pack on my back, looking for things to paint. During the war I drew maps for the Army Intelligence. After a number of years the idea began to dawn on me that packing and unpacking all this junk, in addition to toting it all over the Cape, was irrelevant to my purpose. I became convinced that this was definitely doing things the hard way. Following this revelation my daily sorties were unencumbered except by a small sketch book of the lightest design known, and a specially constructed Duralumin fountain pen. The decision was a good one, I felt less tired, and had greater powers of concentration. My standing in the local chess tournaments, with Ambrose Gring and Charley Winter rose a point or two. Further confirmation as to the excellence of this stream-lined decision came from the pictures I made following it. It seems that in all this tramping around with full equipment I had actually learned something. All that was required to cash in on some of this information was to stop lifting things up and putting them down for a while. I have scrupulously followed this discipline ever since.

In abandoning the weighty apparatus of the out-door painter I did not at the same time abandon nature as subject matter. My studio pictures were all from drawings made directly from nature. As I had learned in painting out doors to use a conceptual instead of an optical perspective, so, in my studio compositions, I brought drawings of different places and things into a single focus. The necessity to select and define the spatial limits of these separate drawings, in relation to the unity of the whole picture, developed an objective attitude toward size and shape relations. Having already achieved this objectivity to a degree in relation to color, the two ideas had now to be integrated and thought about simultaneously. The "abstract" kick was on. The culmination of these efforts occurred in 1927–1928, when I nailed an electric fan, a rubber glove and an eggbeater to a table and used it as my exclusive subject matter for a year. The pictures were known as the *Eggbeater* series and aroused some interested comment in the press, even though they retained no recognizable reference to the optical appearance of their subject matter.

In May 1928, Mrs. Juliana R. Force of the then Whitney Studio Club, bought several of my pictures. Having heard it rumored at one time or another that Paris was a good place to be, I lost no time in taking the hint. With one suitcase I hopped a boat and arrived in the center of art and culture in the middle of June. The rumors were correct, and I felt immediately at home on arrival. I had also brought along a packing case containing two of my *Eggbeater* paintings, just in case someone might be interested. This was opened at the Customs and a question immediately arose as to their nature and purpose. Unable to converse, I intuitively gathered that the works were suspected of containing secret codes, possibly associated with some plot against the welfare of the Republic. After an hour or so the chief inspector arrived and politely inquired what was going on. Addressing me in English he finally explained that it was necessary to know what these things were, and why I had felt obliged to import them. Searching for a definite answer, I explained that they were paintings executed by me in the style of Cubism. I further explained that it was necessary for my artistic serenity to have them about at all times as a source of inspiration. I had struck the right note—"Ah, Cubism," he said, "but of course," and signed an immediate release. This pleasantly terse exchange confirmed my view that I had come to the right place.

I arrived armed with access to a studio located in an alley, at 50 rue

Stuart Davis

Vercingetorix. I paid three months rent in advance, twenty dollars, and holed in to remain for over a year. The studio consisted of a fair-sized room with sleeping balcony at one end and a large side-light. Water and other conveniences were located further up the alley. An alcohol stove constituted the cooking facilities, and a coal stove supplied the required heat. An electric light hung in the center of the room. These facilities might have been considered a bit inadequate in New York, but over there the question didn't come up. There was too much to see and think about outside.

I immediately contacted Elliot Paul, a Gloucester writer friend, and then editor of *Transition*, a magazine of art and literature. He had lived there for several years and gave me a personally conducted tour of the sights. He wrote an understanding article about my work, which was published in *Transition* with reproductions. I had the feeling that this was the best place in the world for an artist to live and work, and at that time it was. The prevalence of the side walk cafe was an important factor. It provided easy access to one's friends, and gave extra pleasure to long walks through various parts of the city. The absence of American drive and tempo was not missed. There was so much of the past, and of the immediate present, brought together on one plane, that nothing was left to be desired. There was a seeming timelessness about the place that was conducive to the kind of contemplation essential to art. There was no feeling of being isolated from America, as I met practically everyone I had ever known at one time or another during the year. I produced a number of pictures and sailed for America with regret on August 1929, on the maiden trip of the *Bremen*. On arrival in New York I was appalled and depressed by its giantism. It was difficult to think of either art or oneself as having any significance whatever in the face of this frenetic commercial engine.

This is not to say that it was my desire to remain planted in France. On the contrary, at the time of leaving I already had the idea that six months more would be about enough, providing frequent returns were possible. As an American I had need for the impersonal dynamics of New York City, and set about making several paintings in which scenes of New York City, Gloucester, and Paris were juxtaposed.

In 1933, the perpetual and specific kind of economic depression, to which the artist had learned to innure [sic] himself, took on a new character. Even the sustaining hope of hypothetical "miracle" sales was dashed. I arrived in New York City from Gloucester on Xmas Day 1933, and the next day enrolled in the Public Works of Art program. From then until 1939, through the W.P.A. Art Project, with its paupers oath, I painted for the Federal and Municipal governments. Two murals were included in the process. This accounts for the scarcity of available or privately owned works by myself during the period. Another contributing factor was the prevalence of meetings, petitions, picket lines, arrests, Artists' Unions, and the Artists' Congress, in all of which I enthusiastically participated. At one point I was editor of *Art Front,* a lively Artists' Union magazine.

In 1939 I was eliminated from the Art Project because my legal period of tenure had expired. Having no money I did the conventional thing—hired a studio and devoted myself to painting. I conducted art classes at the New School for Social Research, which I still do, and had private classes in my studio. I carried on a side-line of public controversy in the press and magazines whenever some misguided individual came out with ideas tending to further confuse the topic of Modern Art. I also was a member of the Artists' Committee and Jury for the "American Art Today" exhibit at the New York World's Fair in 1939, of which Holger Cahill, able director of the Federal Art Project, was also director. I also designed a mural 45 by 140 feet, for the Communications Building, since destroyed, and did a double-page color preview of the World's Fair for *Harper's Bazaar.* I had a one man show in 1943, for the first time in nine years, at Mrs. Halpert's Downtown Gallery. Unknown to me, Johnny Hammond, jazz entrepreneur, and Bill Steig, *New Yorker* cartoonist, hired a three piece ensemble of first class Negro musicians for the opening. The assembled multitude viewed the pictures to the accompaniment of le jazz hot. Mildred Bailey, famous jazz singer, who came as a guest, did a couple of numbers. A good time was had by all, and the exhibition was acclaimed a success. Before closing this synoptic chronicle I want to comment on a situation with which the "abstract" artist is often confronted. In spite of the wide acceptance achieved by modern styles in painting, there still remain a number of people who are continually puzzled by them. "What is it?" and "What does it mean?" are questions extremely familiar to the modern artist. There is no simple answer to these pesky questions because in reality they are not questions about art at all. They are in fact demands that what the artist feels and explicitly expresses in his work be translated into ideas that omit the very quality of emotion that is the sole reason for its being. In this process the preconceived idea of the questioner emerges to take the place of the idea expressed by the picture. But in the face of this certainty the artist always succumbs to the attempt to answer questions that have no answer.

Take a still life of apples by Cézanne for example. What is it? It is an oil painting on canvas, having a subject matter of some apples on a table. But the Apple Growers' Association has undoubtedly used oil paintings of apples on a table in its advertising campaigns. The two subjects are the same but what is expressed in the two similar subjects has nothing in common except subject. The expressive purpose of the pictures is entirely different. One is art and the other has the purpose of setting in motion a train of thought calculated to incite the spectator to rush out and buy some apples. The apples in Cézanne's still life on the other hand leave the salivary glands unaffected. It should be noted in passing that the commercial painting is not inferior in manual skill to the Cézanne, and far surpasses it in optical verisimilitude. What then does Cézanne's painting mean, and why was he so careless about the specific optical facts of these apples? Because his concern was to realize and express his whole sense of unity and meaning in nature. He chose the apples as a particular example of nature and strove to realize their form and color as related to his emotional and philosophical sense of what was true of all form and color. His work means that a man of certain temperament, living in a certain cultural environment, arbitrarily chose to give importance to this kind of spiritual activity as a living value. He devoted all of his time to its cultivation, and cared nothing for selling apples, or paintings either for that matter. When we say that his pictures are great art we mean that the kind of spiritual synthesis which created them, and which is evoked in us by them, is something of great value in itself to be cherished as a potential in spiritual life. Something which we can also cultivate and realize in ourselves. Cézanne did not achieve his stature in a few months or years; it was developed through decades. Similarly, appreciation of what his work means can not be written off in a formula to be assimilated in a few weeks in a classroom. The answer to the question "What does it mean?" will come from much looking at good pictures rather than answers received to the question.

But experience teaches me that the questioner will not let the matter drop here. "Well and good," he will say, "but Cézanne at least painted things that can be recognized as apples, trees, people, however cock-eyed the drawing. What about abstract art where there is no subject matter?" In the first place let me say that the purpose of so-called "abstract" art is basically the same as all other art, and that it always has a subject matter. In fact the difference between "abstract" and "realistic" art is precisely one of subject matter. It would be more accurate to say that it is a difference of aspects of the same subject matter. The "abstract" artist lives in the same world as everybody else and the subject matter available to him is the same. People who will point to a picture and say "that is a picture of a tree," will look at the parallel black lines in a Mondrian painting and say, "What is it?" They will say this in spite of the fact that without a profound awareness of the distance between two points, and the spatial phenomena associated with it, they couldn't leave the house without being run over. By temperament and historical environment Mondrian was moved to choose other aspects of available subject matter than Cézanne. His purpose was basically the same, to realize a synthesis of his spiritual experience. He chose more general terms to accomplish this end, but his art remains a direct sensate expression in which common experience with form, color, and space in nature was the subject matter. His conceptual resolution of this experience has not destroyed its origins but has equated and given them permanence on another plane of perception.

But the development of "abstract" art has not been merely a matter of temperaments. It is the reflection in art of that attitude of mind manifested in scientific materialism by which the world lives today. Through science the whole concept of what reality is has been changed. Science has achieved the most astounding "abstract" compositions, completely "unnatural," but none-the-less real. Every child is aware of this and every popular periodical dishes out romance based on "abstract" ideas. If a petroleum monopoly is cheered for exploiting the "cat-cracker," wherein crude oil is metamorphosed into products that have no counterpart in nature, why should the artist be questioned for finding new realities in his subject matter?

If it is all right for Junior to be nourished on a diet of "Superman" jumping over Radio City, the interplanetary gadding of "Buck Rogers," or the sadistic orgies of "Dick Tracy," why should the modest meddling with the obvious natural fact by the "abstract" artist cause a lifting of the eyebrows? Also, who would buy a radio with a set of "natural-looking" false teeth set into the loud speaker. But people who take the fantastic, and often monstrous, social phenomena now going on all over the world in their stride are thrown into a panic of emotional insecurity when confronted with "abstract" art. The explanation of this is that their interest in art plays such a slight role in their lives that they have no experience on which to base judgment. They retain a grade-school concept in which some vague idea about the *Mona Lisa,* or Millet's *The Angelus,* are the eternal norms for art. In reality a lot of things have happened since then, and Modern Art has met the dynamics of contemporary subject matter on its own terms. It has kept alive the faculty for art experience in a difficult arena. That's what it is, and that's what it means.

Stuart Davis

II excerpts from the notebooks of stuart davis, with diagrams and sketches

Man On an Ice Floe *Gloucester, 1918*

1. One kind to describe a sentimental aspect.
2. Another kind to express the emotional value of related forms.
3. One kind to diagram associated ideas.
4. Another kind to express physical corporeality of associated ideas conceived in weight and light.

The difference between the tradition and ultra-modern expression.

Tradition takes physical reality for granted. It is considered sufficient to place oneself before an object of nature and record its emotional reaction in terms of related forms. Ultra-modern expression takes the whole scope of many [consciousness] as its field and in the plastic arts has as its object the expression of the mental scope in plastic form. It is therefore obvious that while the means of expression remain the same (colors, cubes, and shapes and textures) the subject is entirely different than heretofore, and as a result the finished expression has a very different aspect than one is used to expect from a picture. The confusion lies chiefly in being annoyed because this formal presentation is not obviously a chair or a landscape. The answer is that this picture is not a landscape because its subject is not a landscape. Its subject was a mental concept derived from various sources and expressed in terms of weight and light which is the language of all visual art.

Cubism is the bridge from percept to concept. A cubist picture is a concept in light and weight of a specific object in nature. It is from that only a step to the expression of a concept of diverse phenomena, sound, touch, light, etc., in a single plastic unit. 14th century demanded plot relationship of subject. 1870 to 1918 demanded plastic relationship of subject. 1918—demands plastic expression of mental scope.

A R T *December 30, 1922*

A work of art should have the following qualities.

It should be first of all impersonal in execution, that is to say it should not be a seismographic chart of the nervous system at the time of execution. It may be as simple as you please but the elements that go to make it up must be positive and direct. This is the very essence of art that the elements of the medium in which the work is executed have a simple sense-perceptual relationship. The work must be well built, in other words. The subject may be what you please. It may express any of the qualities that man is capable of perceiving or inventing. It can be a statement of character or a statement of pure abstract qualities but in all cases the medium itself must have its own logic.

Painting is by its very nature an art of color. That is the material with which it builds and when in the effort to get away from the maudlin representations of our predecessors the modern artist uses materials other than paint he is not making a painting but something else. There is nothing wrong with this except that if it is done at all it should be carried to its logical conclusion in which case we have a kind of new art of the bas-relief in materials of the day. Then the question arises whether anything has been gained by this change of medium. I think not. We can enjoy the art of the Greeks as much to-day as any modern work, and from that it is only logical to suppose that a piece of work made today as good as that made by the Greeks would be equally entertaining. There are many artists today who loudly assert that the art of painting is a dead art. While it is easy to see how one might get this reaction from viewing the masses of puerility that are produced in such quantities, yet I do not believe that the statement is actually true. Modern psychology may deny the very existence of art as a factor of importance in the community but that is another story. The fact of the matter is that painting occupies a position of great importance in modern life, as I believe it true that more graphic work is being done today than at any previous time in the world's history. And it also seems that a man like Picasso is an artist of sufficient vitality to be interesting to any age. What then of the ideas about the superiority of the work that is being done by the younger generation in Europe? They it seems are insisting on an absolute purity of the material elements that go to make up the picture. Is this in any sense a negation of the validity of the medium of paint? No, it simply means that the newer generation is intensely interested in expression and that they want their work to be conscious art comparable to all the good work of the past and know better than to try to achieve that quality by imitation either of the old art or of nature. The medium of paint is just as susceptible of creative use today as it ever was and the only thing essential is that the artist realize the life of the medium he is working in. Again let it be reiterated that painting is an art of color and that means that a finished work will appeal to the spectator by the coordination of colored shapes placed in logical order on the canvas. The laws that govern the proper application of paint are as follows. First that in all the qualities of the picture there must be a simple sense-perceptible relationship. In the areas of the work for example there must be a unit of area that dominates all the areas, so that one looking at the picture will instinctively feel a simple order between them. He will feel that this area is half of that one and that this one is twice that. In the color the same thing holds, namely, there is a dominant color to which all the other colors bear a simple numerical relation to one another. When I say *simple* I mean that the work must be right in the way I have mentioned and that if the artist combines only a few simple elements correctly he will have created beauty; needless to say if any one is clever enough to carry this order unerringly into the most subtle and complicated relations he is that much more profound. In the illusionary element of *relief* again the law holds good. If a given plane [has] a suggested relief of half an inch then all other planes in the picture must have a simple mathematical relation to that one which we will assume is the dominant plane. In textures, suggested or actual, the same rule holds. In the element of *line* there must be a simple relation of continuity which in one sense is its area. Then there is the factor of *third dimensional balance* that must be taken into consideration. This has to do with the suggested weights of the various planes of the picture. Their weights must be so arranged that if the planes were actual and the picture were placed in a horizontal position they would be in perfect balance like a building. Of all these elements that go to make the painting there is naturally one that will dominate the others. In different pictures different elements will dominate. In most cases the dominant element is strong enough to dominate and make seem orderly lack of order in the other elements, just as in a jazz band the powerful rhythm holds together the most unrelated excursions of the individual pieces. In a word a work of art can only exist as a consistent unit with its own logic.

A partial definition of a work of art might be,—an organization of units of a given medium which have a positive relation one to another which is satisfactory to the sense of equilibrium. This is quite apart from the subject that is carried by the organized unit. Needless to say works of art will be valued by different persons according to their respective temperaments so that all talk of a standard, except one of the most elastic nature, is out of the question.

The artist must, in order to produce his best work, be a conscious master of the medium in which he works. By means of this knowledge he is able to effect the translation of the image in his mind into the objectivity of his medium with economy of effort and is able to attain the maximum reality of his subject in that medium.

Every medium of expression has a life of its own which must be respected in order to get the best results. For this reason any expression which aims at actual reproduction of nature courts failure because in gaining a questionable illusion the actual life of the work, which is in the material out of which it is constructed, is lost sight of. In painting, paint, and in sculpture, stone, are the actual body of the work just as the body of human is made of flesh and blood and just at that point where the body of the work is sublimated to the idea beyond the sense perception of the observer it dies as a work of art. What this point is will differ with different tastes but that it exists is unquestionable.

Knowledge of the possibilities of the medium I would call technique, an entirely different quality than craftsmanship which is a matter of control of the hand. A man with a knowledge of technique in the sense in which I use it would be sure to produce works of some artistic value whereas a craftsman could be the best of his kind and still fail to produce a single work of artistic value.

The subject of a work of art may be of the most trivial nature or it may be of the highest moral and social significance but in either case it is of secondary importance from the standpoint of the artist.

I see all expression in terms of color. The word COLOR includes, AREA, PLANAL BALANCE, TEXTURE. A work is built by the superimposing of colored planes. For example in a black and white drawing the black line used is primarily a visual actuality because of its color. Secondly it has a certain area the size or extent of which is determined by the color of the paper, white. If you use black on a white paper you will use it in different areas than you would yellow even though in both cases you are expressing the same thing. In a word any graphic expression is the result of the use of color which in turn brings in the element of area which in turn involves the principle of third-dimensional balance. To go back, SUBJECT is nothing from the standpoint of the execution and yet it is the factor that starts the machinery of the execution to work. Consequently any subject is permissible though it be of no greater corporeality than abstract ideas but it will only be successful as a work of art if it submits to the above stated propositions for the reason that the above stated propositions are the flesh and bone through which the idea can have corporeal existence. The practical advantage to be gained from a recognition of these propositions is that the artist will see his inspirations immediately in terms of the medium in which he works and the result will be a clarity and precision that could not be gained in any other way. I believe that very few artists are aware of these facts and that most artists becoming conscious of them would find their work greatly improved.

The elements of color (which includes everything) that go to make up a painting must be correctly presented according to the laws previously stated but their psychological effect on the spectator will only be effective when those color elements are the exact analogy of a sharply felt reality in the mind of the artist. Quite obviously the perceptions of the artist are foreign to most people, in fact it might be said that his audience is restricted automatically by the very quality that makes his work important, namely, its perception or appreciation of values overlooked by nearly everyone. In music, which is by its nature or perhaps

Stuart Davis

merely through convention, abstract, the audience of the artist is larger than in painting—larger, but not really large. The thousands of people that yearly attend the concerts are made up of those who go to hear works that they and their ancestors have heard for generations. The elements common to all music, rhythm, harmony etc. are more readily felt by people in general than are the elements that go to make up a painting, but even at that as soon as a composer elects to use harmonies other than those in vogue for a hundred years his music is not performed at the big orchestral concerts until fifteen or twenty years after its conception when its novelties have become more or less familiar through various channels and even then it is usually met with laughter or anger by the audience, in accord with everything except appreciation. Art is never appreciated early or late except by a few people. The comparatively large body of persons who in some manner every year go out of their way to see or hear works of art are absolutely immune to its messages. Their appreciation of it is based on what some one who knows nothing about it has written [about it] or on the price paid for it or on some act of the artist which has been given newspaper space, on everything but genuine understanding.

ONE PICTURE IS BETTER THAN TWO.

ART IS ART, that is to say, a work of art can only be such by intention and a work of art no matter how slight is superior to a complicated piece of anti-art.

VISUAL ART EXISTS THROUGH LIGHT, whether in black and white or in color one is always dealing in light.

LIGHT, WEIGHT, COLOR, THESE ARE ALL SYNONYMOUS TERMS TO DESCRIBE THE SAME QUALITY OF LIFE THAT MAKES A PICTURE LIVE.

MATERIALS ARE QUITE NEUTRAL IN THE CREATION OF ART.

THE INTENTION OF THE ARTIST IS THE THING THAT MAKES THE PICTURE.

ONE PICTURE IN A ROOM IS BETTER THAN TWO.

THINGS THAT WON'T MAKE A WORK OF ART ARE MONEY, HARD WORK, SYSTEMS OF PROCEDURE, PRECONCEIVED TEXTURES, IMITATION OF NATURAL OBJECTS.

THE THING THAT WILL MAKE A WORK OF ART IS THE INTENTION ON THE PART OF THE ARTIST TO MAKE A WORK OF ART AND NOT SOMETHING ELSE.

ART IS THE THING THAT IS NEEDED AS A LIFE FACTOR AND THE MORE OF IT WE HAVE THE BETTER IT WILL BE.

Intention is the motive power of achievement. Without the intention to do a certain thing it will never be accomplished. It is necessary to be as conscious of your goal as possible. A RATIONAL technique must be developed, meaning a technique that will achieve (when fired by intention) the particular kind of work that you regard as worth while.

There is PAINTING and there is DRAWING (their actual difference is really only one of weight, but for convenience we regard it as though they were separate functions). In making a drawing with black ink on a white paper the original surface is still dominant even after the drawing is finished. That is to say one has simply made some superficial scratches on the surface of a white plane without destroying the original strength of that plane. This is sound procedure but when it comes to the use of colors it becomes more complicated and as a result most paintings are bad. They are likely to start out well with a few simple color statements that are sound but when the process of elaboration starts the original statement is compromised and the picture has lost its chance of being good. The reason for this is perfectly clear and a recognition of it will enable the painter to avoid the prime departure from the laws of rational technique or common sense in other words. To begin with a painting is not a mystery, it is an object made from paint. The paint is the body of the picture and has a certain beauty in itself. This beauty in order to exist must not be tampered with too much, in other words the nearer a painting approaches to an actual illusion of the light of nature the more the primary and direct statement of the paint has of necessity been lost. It is necessary to recognize the limitations (physical not emotional) of the medium, to accept them and to make no effort to conceal them. A painting is made out of color which has certain inherent emotional properties and these colors by use in different proportions can be made to express an intended emotional message. That is the fact of painting. The painter has at hand a set of colors just as the musician has sounds and it is his business to compose in the material that he starts out to work with. It is because most painters do not do this that the average painting is so bad, not merely the difference in message but actual stupidity of technique even among those who are regarded as accomplished painters. To begin with we will say you start with a white canvas of a certain shape. By this selection an irrevocable step has been taken in regard to this particular picture. Every shape and color used in this picture is now subject to your initial choice. In this sense we might say that the selection of the canvas is the most important thing about a painting. When your picture is finished the presence of the original canvas must be felt. If it is lost your picture will be bad just as though you built a tall house and after partial completion you started to remove the foundation, naturally the superstructure would fall down. The canvas is the foundation of the picture. Now, the analogy of the drawing in black on white, it is obvious that in a drawing in line that there will be more white paper showing in the aggregate than there is of the sum of the black lines. Here we have balance, THIRD-DIMENSIONAL BALANCE. In a word the superstructure of black lines does not obliterate the foundation which is the white paper. In the average painting on the other hand we have a complete obliteration of the original surface and a resultant awfulness. In water color there may be tremendous superstructure of planes (as in Cézanne) but, and here is all the difference, they are transparent and consequently of little weight, the white paper shows through them all. In oil painting, on the other hand, you are dealing in an opaque and heavy medium and the procedure is of necessity different. If it is used transparently one is not taking advantage of its inherent power and might as well work in water color. Oil painting [is a] heavier medium than water color just as a painted wooden relief is heavier than an oil painting and is the all important factor to be recognized. To draw the oval of a face with pencil on white paper and then to add with pencil the eyes, nose and mouth is one thing. To draw the same oval as a solid pink plane in oil paint, shade it and add the eyes, nose and mouth with a different color on a brush is something else. The innate sense of weight of the artist usually comes into play automatically in the first quick application of paint when he is sketching in his principle planes but when he begins to elaborate and to copy the subject in front of him with its shadows and variations that instinct is suspended and the result is we have a rotten picture. The instinct is sound but the desire for imitation of nature is stupid, and impossible. The physical reality of your oil painting is simply some layers of paint, recognize this and make your effort to arrange in a perfect third-dimensional balance a few colors which have a positive emotional appeal symbolic of the emotion you feel at the time of painting. How that emotion is engendered in the artist is of no importance. He can get it by standing in front of a landscape, figure or still life or he can get it from his memory of one of those objects or it can be the result of a purely abstract idea. At all events it is the emotion that he is communicating in terms of paint and not the thing itself. The more the paint is allowed to retain its potential physical beauty the greater the strength of his statement will be. An oil painting must be composed of a series of superimposed colored planes whose aggregate weight is less than the base on which they are constructed. When a subject comes to your mind you must rationalize it in terms of oil paint and if you do this correctly you have given your emotion its maximum reality in the medium you have chosen.

January 31, 1923

The first law of artistic beauty is to work with an appreciation of the medium in which you work. Its possibilities and its limitations.

We are immediately concerned with the medium of paint.

Paint is color. It is thin, fluid. One does not make architecture out of a thin, fluid material. And if sculpture is desirable one turns to stone or metal for his material. The obvious deduction is that a painting by its very nature should not attempt illusions of profound weight, relief, etc.

In translating a subject into paint it should be thought of in terms of thin washes of color. It is by a proper adjustment of these that the best results can be obtained.

If our theory is carried out the resultant work should move the spectator primarily by means of a combination of color in various proportions. There is nothing else to move him. Consequently, all illustration and story-telling aside, a work should be composed of vertical, horizontal and diagonal units of color.

The Assyrians glorified their king in art; the Greeks found a common ground in the glorification of the body; the Gothic artists united on a mystical satire; the Italian artists of the Renaissance made art in the image of worldly riches. They were all slaves; all using their art for the glorification of some extraneous power. Democracy is the cry of the world today. The artist must express the plain man, even if that plain man be himself.

Every picture is visible because of light and dark.

It can be white light or colored light. The same laws hold good in either case.

The doctrine taught by some teachers that the working ground must always be white is a fallacy. It can be white or it can be colored according to the will of the artist.

A painter deals in light.

If he is working in colors every color that he puts on the canvas represents a degree of relief or recession.

There is no such thing as a two dimensional picture. For if it has not at least two tones it cannot exist and the mere presence of these two tones means that a statement of light and shade has been made. Light and shade means third dimension. The most that can be said is that a picture has much or little third-dimensional quality.

All this makes it clear that a picture must be sound from the standpoint of light to be good. By thinking of the work in these terms it seems that it should make for better work. More simplicity and less errors.

February 26, 1923

1. In applying the colors to the canvas one is making statements of advancing and retiring planes (quite aside from overcutting forms which is representation of advance and retreat).

Stuart Davis

2. Now the impulse is to paint in this most direct manner in an *actual* and not an imitative way.

3. This means the illumination of all perspective—all *illusions* of distance reduces the work to an arabesque of pure colored shapes.

4. Why is this a desirable procedure?

5. Because it produces a result that is a complete thing in itself. It arouses emotion in the spectator because of what actually exists on the canvas and not by what is suggested (or it may be just what the procedure suggests—a mathematical feeling that it is regarded as good).

6. This latter statement is not necessarily true because it is possible that such a way of painting might be full of human emotions. The thing about it that I understand clearly is that it makes for strong, simple design and color which I arbitrarily regard as superior to weak design and weak color which results from the thousand compromises necessary to realistic transcripts.

7. My reasoning leads me to believe that there should be no modeling at all in the ordinary sense of the word but that every color should be a flat plane of a definite size and shape.

8. The completed picture should be an organization of positively related units in size, color, shape and planal relationship.

9. This attitude if clearly understood will give a direction to the work of the artist who uses it that I believe is a good direction.

10. Harrison Fisher heads and this ideal are incompatible.

11. This ideal has nothing to do with social satire or story-telling illustrations. It is the antithesis of these qualities.

The Subject   *March 2, 1923*

The subject must be visualized instinctively as a colored shape of a certain size. This represents the entire process of painting so far as I can see. The elements that go to make the picture on your panel are ----- SHAPE, COLOR, and the SIZE of the colored shapes in relation to one another and to the size of the panel. (Direction and planal relationship we will leave for the time being. [I am] not quite sure of their place in this scheme. They may be included in the foregoing elements.)

I want the picture to be simple.

I do not want any illusions of light in the accepted symbolism to creep into the painting as I desire the light to be the actual light of the color itself. I want to recover the primary sense of vision.

All natural perspective must be eliminated because this is an illusory element which compromises the purity of the expression. (Overlapping planes such as those employed by the Cubists are illusory perspective and must not be employed.) This seems to make the ideal picture which we are projecting take shape as a kind of picture writing or hieroglyph. There is this distinction, however, that the hieroglyph expresses an idea moving in time, a succession of images, while the picture I have in mind will concern itself with the expression of static form. The colors that are laid on the panel must BE the picture. They must have a simple obvious relationship as to size and shape which will be the result of the correct evaluation of the color and shape factors of the original simplified. The method of procedure in making such a picture will be somewhat as follows - - -

First the emotional reaction to a given object or group of objects. Second a conscious analysis of the elements in the object that were responsible for the emotional stimulus (analysis in terms of color, size and shape). Third a workmanlike execution of those elements in color on the panel.

March 5, 1923

1. The visual sensation is the result of light on three-dimensional form.
2. Sculpture is the form.
3. Painting is the light.
4. A painting at its best is an emotional chart of light.
5. It can be colored or black, grey and white.
6. Macdonald-Wright made some pure color progressions but they were used to describe complicated planal relations and as a result there was a lack of *actual proportion* in them. It was the old story of "a picture of something" instead of being a complete visual unit in itself.
7. My theory demands purity of expression. It demands that a work executed in paint stimulate the observer visually through the arrangement of color tones in definite proportions. This eliminates all copying of natural effects as the colors are laid on in proportions that are ideal and have no counterpart in any natural object. The proportions of the color must be to the end of color and not imitation of nature.

—Quite obviously your painting is not the same material as the original objects. In the first case you have three different kinds of materials in three dimensions, in the painting, one kind of material in two dimensions. This is the life of your painting—paint on canvas, and it is my contention that when you try to create illusions with it that you weaken its potential power as an emotional stimulant. In making a

Stuart Davis

painting the actual qualities at your disposal are—the color scale, shapes and relative size, and I believe that it is by the positive use of these factors that the greatest force can be obtained and consequently the closest approximation to the strength of the emotion originally felt.

This method eliminates representation altogether and it is this point that is the thorn in the side of the public and of most artists. If you admit the original premise that painting is a purely visual art then you must admit my conclusions from that premise for they are logical.

Cézanne tried for years to paint things just as they looked to him. There is no comment in his paintings except about light on form. But in order to achieve this he resorted to strident simplifications of shape and color and he employed illusion third-dimension which I believe is a weakness. It must be a weakness because it does not really exist in the painting except as illusion and I maintain that it is better to frankly admit the limitations of a two dimensional medium and to develop it to its utmost along that line. If you want three dimensions, use sculpture which is a real three-dimensional medium. A visual work of art is great in that degree to which it approaches the natural phenomena of light on form. The fact that it can be used to tell stories is not a proof as most people think that it should be used to tell stories. All visual art is an abstraction because it seeks to express a natural complex fact in a more simple medium. Sculpture probably approaches nearer to nature than painting because it has actual three-dimensional bulk which is the dominant fact of matter but still is a very limited medium compared to the multiple mediums of nature. It is obviously not nature and should not masquerade as such.

Well then, it is the aim of the visual artist to create in a spectator through divers mediums an approximation to the optical sensation that he has received from a given object and in view of the foregoing argument we admit that to recreate the natural objects in paint is a physical impossibility. The course then obviously is to realize the limitations of the medium which you are using, make no attempt to conceal them, and to build as strongly as possible with what you have. The natural objects have become paint, it is paint that is to move the spectator. Well then, let us be sure to move him by the potential beauty of the paint and not by paint echoes of nature more or less correctly copied in a simplified way. The sentimental mood has for some time been the aim of music and painting. This is weakness because of its unreality, because it deals entirely with the imagination and not with facts. Its ideal is a semi-conscious state of memory which it offers as a happy state. This is obviously weakness. The stimulating media of painting or music are weakened by this ideal because the stress is laid on something outside themselves, the potential strength of the musical note or color is sacrificed to psychological utility. I mean by this that a given color will not be appreciated because of its relative size and strength in the composition but because it suggests a remembered visual impression, familiarity, sentimental attachment, etc. While admitting most readily that the function of art is the restatement of natural sensations I separate from the majority as to the best way to do it. The sense stimulation is felt and recorded by the brain but when it comes to giving it objectivity in a medium different from the original stimulating source the trouble commences. You are stimulated we will say by the sight of three red apples in a white bowl that rests on a green cloth and you desire to make a painting of this pleasurable sight. . . .

The Piece-Work Picture *1923*

All impressionistic work is piece-work and lacks a unifying principle.

It is too personal. It separates the individual from all the rest of the universe and that is weakness.

The more one is immersed in unity the more strength one has by the very nature of the situation.

To draw is to make a shape and a movement in time.

Every unit that goes into the picture should have a positive mathematic value. The picture should not attempt to be nature but a conscious parallel construction that interprets nature in terms of the understandable.

The whole thing brings on the equation between the "idea" to be expressed and the "form" the expression is to take.

The form must be complete in itself but it must be set in motion by natural forms which are the stimuli but are not the art work. This is a very difficult problem, how to follow the initial impulse and at the same time ignore it.

Inspired chess play or sound chess play or correct chess play are all the result of the ability to see a situation that will occur in four or five moves and to judge its value as a winning or losing position. One can arrive at this kind of chess play by study of the game so that situations group themselves into classes. By this means one is able to make quick judgments as to the value of a given position simply because one has previously analyzed the position or a similar one and knows what will happen.

You may feel this way about it. You want to do public work. That is, you are not satisfied with the hermit life of the modern artist. In order to do public work it is necessary to have two qualities. One must be a master artist and he must execute ideas of public interest. Not satires or jokes but must have a genuine appreciation of simple natural phenomena.

March 9, 1923

The effort of all painters is to shock the spectator by means of his color and design into reexperiencing the emotions that caused him to execute the painting. I am speaking of visual painting not illustration where the intention is to tell a story. The question naturally arises as to how to best express the emotion felt in paint. Up to date, the most successful method has been to copy the original stimulating object as closely as possible (the simplification that occurs in the type of work referred to does not run counter to the statement that the prime motive is to copy the original because the good imitationist painters have sense enough to allow for the limitations of the medium). It is now felt by many people however that this method of producing the sensation of reality has been developed to its utmost and that if we are again to experience visual pleasure in the medium of painting it must be in a different way. I believe I have arrived at such a method by the following logical process.

In the first place we must inquire what a painting really is and what are the mechanics of its emotional faculty. The answer is that a painting is composed of colors of different areas laid on a panel of certain size and shape. That is all there is and consequently the emotions that are felt on the contemplation of a certain painting must be the result of the combination of colors that the artist has put on the panel. Admit this and there quite obviously is no other course to follow than to work consciously in units of color of definitely related areas. My method demands that you divide the panel on which you are going to paint into certain subdivisions that are of visual value, for instance, on an oblong panel you might divide its length into four parts and its width into three parts, then you have a simple unit of proportion on which to base your areas. The emotion must then be interpreted in terms of color occupying a given proportion of the area of your panel and those proportions will all have a relationship easily appreciated by virtue of the common unit by which they are all measured. In the plan mentioned above all the colors will occupy areas which are either multiples or divisions of fourths or thirds. By this method it is possible for the artist to express himself completely in terms of the medium he has chosen and the result should be one of greater potential emotional power than a painting in which the artist made a series of compromises with his medium in his attempt to copy the exact values of a given local object. One method is a faint echo of the original stimulating object, while the other, better one is a frank translation of the original stimulating object into terms of the stimulating values of the medium of paint.

It is important for the artist to realize the physical nature of expression in paint.

In order to find this out we ask the question, "What qualities are common to all expressions in paint? What are the qualities that are automatic and inescapable?"

The answer is - - - TWO-DIMENSIONAL AREA and LIGHT AND DARK which is three dimensional illusion.

These are the two qualities that are the physical facts of painting. They are automatic and inescapable and it is by the varied combination of these two qualities that a work of art is produced.

These qualities are the property of painting and have nothing to do with natural proportion and natural light and shade.

Painting is the vehicle for the expression of an ideal.

An ideal is a mental concept, an evaluation of natural material.

It can be the Greek ideal of physical health and logic. It can be the ideal of the Middle Ages of the Holy Virgin. It can be the ideal of the Renaissance of wealth and richness. It can be the ideal of the present day of Democracy or every man a law unto himself, personal expression, Expressionism. The ideal, what a man says, what he thinks is worth while, are subject to constant change but the method of the expression of that ideal in paint is a constant quality.

The art school teaches ideals and not painting. They teach you to look at things as physical facts or they teach you to see them through the eyes of some dead idealism. The teaching of the study of nature as a quantity without relation to the perceptor, to measure it with a ruler, is an ideal, an evaluation of what is worth while, as much as the teaching of the Greek ideal. Painting should be taught in the art schools and not ways of looking at things.

The only vital principle today, bad or good, is the ideal of democracy, every man is the equal of the other hence the man's personal reaction[s] to a given scene are the ideal. He has no standard of what is worth while in a given scene except the way he happens to feel about it at the time of perception. There is no common idealism to-day except this one of the right of a man to do as he pleases.

The Process of Painting *April 20, 1923*

The process of painting is as follows:

One is stimulated by the visual contemplation of certain natural objects in the desire to duplicate the sensation of pleasure by the process of painting. The question then arises after many futile attempts to do this, How to do it. Which question leads to an inquiry into the physical properties of the medium of paint. What are the possibilities of expression in paint?

The analysis yields the following observations:

A painting is a collection or complex of colored tones of definite shape and size, that is all. Every thing that is expressed through the medium of painting must live through these properties of size, shape and color. Further we observe that the only actual physical reality (or let us say its most powerful appeal) of a painting is the relation of two-dimensional areas, these are real. Here is actual two-dimensional space that has the power to affect us emotionally. And the colored tones that mark off these spaces, what of those? The colored tones are simply greater or lesser degrees of light reflection, which means three-dimensional form. That is to say the only way in which three-dimensional form exists for us visually is by the phenomenon of light reflection, planes further away from the source of light receive less light and that is for us a symbol of a difference in planal position, or in other words the third dimension. It therefore logically follows that in placing on the canvas colored tones of varying degrees of light reflection we are symbolizing three-dimensional form, or making the statement planal angularity. So here we have actual two-dimensional space and an illusion of a third dimension as positive properties of painting which are constant and inescapable. Any haphazard stroke placed on the canvas can be described as to two-dimensional space extension and as to the degree of depth in relation to the plane of the canvas that it suggests.

Some one will now doubtless arise and say "True, but what of it?" to which question it is necessary to make the following reply:—A painting is a painting. It is not the object which inspired its creation.

The painting only lives and has force to stimulate emotion through the properties described above which are its body. Therefore these properties must be respected and consciously ordered so that the painting may have life. To begin with you have a flat surface of definite proportions, this is the base on which your work is built and its presence must be dominant in the finished picture or else you have destroyed the fundamental physical fact of your work. And yet this is precisely what the painter who tries to copy nature always does. By imitating the three-dimensional facts of his subject in paint he gets two-dimensional disorder which is death to the most potent quality that a painting can possess. He inevitably destroys the flatness of the surface that he is working on and his completed picture is, apart from his subject, the description of a geometric solid which has not even the virtue of being simple like Cézanne. Any painting is the description of a three-dimensional surface, can't be anything else, but that surface should be a head-on view of an incised plane and not an exaggerated symbolizing of forms in perspective. This is so because in the effort to create the reality of nature the reality of the painting is lost.

Now the question is, to what extent is it necessary or desirable to have the forms of the picture comparable to natural concrete forms? Logically, every stroke that goes into the composition of a picture should be an integral of size, direction and depth and if this is admitted verisimilitude is not only impossible but irrelevant. This makes painting an art of construction for the purpose of direct visual pleasure as opposed to what it always has been, an art in the service of church, politics, bourgeois family life or art.

A picture must have unity, singleness of idea. It must be ONE thing and not TWO things.

In color the way to achieve this unity is to have a dominant color and to see that it is a visual dominant and not merely a theoretical one.

Many artists who use the Marratta and similar color systems believe themselves to be using a palette that automatically achieves color unity through a dominant color that runs through the whole palette. Theoretically this is true but actually it is nothing of the sort.

Color dominance is inseparable from area. Unless that color which is to be dominant occupies more area than all the other colors combined it is not dominant. They might reply that in as much as their whole palette is keyed up to a certain color that color is present in all parts of the canvas and that its area of occupation is large. True enough, but the original vitality of the color is so compromised by the endless process of mixtures through which it has passed that its visual presence is non-existent.

Any color system that is not based on the visual effect of color is of no use in painting however true it may be from the standpoint of logic.

A painting either exists as a visual fact or it does not exist at all.

No work of art can be true to nature in the objective sense. The nearer it approximates the natural appearance of objects the more it is likely to be far away from art.

A work of art is an orderly construction in a given material.

Nature is an orderly construction in millions of materials.

Little order and big order.

The one is not the other. It is only a parallel system.

The deduction from all this [is] that one must commence with a realization of the limitations of his medium. Until that fact is well understood no art is possible.

It is better to make a slight work of art than to achieve pretentious non-artistic constructions.

The element that the painter deals with is LIGHT.

Stuart Davis

It can be roughly divided into three degrees, light, medium and dark. All colored light can be classified as above.

These three divisions are not permanent qualities but are relative. Thus it is impossible to assign a definite category for RED which by its nature is Dark. If a red plane be placed on a white background the red will have the relative value of dark. If it be placed on a complementary green background [their] light and dark value may be said to be equal. If it be placed on a black background its value will be light. It must be understood that these values are the visual and not the scientific ones. Since we are dealing with a visual fact visual values are the only ones that apply.

I believe that a picture should be thought of in terms of light and dark with the secondary consideration what color the light is.

A plane composed of the twelve color divisions of the palette laid together in stripes would be a positive light and dark statement. The twelve colors have great light and dark range one to another but the placing of that plane on a white background would render their several differences nil compared to the tone of the whole plane as compared to the white background. Therefore in doing this the artist has merely made the simple statement of two major degrees of light although one of the degrees is composed of twelve different tones.

1923

Realism in the sense of trying to reproduce optical effects whether of the Bouguereau type, which seeks to represent the human figure as it appears in the clear, even light of the studio; or the Whistler type which represents the human figure as it is seen at dusk or twilight, is bad. It represents a low vitality. There is no big ideal involved, none of the evidence of a strong will to live such as appears in the work of the Egyptians and the Greeks. This realism is a type of art which shows the painter to be satisfied with the most trivial matter to which he attaches a sentimental importance, or endows it with an anemic human quality.

The best man is he who has a large view of life, is not befooled into giving to small matters an importance that they do not possess. His ideal would center around man as the highest product of nature within his horizon and his thoughts and feelings about man would be the product of his natural abilities without any myopic distortion. The Greek, judged by his sculptors, conceived man as a noble animal, a healthy, happy animal who was sufficient unto himself and a person well worth while admiring. Their art is not realistic in the modern sense. While they use the physical facts of a man's body with far greater thoroughness than many modern [artists] they at the same time endow this local phenomenon with a feeling of its relation to their mental scope that makes it important and powerful. In a word he is conceived as a part of a scheme (and a noble part) and not as a static entity existing by itself without relation to time or place. Your modern artist on the other hand at his best conceives man as he would an apple (at his worst as a sentimental character whose entire reason for existence lies in his temporary social relationships with his fellow man). By the modern artist he is conceived as a chemical phenomen[on] without aim, purpose or destiny but simply as a chemical unit of more or less interest. The modern artist represents man in this manner because it is the general thought of the world at this time and the artist is a part of his time and is inseparable from it. It seems to me that this is a condition of stagnation that is deplorable but that awaits other solution [than] any that has been offered up to date. What is needed is a new unifying impulse that will bring forth a new interest in life.

1923

In the Van Gogh type of landscape the COLOR was SIMPLIFIED. Now it becomes necessary to simplify the planal structure.

In doing the planal simplification a certain BALDNESS was the result which took interest away from the picture. In the color simplification interest was added to the picture.

I believe the reason for this was as follows————

In the color simplification the natural outlines of the objects were adhered to and gave a variety to the picture to which the added intensity of the simplified color gave further interest. In a word the simplified color picture had practically all the detail and variety of the ordinary impressionistic painting with a greater color intensity. The planal simplification on the other hand was so drastic that practically all the interest of the natural object was lost and the only remaining feature was a too simple formal combination. As a result the work while theoretically correct does not hold the interest of the spectator. To remedy this defect a revaluation of the meaning of the phrase "Planal Simplicity" is necessary.

To begin with the object of doing the painting in the first place is not to construct an abstract figure but to get on to the canvas in a direct and positive style the actual shapes and colors of the objects that inspire it. Therefore while it is necessary to have a dominant simple planal combination as a base just as there is a simple and dominant color the planes should be carried on into minor variations which brings the picture closer to nature. In a word a true realism.

The method of procedure in work of this kind is as follows————

Stuart Davis

DRAW with a piece of charcoal your design just as every one does only instead of a simple map of the objects in front of you let your drawing be a complete planal statement with a positive scale of relief. The result is that you have a simplified statement in paint of the natural objects of great clarity and at the doing of it have not eliminated all recognizable formal sensations.

This is not an arbitrary symbolism but is based on the actual meaning of the colors.

Color is a symbol of light.

Light gives us our visual sensation of relief.

Therefore color is the only relief possible in painting.

A symbolic relief.

The minute imitation of relief is used the potential power of the color is destroyed.

The subject should be evaluated in terms of relief which is the natural phenomenon that we react to, this conception should then be given expression in paint in terms of advancing and receding colors as the paint equivalent for actual projection.

Notebook sketch, 1926.

Notebook sketches, 1926.

Stuart Davis

Notebook sketch, 1926.

Notebook sketch,
Paris, *ca.* 1928

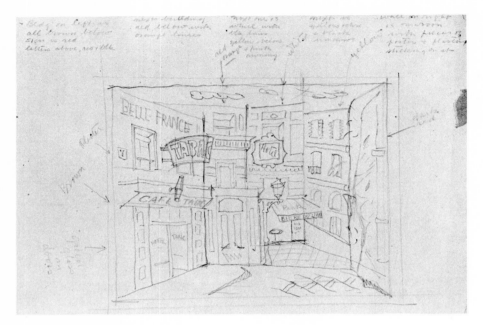

Notebook sketch, Paris, *ca.* 1928

Stuart Davis

Daybooks (*ca.* 1931–38)

Ca. 1931–32

A point of importance in regard to my color theory is that the outline of any given color spot is part of the contour construction of the composition. Color used without regard to this obvious function can certainly not be used correctly. Whatever characteristics may be inherent in color the above mentioned certainly come first.

1932

The artist goes to nature to draw. In nature he sees a series of accidental combinations from which he selects. He is selecting accidents just as though he selects from a series of random lines on a piece of paper which have been drawn by himself.

This is the *subject* of painting. The mode of expression is by means of angular variation. From any given point the line moves in a two-dimensional space and is continually creating space relative to all existing points which is either expansive or contractive according to the point of observation. Relativity, knowledge of this fact, and the ability to visualize the logical correlatives of a given angle allows the artist to *see* the *real* angular value of his drawing as opposed to associative value.

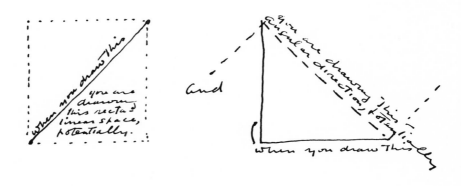

A drawing or painting can only be understood physically by its arbitrary point relationships as determined by parallel coordinates. All drawings have point relationships. Yet some are good drawings and most are bad.

If point relationships were the only requirement to achieve interest, any random marks on a piece of paper would be interesting which we know they are not. Therefore there must be some particular kind of point relation which is good.

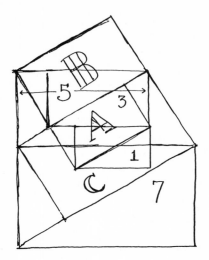

Study good drawings to find common point relation characteristics. If there is a type of point relation [that] is good as opposed to a type that is not good, then this knowledge can be used on nature itself. One can supply the points which are lacking in a natural scene which is uninteresting and make it alive.

Definitely understood are the ideas relating to drawing as follows: that anybody can *see* an interesting subject in nature. That none can draw it effectively. That a drawing is a real thing, equal to but *not* a replica of the subject in nature. That the anatomy of the drawing is *two dimensional*. That the *only* possible [thing] to be achieved in drawing is a numerical variety in the two-dimensional elements. The indivisible second unit is the triangle. The only possible optical fact is a change of direction which automatically creates a closed circuit, the [?] as any points on the two directions have continuous directional relation to each other.

Further, that there is a "specific" angular *contrast* which is fundamental to the most diverse subject matters (this contrast constant may differ with different artists or different groups of artists but will remain the same to the same artist).

Optical interest is an intuitive observation of simply and clearly related rectangles. The observations can be drawn by drawing the rectangle itself or the diagonals or curves subtending one or more sides of the

Stuart Davis

rectangle or the diagonals. The analysis of the intuitively perceived complex must be made in terms of one areal (angular) contrast at a time. When possible, let the rectangular principles assume associative shapes of common experience. Draw the co-ordinates not the natural deviations.

A drawing is never nature. Therefore it is necessary to arbitrarily define space in terms of a standard and its variants, the 90° angle. The object of drawing is to build up measurable angular variations. Through these variations, which are the language of graphics, the artist must communicate with people. As the area of a surface is the NUMBER of times a unit area goes into it, so the only possible graphic description of a visual sensation is through the *number* of times a unit occurs in a complex. The *unit* of drawing is an angular contrast.

  *This is a graphic expression of an angular contrast*

Stimulation occurs through the comparison of *like* elements, the areas *A* and *B* which are *like* in their common birth from the angle but dual in their direction (through change of angle) from a common point. Diagonal *A* and the dotted line create the duality and contrast which is variation.

There must be *real* geometrical variety in the drawing. Through what sequential units can it be achieved?

The unit observation in nature must be a contrast, a comparison. A comparison of what? Indivisible triangular units . . . or are the observed contrasts the result of the comparison of triangular complexes such as rectangles?

The shape is always an accident of a point-to-point change of direction. It would therefore seem that the unit of observation should be simply a directional comparison with relation to a preceding or assumed direction. The right angle is the easiest directional standard of comparison.

. . . . The picture can't be a mystery because it is composed of angles and all angles are measurable [see the illustration on page 58].

Is a mechanical explanation of a picture possible? It may be possible. Then what makes one picture different from another? What makes one machine different from another?

Any machine can be thoroughly understood and yet they have an unlimited variety. Machines differ one from the other to suit their relation to the work they have to do. Pictures differ to suit *their* work. What kind of work does a picture do?

A real variety in terms of direction would be one in which the lines do not duplicate each other

If an ideal sequence be assumed, as standard such as ⟶ a right angular extension of all points, we have a numerical complex of real directions but something necessary is still absent. What is it. In view of the fact that it satisfies the definition of drawing (an angular variety) why is it not satisfactory?

Because it is a thoroly comprehensible progression? Hence offers no illusions or "variety"?

The picture is a fourth-dimensional observation which simply means that it occurs in Time. The unit of Time is the triangle which is assumed to exist outside of Time, in other words it is an abstraction and does not have reality until set in motion by duplication. A triangle could be analogous to a second of Time.

The picture itself could be called a Duration of so many seconds of Time (Einstein has said that space is a fourth dimension). Therefore we must build the picture with four coordinates, thus:

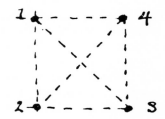

Stuart Davis

The objective of painting: to draw observed optical sensations in two-dimensional terms.

Therefore, our subject is not that which we see in front of us but a limited and arbitrary analysis in two dimensions. Therefore, if one says, "Why must I draw triangles etc., why do I have to visualize in these terms when they are not in the subject?," the answer is that they may not be in the subject but they are most emphatically in your painting. If an artist cannot visualize a simple geometrical relationship how can he pretend to a more complicated one. The answer is that he tries for complication through ignorance and gets a stupid result. The hypothesis states that *any* agreeable optical sensation may *only* be approximated two dimensionally by means of the arbitrary division of the 360° into definitely simplified groupings, 90, 60, 45, 30, for example. Such a simplification of the possible directions, from any point, gives you a *limited* choice as to *where* the color is to be placed.

All artists have some limited or spaced color-tone system which simplifies selection of the color tone for any area. Such a system however tells you nothing about *where* the tone is to go or how large it is to be. Given an area to start with, the next addition must have a specific angular relation to the already existent points. If these angular variations are limited the choice becomes simpler and an understandable relation is set up in the design which makes it capable of simultaneous comprehension.

Color, in Nature, groups diverse angles and puts them on the same visual plane. It simplifies and suggests a large order which enumeration of the objects in the scene would leave orderless.

On seeing an interesting scene in Nature, the artist has intuitively visualized a simple angular relationship. The vision has nothing to do with the specific objects that make up the scene and cannot be captured by copying those objects. The vision is a comprehensible angular complex and can only be understood in geometrical terms.

The optically agreeable is specifically related to simplicity of angular variation. This is not merely a phrase but a fact which can be comprehended and used to draw faultless pictures.

One constantly glimpses the character of the intuitive selections of scenes made in walking around. Their common denominator is analogous area which in turn is the result of angular simplicity.

The good picture is optical geometry. But more than, or rather through that geometry, the artist may express his sense of numerical variety. Which is a way of saying angular variation.

It is even possible to have a set formula for a good picture. The formula capable of adaptation to various associational ideas.

As in music, the blues, a set form, are always good and one might

say that they express everything that can be expressed. A series of formula pictures carrying a sentimental association is possible and would be desirable.

The formula can only be arrived at through wholesale observation of nature and intellectual selection of the common denominator of varieties . . . which can be rationalized and used over and over again with success. It is of course not present in just any subject at all, but awareness of its character will allow the artist to see it when it is there.

September 20, 1932

When we see in Nature an "interesting" subject it simply means that we have seen an accidental space definition which corresponds obviously to geometry and is therefore comprehensible.

Comprehensible doesn't mean that we immediately see all the relations but it means that we detect the absence of confusion and hence infer system or order and we hasten to draw it because we feel that it is something we can master. This is the normal, wasteful process. Much superior is the method whereby we carry our system with us and impose it on the subject.

This system is the realization that all observations are triangular in character. That no definition of space is possible without triangulation. Also that observation exists in time and hence is sequential in character. Therefore our picture is a number of triangular observations, simultaneously presented.

From any two points we draw straight lines whose juncture forms a third point and establishes length ratio. With the two origins as constant reference we draw other straight lines which establish new points and thus we have our space complex resulting from direction changes.

Stuart Davis

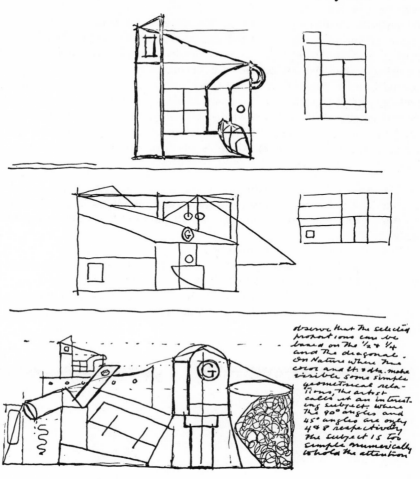

Aug. 3, 1932.

observe that the selection proportions can be based on the ½ + ¼ and the diagonal. On Nature where the color and lt. + dk. make visible some simple geometrical relations, the artist calls it an interesting subject. Where the 90° angles and 45° angles are only 4 + 8 respectively the subject is too simple numerically to hold the attention

1932

There is a rational distinction between good and bad drawing. It is possible to know how to go about making a good drawing.

It therefore logically follows that all of the drawings of a person who knows how to make good drawings will be good. Experience has shown this to be true.

Good drawing is an attitude of mind in which the artist directs his efforts to the accomplishment of a good drawing and is not side-tracked by other considerations such as—whether someone will like it, whether it is salable, whether it looks like this subject etc. His attitude of mind will concern itself with a physical analysis of the subject in terms of two dimensions. Further he will always be aware of the truth that this subject is an intuitive selection from the space complex before him. And further he will direct as far as possible his intuitive selections by the knowledge that such selections are of necessity composed of length comparisons in pairs. That all the space of his subject is of equal value and its interest is always due to contrast of length or rather comparison of two lengths. With this knowledge he will direct his observations to the conscious (as far as possible) selection of length comparisons and by so doing will have data which is of direct utility in picture construction.

The usual methods of painting exhibit an insensitivity which is disagreeable. The total disregard for drawing and the intense concentration on mirror-like reflection remove nearly all painting from the sphere of taste.

They are repellent as a wooden bed.

To escape this heritage a taste for drawing or material must be cultivated so that we may judge directly what we are seeing.

The drawing of the past had as intent, illusion. Because of this it is subvisual and not operative in the spatial sense.

Notebook pages, 1932.

Stuart Davis

Gloucester, 1933

Visual space is regarded as an alternation of black and white particles in a gray medium. The gray medium has no shape. The gray medium is only understandable to us when we arbitrarily impose on its discreteness or particularity.

Thus our concept of form is a picture of the character of our own understanding.

We arbitrarily define where there is no definition. We define in terms of triangular ratios.

We are not able to solve this complex.

The concept of a single direction automatically involves three. Thus, if we say the direction is East we are comparing it with a North and the angle between the two is the third direction. Thus, the triangle is the unit of the concept of direction.

I want you to get some idea of the facts (physical) of painting. By physical facts I do not mean permanency of colors. By physical facts I mean the two-dimensional division of the surface on which you work. I mean the cultivation of the ability to quickly disassociate the associational and relative values of any subject from its two dimensional structural reality. This is necessary because your picture is a two-dimensional reality at all points of its conception, execution and finish, and to consider it in any other manner is to deal in fantasy.

Also, I have not a mathematical formula for dealing with this two-dimensional space expression because I have never felt that it was important. I have always felt it to be much more important to simply cultivate the sense of two-dimensional space emotionally.

We know that Giotto laid out his walls mathematically as recorded by Cennino Cennini, but whether he carried this ratio beyond the primary divisions is not stated. There must be no preconceived idea of what a picture is to look like. For example, the labeling of Cubism as experimental by numerous persons means nothing more than [that] they find the Cubist pictures unlike some other type of picture they have in mind. Therefore, give your picture a chance. Don't be too sure it is bad, when you may have merely noted its failure to correspond with some preconceived type. Your failure may exceed in interest the ideal you failed to achieve.

It is impossible ever to know what makes a picture good. We can know only that its execution is clear or confused. We may understand it in terms of a geometric or mathematical parallel and [on] such appraisal of our emotion is the painting itself.

Therefore we start without a preconceived emotion. The emotion is in us. We can never understand it, so we forget it. We devote our attention to things we can understand. Things that we can measure. To understand anything we must arbitrarily define or limit it. In painting, such definition consists of saying, this space starts here and stops there, and as it is easy to visualize a defined space as a square, we can mentally compare the irregular enclosed space of our subject with a square of the same size and more easily measure its character in this comparative way.

All ideas of "painting quality," "volume," "third dimension" are names of subject matter and are not helpful in increasing the sense of picture reality.

Visualize the subject objectively in terms of sequential area alternations (black and white) but in doing this it is necessary to visualize the abstract relations thus obtained as natural visual forms of common experience. Or, in other words, a group of these abstract area alternations are made to create an associational form, which, however, may not be the form from which it is drawn.

Visualize abstract area groups which have analogy to simple visual naturalism.

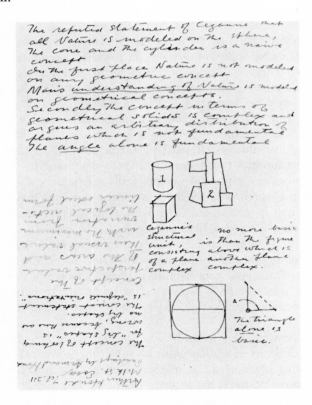

Daybook page, *ca.* 1933.

Stuart Davis

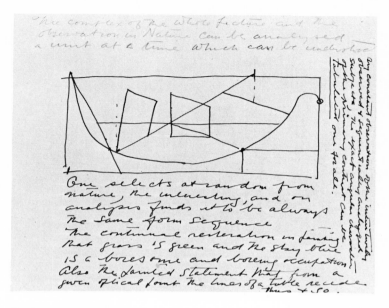

The complex of the whole picture and the observation in Nature can be analysed a unit at a time which can be understood

One selects at random from
nature, the interesting, and on
analysis finds it to be always
the same form sequence
The continual reiteration in painting
that grass is green and the sky blue
is a boresome and boreing occupation
Also the labored statement that from a
given optical point the lines of a table recede
thus ↗ ↘ ↘.

Daybook pages, *ca.* 1933.

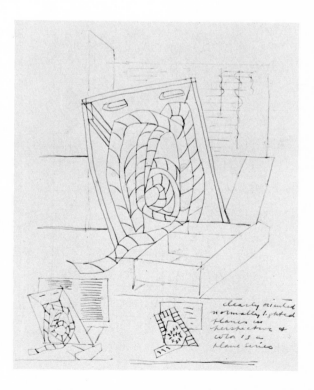

clearly outlined
normally lighted
planes in
perspective &
who is a
plane series

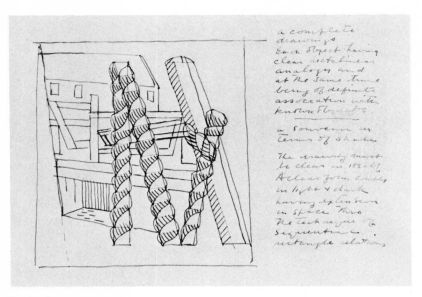

Daybook page, *ca.* 1933.

Daybook page, *ca.* 1938.

Stuart Davis

Reality in art is composed of shapes and colors.

The artist must direct himself consciously to manipulate these objective elements.

Shapes and colors are of two kinds:

Objective	1. Local shapes and space shapes
and	
Subjective	2. Local colors and space colors

The sense of reality which the artist has only exists in terms of shapes and colors.

Then there is the geometric shape and color of the two dimensional medium of painting itself.

The local and space shapes and colors of perception are evaluated in terms of the geometric shapes and colors of the medium of expression. Therefore, what the artist is concerned about is the observation and record of shape and color by means of an ideal shape and color scale.

The point must be made here that the observations of the artist are not concerned with the ideal shape and color scale but with the shapes and colors of objective and subjective experience.

Thus, the Meaning of art does not lie in the ideal scale even though it is always by manipulation of the scale that the expression of reality is achieved.

The meaningful positions of the geometric scale are only accomplished by first observing a position of local and space objects and colors to which the geometric shapes and colors are then made to correspond. (It should be noted here that sometimes an aimless manipulation of geometric elements may result in a meaningful design. But, again, it only becomes meaningful when it refers to something outside itself.)

It therefore becomes established that the artist is always drawing and composing shapes and colors which refer to natural environment. Recognition of this one point alone does away with a lot of mysticism about art. Then all of these local and space objects and colors have their ideological meaning too.

By ideological meaning I mean values other than physical, values having political, social, entertainment significance. This ideological content is present in all art. It is the "story" in the moral or didactic picture. It is the "mood" in the modern art of individual expression.

Art, then, is a triple unity of geometric form, objective form, and ideological form. With the knowledge of the reality and meaning of art the artist can approach his problem objectively. He can systematically record by going to nature without prejudice and selecting the shapes and colors of which its character is made. Second, he can consciously select the suitable objects associated with a purposeful idea and then construct them in their proper shapes and colors. Third, he can manipulate geometric space experimentally with the hope of finding new synthetic forms.

Stuart Davis

||| murals

Mural for the Hall of Communications, New York World's Fair (working notes and diagrams) (1939)
Stuart Davis

World's Fair Mural

Length	136 feet or 1632″
Width	44 feet or 528″

Scale of drawing 1 inch to 54.4″

30″ × 9.75″

Width of basic line in final mural
3.4″

1/8/39

Content and Form

1. Quality of a flat surface decorated by hand
2. A real three-dimensional space harmony
3. Ideological direction is spatial study of the principal forms connected with the historical development of the various branches of communication.
4. The Social Expression is to create a unified emotional response to the physical aspects of a specific group of objects as perceived through the mood of the artist.

   The story of the historical development of the means of communication is the story of the mechanical and electrical objectification [of] the human eye, ear, voice, and bodily motion.
   This objectification process has taken the following basic forms:

Organized Speech—Language
Writing and Printing
Drawing and Painting
Camera and Motion Picture
Television—Telegraph
Song and Music
Telephone—Radio
Phonograph

Therefore the composition should be composed of the forms of the various apparati which constitute this objectification.

1. *Speech—Language*
   the human mouth
   shouts
   speaking trumpet

megaphone
post horn

2. *Writing—Printing*
   the human eye
   written and typed words
   the alphabet, ancient and modern
   newspapers, books

3. *Drawing and Painting*
   the human eye
   brushes, easel, palette, pencil

4. *Camera*
   the human eye
   film
   the sun
   artificial light

5. *Sound Motion Picture*
   the human eye and ear
   the cameras
   arc lights
   electric switches
   the written script, letters
   the phono-disc
   the loud speaker
   the movie projector
   the film

6. *Television*
   the eye (and ear)
   special lights
   the scanning disc
   the electric eye
   infra-red ray

7. *Telegraph*
   the eye
   printing—type
   telegraph blank
   ticker tape
   telegraph key

8. *Song and Music*
   mouth and ear
   musical instruments
   bars and notes

9. *Telephone*
   mouth and ear
   electric robot and electric ear (A.T.&T.)
   telephone instruments
   scrambled words
   teletype—sound vibrations on a rod or wire

Stuart Davis

weather charts
news—headlines
teletype tape
10. *Radio*
the ear
spark coil
antenna
directional antenna—S.O.S.
radio waves
vacuum tube
radio receivers
microphone
music
11. *Phonograph*
the ear
phonograph records
discs
dictograph
12. *Postal Service*
the eye
post-horn
stamps
letter box
pigeons
pony express
stage coach
post cancellation
mail bags
airplane
13. *The Hand*
the eye
semaphore
hand language—signs
smoke signals

History of Communication is mechanical objectification of the human Eye, Ear, Voice, and Hand.

Voice—Ear

Human Sounds
Words
Language
Drum telegraph
Hilltop telegraph by shouting
Whistling telegraph
Letters on hilltop seen by telescope

Telegraph
Speaking trumpet
Megaphone
Telephone
Telephone cable
Telephone, typewriter, or teletype,
    police, weather, news
Overseas phone
Scrambled sounds
Electric robot talks to electric ear (see A.T.&T.)
Wireless telegraphy
Spark coil
Antenna—directional antenna
S.O.S.
Radio waves
Vacuum tube
Commercial broadcasting
Sound movies

Speech—Sound
Words—Language

Drawing
Sign language
Gesture signs
Beacon fires (King Agamemnon)
Smoke column signals (Indian)
Drum telegraph
Hilltop telegraph by shouting
Whistling telegraph
Sun reflected from shields telegraph
Men in sight of each other who communicate by change of position of
    arms, legs, body
Semaphore
Pigeon messages

Torch as a symbol of war
Palm or olive branch as symbol of peace
Rose symbol of love
Alphabet (pictures represent syllables or sounds)

Postal service
Runners
Donkeys or horses in relay
Camels
Messages on clay tablets
Papyrus
Parchment
Rag paper (12th-century Europe)

Stuart Davis

Roman postal system of government
Early ink has to be used with brush
Postal communication stopped in Middle Ages
Revived in Renaissance
German "butcher post"
Cattle merchants' "post horn"
Paris, house-to-house mail service 1635 A.D.

Government control of post
Queen Elizabeth in 1591
Cromwell in 1657
Centralized post offices and official postmen
Penny post established in London 1680
4 to 8 deliveries a day in London
1711 Post Office Act coordinated postal service between England, Scotland
    and colonies
Stage coach service 1800
Post horn still in use
Pillar type of mail box
Pneumatic tubes
Stilt walkers delivered mail in second-story windows in S.W. France
Letters and newspapers only were carried but in 1848 a book post was
    established in England to aid education

Post card—Austria 1869

Postman in 17th-century America was
    a servant
    a friend
    a merchant
    a peddlar
    Indians
    sea captains
First established post service was in Massachusetts in 1638

Robberies frequent

1794 U.S. Post Office Act passed
Low rates to combat bootlegging
Fastest delivery
New roads and post offices
A social service and not a profit plan
Pillar boxes and drop boxes
Pony express
Finally outmoded by Overland Telegraph Co. in 1862

Railroad mail coaches
Mail bags
Parcel Post international 1875

Parcel Post in U.S. 1912
Auto Mail service 1914
Air Mail service 1911

Floor trucks
chutes and floor wells
pneumatic tubes
dog sleds
steam and electric trams, speed boats, airplanes
postmarks, stamps
400 years from first crude ideograms to the high-speed written idea of
    today

Electricity

Thales discovered magnetic amber but *visual* telegraph was developed first
Then the telescope allowed development of the semaphore
Letters on hilltop seen by telescope
Claude Chappe semaphore 1791
Bar of wood with 2 wings produced 192 signals
33 signals a minute
Early electric apparati
All early forms of electric telegraph
Cables
Ticker system (Commercial news)
Automatic telegraph typewriter

Telephone

Speaking trumpet
Megaphone

Vibrations of rod, string, wire carry sound further than the air
Word "telephone" in use by 1796 came from Greek meaning the trans-
    mission of sound by trumpets

Human Ear—the spoken word
1st private phone 1877
also news dispatches
and 1st public exchange
P.O. took over trunk system in 1892
Telephone cable
Telephone, typewriter (teletype) connected by electricity to another so
    that typing on one produces same message on the other, either on tape
    or stationery
Used by police departments
Weather reports—Department of Commerce
Newspapers

Press Associations

Teletype has 12,000 subscribers who can write directly to each other just as you can call anyone on the phone

Extensive telephone use has cut down ruralism to 44% in U.S.

Overseas telephone has a device which translates words in unintelligible sounds and insures privacy. It is put back in proper order at its destination

Electrical robot talking to electric ear is being installed with new transmitter for new type of telephone hand sets

Wireless Telegraphy

Spark from coil set up currents in another coil which traveled with the speed of light

These waves could be reflected by metal mirrors and focused by lenses of pitch. Unlike light waves they made no impression on the eye

Aerial mast or antenna

Spark gap—2 metal balls
   glass plate condensers
   transformers

Ships equipped with wireless

SOS

Directional antenna (fog)

Underwater sound signals

Radio beacons

Radio waves travel in circles

Crest of one wave to another is the wave length

Commercial broadcasting

Advertisement

Music

Sports

Hygiene

Weather

Politics

News

Television

Pictures and writing by wireless

Selerium is electric eye

The human eye

The photo electric cell and thermionic valve amplifier

Infra-red rays see through fog

Printing

Written public announcements

1st published newspaper in Germany 1609

Governments of 17th and 18th centuries frowned on these newspapers because they threatened their authority

Free speech—democracy—as a result of mechanical development

Development of the press was slow because of this

Books
Alexandrian scribes
Medieval copyists
Babylonian seals
Movable type—China—1050
Tin type—1314
Type-setting machine, wooden type
Printed book popular first in Germany by 1700
Printing press 1424
Cylinder press 1812
Electrotype
Automatic folder
Rapid printing brought new interest in literary and art circles
Pocket magazines
Hand bills

Increased speed of communication in radio, airplane, streamlined auto, railway engines, etc., created lively spirit in printing

Letters

Printing—relief
  offset
  gravure
Lithography—parent of offset

Pictures

Advertising art
The camera
Use of pictures dependent on technical development in engraving and printing
Positive photostat print of drawing facilitates speed in development of the drawing by changes, etc.
Sheets of cellophane used in animated cartoons
Vacuum tubes
Moving picture (camera)
Magic lantern
Film
Sound movies

Stuart Davis

<table>
<tr><td>

Data lacking

1. Postal Service
   more material needed

2. Printed Word
   modern printing Machinery
   old fashioned printing machinery
   Type faces

3. Telegraph
   more material needed

4. Telephone
   ~~Telephone poles, wires, & insulators.~~

5. Motion Picture
   Film strips

6. Radio

7. Television

</td><td>

Data on hand

Eye	Weather instruments
Ear	Letters
Mouth	Chinese
Hand	Babylonian
Signal Flags	Egyptian
Mechanical Semaphore	English
Flag Semaphore	Printing
Movie "Shots"	Newspapers
Parade torches	Books
Smoke Signal	Post Office
Flares and Smoke	Mail Bags
Stream lined autos	Rural Mail Boxes
Auto License Plates	Pigeons
Stream lined train	Mail Coach
Airplane	Radio
Drum telegraphic	Circuit diagrams
(See african drum records catal.)	Microphones
Siren	Parabolic mike
Radio Loud Speaker	Television cameras
Phonograph + Disc	Panels
Musical instruments.	Antenna Towers
	Sound Movies
	Winding Spools
	Projector
	Flash lights
	Telephone
	Earphones Panels
	Early Telephone Sets
	Modern
	Switches
	Antenna Towers

</td></tr>
</table>

1/9/39

Procedure in Construction of World's Fair Mural

1. Collection of factual visual material
2. Theoretical formulation of function, character, and technique of mural
3. Selection of individual elements, from aesthetic standpoint, which are to be included in the design
4. Aesthetic designing of these elements
5. Inductive composition of these designs to produce new space objects

1/9/39

This mural must incorporate all the objective aesthetic principles which I use in the architecture of an easel painting. These are:

1. The real third-dimensional nature of the medium
2. Local objects and space objects such as

objects in perspective
objects on a single plane isolated
objects and their space relations
geometric objects and free objects

3. The principle of the discontinuous nature of perception, which involves the limitation to one relation at a time
4. Each relation must be visualized completely as
    1—real extension in two-dimensional space
    2—real extension in tone-color space
    3—as a geometric object
    4—as a free object
5. Composition

Can develop deductively or inductively. That is, the nature of the parts can be determined by a space-object which is determined geometrically

or

The nature of the geometric space-object can be determined by the accumulation of the individual parts.

In practice, both of these methods work dialectically to produce the end product which is a unity of opposites.

This mural has an ideological content which dramatizes the development of communication between men. Such a theme can be expressed in many ways and with different scopes.

In this case the requirement is to express the idea in a single panel in a decorative form.

The technical information relating to the idea is supplied by other mediums in the same building.

The function of this mural then is concerned only with the aesthetics of the subject. It must convey to the spectator a feeling or a mood which will be remembered by [him] as beautiful or emotionally pleasant and stimulating. In recalling this mural the spectator will not remember dates, costumes, materials of construction, correct historical sequence, or factual information; but he will have a pleasant and stimulating recollection of shape-objects in space in relation to each other.

The value of this kind of expression to the communication industries is that it implants the consciousness of their value on the plane of aesthetics in addition to the other planes of consciousness which have been impressed by more appropriate means.

A comparison of the function of this mural may be made with the theme music of the World's Fair itself.

This music in no sense contains nor expresses the multiple facts or significance of the World's Fair. All those aspects are expressed in a

Stuart Davis

thousand other ways, but there is yet a good reason to have an official theme-music. It is something simple that can be remembered in association with all the other experiences which the visitor to the fair will recall.

The same can be said of the official colors of the fair. They do not contain any factual expression of the aims and meaning of the fair but they are a symbol of it to which the factual memories are attached.

Therefore, in designing this mural the only thing to work toward is a personally felt design which has a real physical variety of space, conceived around the objective forms associated with the mechanical extension of the senses of sight, hearing, and voice of man; which is the history of the growth of the means of communication.

1/10/39

This mural has a specific character, a specific intention.

It is important to know precisely what this character or quality is so that one can describe what it is and what it is not.

First of all it is a work of Art. The word "Art" is used in the sense in which it refers to "Fine Arts."

Now "Fine Arts" also requires definition.

"Fine Art" means a work which is beautiful and its beauty is the result of the physical order of the elements within the work of Art. This means that a work of Art is complete in itself. It is an end in itself and not a spur to action but to contemplation.

One thinks of nothing in a work except the regularity and variety of the different relations in it.

The pleasure one derives from varieties is an end in itself. It is a pleasure which comes from the experience of order and complete understanding of a specific aspect of nature.

The quality which is common to all works of Fine Art throughout history is the existence of a real physical order in the space of the material of expression. This doesn't mean that there is some single kind of order which is the real "Art order."

Every Art order is different. "Art order" and "real physical order" are synonymous. The work of real Art expresses nature by analogy not similitude.

So this mural whose subject matter is the development of the means of communication through the ages, can only be a work of Art by my consciousness of what a work of art is and my purpose to make a work of Art instead of a work of information.

Therefore I will this mural to be a work of Art made of spatial elements associated with Communications. I will it to be simple and easy to remember. Its tone-contrast is limited to white on black. The black is basic.

The design must be placed on this huge space as though it were a sketch on a sheet of typewriting paper. Mechanical lines should be avoided.

The dialectic of its creation should be studied. The alternation of the deductive (geometric) method, and the inductive method must be properly played against each other.

The electric globe becomes a circle and the circle becomes an electric globe again, but a changed one.

Objects are produced, visually, by the movement of color through space. Therefore, an intuitive color concept is at the same time a concept of form.

Form and color are a unit. In the case of this mural the pre-conception of a black ground with white lines on it automatically is an idea of a certain kind of space.

The raw material of the subject matter must be looked at with relation to these limitations. Therefore this mural will represent the courage and simplicity of an artist who has contemplated certain historical forms.

Its social message is one that any person would like to be able to say for himself. It is the expression of a digestion of chaos and its assimilation in personal terms. Thus, it is an expression and affirmation of the rightness of personality and the center of truth in man's own self.

1/15/39

A real interval harmony.

An idea in intervals (through creative leaps). This involves awareness of:

1. The tone contrast being used
2. The spatial "common sense" balance of what is drawn as a whole
3. The direction, length and geo-local character of the line used
4. The area which the line defines
5. The character of the object drawn
      A—Perspective space-object
      B—Local plane-space object
      C—Super loco-space objects
6. One relation at a time
7. The size-shape, tone-intervals
8. Inductive and deductive compositional dialectic
9. Visual fantasy is not out of place

The order of art is a topographical order which involves:
Direction—Position
Length—Size

Shape
Tone

1/18/39
Space
Perspective Objects
Local Objects
Both are composed of unit areas which make up the object by their

1. Direction-Position
2. Length-Size
3. Shape (imaginative)
4. Tone (contrast)

The objects are size-shape-tone objects.
They have real two-dimensional reality.
They express real three-dimensional reality.
The construction of objects is a dialectic process alternating between the inductive and deductive system.

1/20/39
Point One
There *is* an aesthetic order as opposed to a non-aesthetic order.
Point Two
There *is* a right and a rational way to approach the composition of an aesthetic work.

In composing a picture each step of development is dependent on visualization of a specific set of directions, sizes, shapes and tones, which represent the new object. This visualization is then related visually to the already existing adjacent object. The super-space shapes develop inductively in this way.

Notes

January 25, 1939
The subject matter of art in painting consists of local objects in space.

The expression of this universal subject matter is achieved through graphic symbols which occupy a real two-dimensional space. Recognition of this fact is crucial to the creation of Art. Art is a real topographical order in two dimensions. This order is not an ideal order. It is always a unique and concrete sequence. The local objects in space of nature are transformed in Art to conform to the nature of the medium of expression. In painting this means that an analysis of the objects of nature is made in terms of:

1. Position—Direction
2. Length—Size
3. Shape
4. Tone Contrast

The artist must visualize the objects he wants to draw in the terms outlined above. These objects are of two kinds:

1. Local object shapes
2. Planes in perspective

In each case when he thinks of an object he must think of it in relation to the space-division that already exists on his canvas. If no line has been drawn, then the geometric rectangle of the canvas must be regarded as the existing space division. Then the object which he is about to draw must be regarded as to:

1. Position—Direction
2. Length—Size
3. Shape
4. Tone Contrast

in relation to the already existing objects.

With the drawing and placing of the new object in the composition, a series of new relations is set up which must be regarded as a new space-object. In this entire procedure it is necessary to use the concept of the "minimum interval." This concept is the basis of Art. A minimum interval is the least degree of:

1. Angular Variation
2. Length
3. Tone Contrast

which is visually effective in the scale of the work. This minimum interval is not an ideal concept. Rather it is a concrete concept of a geometric object having all the basic qualities of any other object.

In regard to this minimum interval it is necessary to see it in relation to the spaces which it establishes—above, below, and to right and left —in the existing composition. The shapes which a minimum interval leaves after it has been drawn are a part of the interval itself and must be so regarded.

Drawings and paintings which are not Art have no "social content" as Art. The social content of Art is always simply Art itself. The social meaning of Art consists at all times of an affirmation of the joy felt in the successful resolution of a problem. This expression has social meaning because it gives concrete proof of the possibility of establishing order in certain aspects of man's relation to Nature. Such expression is a moral force and provides courage for life to those who experience it.

Illustrations, cartoons, story-telling murals, etc. are not Art because, in the last analysis, they do not even try to be. Their function is not to establish certain concrete relations in a given medium, but rather to stimulate action in other fields.

The social content of these types of expression is not a moral force.

1/30/39

There is a definite line between Art and Non-Art. It is necessary to establish this fact so that the use of the term "Art" can have a precise meaning.

In general, the term "Art" is used to describe all sorts of dissimilar qualities. If a precise meaning be assigned to the term "Art" it will also allow the development of proper terms to denominate [sic] the various other different qualities which are now loosely and erroneously termed "Art."

The precise meaning of the term "Art" is generally understood by artists and critics, but a verbal definition of its limits that is satisfactory has not been made.

Such a definition, to be adequate, must be broad enough to include all the manifestations which occur on the side of the line which distinguishes Art from Non-Art.

Clive Bell's description of the quality which is common to all Art as "Significant Form" has truth in it, but it is too vague to have much value. When an informed person says that a work is "artistic" or "good Art" they are describing a definite kind of reaction as opposed to other kinds of reaction. For example, they do not mean that they have just had an experience which enlarges their mathematical knowledge. Nor has their fund of information about biology, botany, chemistry, domestic science, economics, politics, or athletics been increased. When they say that a certain work is "Art" they mean just one thing and that is an experience of a special kind to which they give the name "Art."

Now it is true that this experience will react on and possibly stimulate experiences in other fields such as economics, politics, etc., but in the present discussion this fact is beside the point, because we are not trying to define the social relations of Art but to define Art itself.

Every human action has repercussions in other human actions but the effect of an action on another action is not the measure of value for the initial act, in all cases.

For example, the execution of a work of art in sculpture may be made to decorate a building which is later found to be unsafe for human occupation. Now the social relation in which this sculpture functions is bad and the building is condemned and the work of art along with it. At this point the sculptor can say that this experience has made it clear to him that the social conditions which allowed the construction of the unsafe building are intolerable. He can say, from now on I am going to devote my Art to the purpose of pointing out to people the horrible conditions which made this bad situation. To that end he proceeds to make works which convey certain information but which do not convey an Art experience. Does this mean then that the sculptor is a bad artist? Yes, he is a bad artist. But does it also mean that his work is valueless. No, because his work may become a factor in making the changes necessary to improve those bad social conditions. Therefore, his work has genuine social value, but, at the same time, it is not Art. Now suppose, on the other hand, that when the building with his sculptural decoration was destroyed the artist had been unmoved by the social conditions which led to the destruction. His attitude toward Art remained unchanged and he continued to make genuine Art without reference to any specific and immediate social problem. Would he then be a bad artist? No he would continue to be a good artist. Or would his work be devoid of social content? Certainly not, because the creation of Art itself is a positive and progressive social value. To denominate works which have an immediate social, political, or economic reference as "social content" Art is a mistake. First, it implies that Art without this immediate reference is devoid of "social content." Second, to call a work which does not have the basic intention of being a work of Art but instead of being a source of information for action, outside the field of art, to call such a work "Art" is to mislead and confuse issues. The "Social content in Art" propaganda by the cultural front of the left has been guilty of this error. At the same time is it possible for a work of art to be Art and also refer to immediate events. But the two qualities are definitely separate. If such a work is preserved by future generations it will be because of its Art content, not its social content. An example of this would be the work of El Greco, whose pictures are valuable today because of their Art without the least reference to their religious symbolism. This statement may be objected to in the following way. It will be said that contemporary admiration for El Greco on the basis of the isolation of his form from his content is a perversion and that such appreciation is one-sided and does not do justice to the full meaning of his art. But I do not accept this objection for the simple reason that it is metaphysical. It denies the existence of an isolated entity. It affirms the existence of the whole and implies the impossibility of knowledge of any part of that. Of course the expounders of this theory do not act on it, precisely because it is impossible to do so. That is why

Stuart Davis

I call the theory metaphysical. In practice they make arbitrary limits and isolations like everybody else but they refuse others the same right.

This is the theory of totalitarianism, and since it is a false theory, its products must be bad. The dogmas of dialectical materialism which assume the revolutionary development of reality and the concept of the unity of opposites and the change of an isolate into its opposite do not in any sense lead to the conclusions of the "social content in art" school of thought. That conclusion is purely political and expedient in character and for the sake of honesty should be so recognized. In fact, the assertion that the works of art of the past cannot be appreciated without full consideration of these social relations is in itself a denial of the theory of dialectical materialism. This is so because it denies motion in the social relations of Art. The contemporary function of a work of Art may rest heavily on qualities in it which are extraneous to its Art quality. The music of Bach and the painting of El Greco would be examples of this observation. These men made their living by references in their art to matters of immediate social import. That was a limitation in the development of the historical epoch in which they lived. The people of that time were moved by the art of Bach and El Greco and referred its meaning to religion. Today, because we are more civilized, because the productive forces of modern industrial society are so much greater, because people have so much more material and cultural wealth at their disposal, we are able to appreciate the profound order of the physical structure of these art works and to study it objectively. We study these works without reference to any other field of action except Art itself.

To argue that this is the attitude of "formalism" or an arbitrary separation of form and content is false because it implies a non-material reality. It implies that the physical nature of these works of Art is unique to their specific social reference to their own time, and that for the work to have meaning both the form and the content of social relations must be understood. But this implied assertion is the very acme of a static concept of reality and therefore anti-dialectical. It means that each form-content unit is eternal and that its meaning does not change. If this were true we would never have heard of Bach or El Greco. But we know it is not true, because while people interested in Art have long since ceased to care about the religious aspects of this work, they care more today about its Art aspects than at any previous time in history.

This does not mean that the student of Art has become anti-social in his attitude toward it. On the contrary, it means that the developing productive forces with their concomitant political form of democracy have enormously enlarged the scope of man's understanding. Instead of seeing in the forms of the past merely a simple form-content relation of Art-Religion, we are able, through our concept of democratic individuality, to see the Art-Individual relation. We are able to appreciate the special personal interests and struggles of the artist, and through that knowledge we gain courage and strength to meet our own. And further, if the meaning of the works of Bach and El Greco was restricted to their form-content relation of Art-Religion there would be no reason for our interest in them because religion is not our concern today. Therefore, it can only mean that the formal relations of these works have another content which continues to have special meaning for us and this content can only be Art. So now we are brought directly to the question, what is Art as distinguished from Non-Art. First, it must be recognized that Art is one of the natural functions of man like eating and sleeping. We know this is so because people of all times and places have made Art. All attempts to describe it as a perversion of some other function such as play, sex, social purpose, are unnecessary and foolish because play, sex, social purpose, etc., are also natural functions of man and are carried on by all people at all times just as Art is carried on. One might as well say that eating is a perversion of the sex instinct. No, Art is not a perversion of, nor an escape from any other function, it is a natural action and sufficient unto itself. It satisfies no appetite but the appetite for Art. The appetite which Art satisfies is the hunger for physical stability in the space of the three-dimensional world. It is the product of real experience in moving through space, by walking, seeing, touching, hearing, and the sense of reality which these experiences bring. No expression which does not satisfy the sense of three-dimensional spatial reality is ever regarded as a work of art by people who have the capacity to experience it. In contemporary swing parlance, it is "solid." Color, light, texture, sound, logic, are all attributes of the spatial sense, and thus the mediums through which it can be expressed include division of a two-dimensional surface, division of a three-dimensional block, division of a sound-time-space, division of a space bounded by logical ideas. But in every case the emotion which is fed by the expression is founded on the experience of the ground under our feet and movement toward a horizon. If it be objected at this point that since there are an infinite number of space experiences, and therefore an infinite number of expressions based on them, and therefore that the definition leaves us without any measure of Art as opposed to Non-Art, I will have to explain further.

A real expression of spatial experience which is called Art only has objective existence through the ordered arrangement of some material such as drawing, sculpture, music, literature. Each of these materials has spatial limitations and characteristics of its own which are different [from] the spatial experiences which are expressed through them. Now expressions can and are made in these materials which are not Art and the reason they are not is because the expressor has not tried or has failed to translate a real spatial experience into terms of real space of the material of expression. Works which are not Art can stimulate you by some clue to take action in some field outside Art, but they never record a spatial experience which stimulates you into seeking new experiences in the field of Art. A political cartoon, a commercial ad, a popular song, or a short story, are usually not Art, but this in no sense means that they do not often fulfill a useful public function. My effort here is not to belittle or to suppress Non-Art but to make a clear distinction between it and Art. Further, it is to call attention to the real social content of Art in contradiction to the false "social content in Art" propaganda which prevails and which is nothing but a plea for Non-Art. In considering progressive social consciousness it is valuable to consider once in a while the fact that its purpose is the betterment of man's standard of living. And an essential part of such betterment in any civilized society is the preservation and development of Art expression. If we are to struggle consciously for social betterment through political, social, and cultural means, we must give proof of our sincerity by preserving the forms of social values in the struggle. If the only means of defeating barbarism or totalitarianism is to become barbarians ourselves, then what guarantee can be given that social betterment of the standard of living will be achieved? Specifically, if to defeat Fascist aggression we must abandon our individual liberties and submit to totalitarian regulation, then let it be frankly stated. Let it be frankly said that Art, Science, and Morals, must be oriented toward the collective security and that individual freedom is at an end, but do not, as is now the case, make propaganda to make it seem that all vital human activity is the product of collective action and that all individual experiment and imaginative projection is anti-social and escapist. Artists today who are struggling under the slogan, "For Peace, Democracy, and Cultural Progress," must not be led into considering these phrases in terms of their opposites, namely, War, Totalitarianism, and Cultural Reaction, because this is the real slogan of Fascism. Freedom of expression in the Federal Art Project must be matched by freedom of expression in all programs for progress. A real work of Art is just as valuable socially today as at any other time and the right to make real Art is worth fighting for. The right to be an artist free from service to any other social function is as much a right under democracy as the right to unionization and collective bargaining for better living conditions. Art cannot develop merely on government support unless the artists who are supported have a clear concept of the meaning of Art. We need more Art production, more Art consumption, through government support, but we also need conscious improvement of the quality of that Art, and this cannot be achieved by the present "social content" attitude of the artists' organizations.

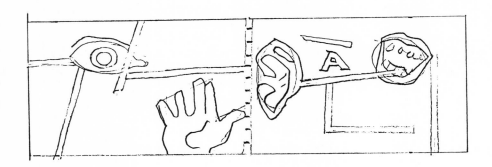

The creative, concrete space-shapes

The Size-Shape-Tone of the Concrete relations

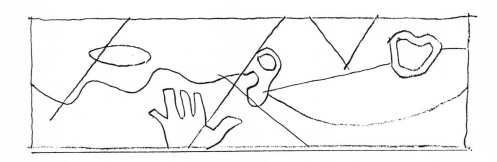

```
          .3235          3.2 × 10
136 / 44.00 00
 3    408
408   ────
180   320
      272
      ────
      480
      408
      ────
       720
```

Stuart Davis

The by concrete shapes are of necessity few
in number and a decision about their
character can be made quickly.

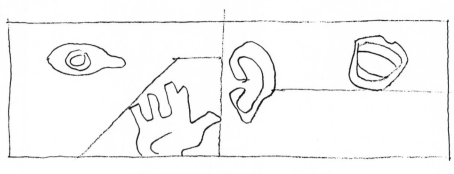

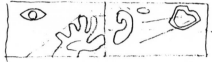

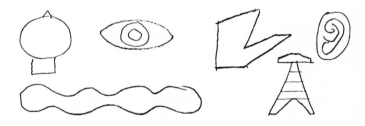

The areas are simple at all times
On the simplest relations they always describe
either, a perspective object or a local object
This is done by   The relations of

not a series of impressionistic
sketches, but a simple
spatial relation with
drastic symbolic re-
duction.

position
size
shape
tone
of the unit area

The symbolism of this mural can be just
as simple and arbitrary as you choose
to make it. Academic art uses obscure symbols.

Mural for Studio B, WNYC (working notes) (1939)
Stuart Davis

3/23/39

My mural painting in Studio B of WNYC is painted in a style which is popularly called, "abstract painting." It represents a series of formal relations which are identified with musical instruments, radio antenna, ether waves, operators panel, electrical symbols, etc. These various elements are presented in an imaginative rather than a factual relationship. It has been my intention to place these various elements into juxtaposition with each other in a way which one often does in remembering a scene or event and the incidents relating to it. In remembering a scene, for example, certain aspects of it are exaggerated and others are suppressed. The scene is rearranged and recomposed according to the importance and meaning which the different elements have had for the spectator. This process of ideological composition is a common experience with everyone. The artist always does it in creating his pictures. In other words we do not simply reflect the things we see, like a mirror, but we compare them, in our ideas and emotions, with things we have seen before and with things we hope to see. This is what I have done in my mural. I have taken elements relating to radio and composed them in a harmonious design of shape, color, and direction. The result is a visual decoration which creates a mood in the spectator, just as a piece of music creates a mood, instead of giving some kind of factual information or instruction.

A mural painting has to be seen over and over again. It is usually a permanent part of the architecture of the building. If it simply tells a story, such as who discovered the radio wave and the date of its discovery; or if it is simply a scene showing a bird's-eye view of a radio station, for example, then its message or particular viewpoint, once learned, is likely to lose its interest because the spectator knows it all by heart. He has no reason to look at it any longer. But if the mural represents a real harmony of color-space conceived [by] an artist then its useful function to stimulate interest in the spectator is certain to continue for a long time. This is so because the story which the work of art tells comes from experiences in the artist which are deep and do not only refer to a single and passing experience.

We listen to the music of Bach today, for example, hundreds of years after its composition, with undiminished interest. Certainly our reactions to it are not exactly the same as those who heard it played in his own day. And certainly some of its musical meaning had a different significance for his contemporaries than they do for us. But there is a meaning in it which transcends different times and different ways of life. There is nothing abstract or unworldly about this meaning. It is very concrete and real and our interest and reaction to it is proof of its very direct relevance to our own lives and interests today.

This subject matter of art which holds our interest beyond the immediate meaning of the elements which make it up is based on experiences which are common to everyone. There is no aristocracy of artists. Everyone is an artist and the great artists of history, who were also human beings, are the proof of this. Their work is the testimony which proves that human beings are artists.

The subject matter of art is always the same in the general sense. In the particular sense it is never the same. The subject matter which is common to all works of art is constructive order and the achievement of it in the material of expression. A painting, for example, is a real three-dimensional space, just as sculpture is. It is composed of real two-dimensional areas, real directional motions, and real tone-color contrasts which advance and retire in the third dimension. There is nothing obscure or difficult to understand about this because it is a type of experience which is common to everyone everyday. When we walk in the street we experience the sensations of moving directionally, defining two-dimensional areas and making optical adjustments to tone-color contrasts. The act of walking, whatever else it may be is also the act of drawing and painting. If in the act of walking we fail to make a constructive, ordered plan in the space we traverse it is soon brought to our attention by a collision of some kind. So in painting the artist who fails to create a real, constructive, and potentially measurable order on his canvas fails to produce a work of art. There are, of course, many other kinds of spatial experience besides walking, but that serves as an example. When we react to a work of art in painting we are reacting to a real three-dimensional order in space which reflects in some part our own experience as people moving in space.

This reaction, it must be noted, is basically independent of the particular objects which are shown in the painting. These objects may be people, landscapes, buildings or machinery, or simple geometric forms, but in every case our first demand of a work of art is that the space it occupies by its three-dimensional definition be a constructively ordered space. If the picture be only some geometric shapes and yet we feel in it an affirmation of constructive order, we are satisfied. If, on the other hand, the picture represents some great historical event and does not have a real constructive order in its definition, we reject it in spite of the importance of the events it portrays. The history of art proves this statement.

A genuine work of art has eternal value because its basic subject matter, constructive order, has eternal value.

Mural, *Allée,* for Drake University (statement and diagram) (1955)   *Stuart Davis*

Allée is a French word meaning an alley or long vista. It is a long painting. Its length over-powered my studio and made a deep impression on my mind. Also, there is another French word with the same sound which means "go." I like this association. I like the variety, the animation, the vigorous spirit which is part of college life. This feeling of energy and vigor was in my mind during the painting of the mural.

Following my first visit to the Drake campus, I carried back to my studio a strong impression of the simplicity and directness of the architecture. I set out to make the mural harmonize with the room. The composition of the mural is vigorous in keeping with its surroundings. The figures in the mural are severely rectilinear. I did not clutter it up with detail, yet there is considerable variety of size and positional relationships.

I remembered the whiteness of the room—its ceilings and walls—the black floors, the blue sky outside those high windows, and the red rectangles of the brick dormitories. Therefore, I decided to use blue as the main color on a white background and chose red and black as the other two colors. I determined to use only four colors. This was a real challenge but I was sufficiently interested and took enough time to succeed. As a result, I feel the mural is more colorful than if I had used many more colors.

Do not look for meanings and symbolism which are not there. Instead, look for the color-space relationships which give the painting its vigorous tone and its structural feeling. The placing of the figures and colors were done with feelings and thoughts which were the product of my interest in life. The meaning of the mural will change as the viewer gives meaning to it.

I feel I was successful in doing what I set out to do which does not depend on events or depicted replicas for its meaning. I tried to achieve simplicity and directness. When I think of a college campus, I think of intellectual issues debated with vigor, of football, poetry, jazz music, of excitement. These were in my mind when I painted the mural. During the longs months the mural was in my studio, I had the notion it would look all right when it was mounted; now that I have seen it in the Dining Hall, I feel that it does.

$$12 \times 8 = 96'' \text{ high}$$

Drake Mural

$$34 \times 1\frac{1}{2} = \frac{68}{34} \quad 3\overline{)408''} \text{ long}$$

$$136 \quad \frac{1}{3} \text{ of length}$$

$$24'' \quad \frac{1}{4} \text{ of height} \quad 4\overline{)96}$$

$$34'' - \frac{1}{4} \text{ of } \frac{1}{3}\text{'s of length} \quad 4\overline{)136}$$

$$24 \times 4 = \quad 12\overline{)96} \quad 8 \text{ ft}$$

$$34 \times 1\frac{1}{2} = \frac{68}{34} \quad 12\overline{)408} \quad 34 \text{ feet}$$

3 Canvases 24" × 34"
are the size of the mural in the
scale of 3" to the foot or 25%

IV specific paintings—meaning and method

Eggbeater Series (1941)* *Stuart Davis*

In 1927–28, I painted a series called "Eggbeaters," which involved a different kind of transposition of values than I had previously attempted. In my pictures of juxtaposed scenes, the units of composition were complex. That is to say, the entire area of a given scene was made arbitrary in shape and fitted against another scene-shape, but the interior of the shape consisted of houses, trees, and sky, much as they appeared in nature. The structure of the picture was imaginative in the juxtaposition of units, but the internal structure of the units was simplified naturalism and little related to the external structure. In my "Eggbeater" pictures, which had a still life as subject matter, I equated all the forms and spaces of the subject in terms of flat, geometric shapes. I drew these planes in perspective, and the result was what I would call a "space-object."

This was a great advance over my previous work from the standpoint of structural integration. The individual objects in the still life were visualized, not in their isolated internal aspects, but as part of a larger system of spatial relations and unity. These pictures derived from an emotional and imaginative perception of an objective matter; they included transposition of sizes, shapes, and colors, and were carried out in awareness of the logic of the three-dimensional color-space of the canvas. They were really pictures of an imaginatively projected object which satisfied certain emotional reactions to form, color and space. The method of construction was based on abstract theory, the picture itself was a concrete visual image, capable of creating direct sensations of form and color in exactly the same way as any accidental association of objects in nature create visual sensations. The only difference between the art image and the nature image lies in the intuitive and intellectual unity which the artist has established in his picture.

Bass Rocks (1942)† *Stuart Davis*

Bass Rocks represents the color and space harmonies which I observed in a landscape subject. It is not a picture of everyday visual aspects; it is a selection of certain relations of spatial order and logic which were actually present in the subject. Casual observation of the scene from

* From a lecture "How to Construct a Modern Easel Painting," at the New School for Social Research, New York, December 17, 1941.
† Statement for Contemporary American Painters Series, 1942, Jack C. Rich, Publisher, 1950 Daly Ave., New York City.

which they were taken would not reveal the elements from which my picture is made. These harmonies only become apparent after study and contemplation of it. I think this its chief value, that it is a record of certain hidden beauties, which are none the less true and real.

Pictures of this kind, indeed all genuine art, help to keep the eye of the beholder alive, force him to make observations, and give value to, aspects of nature which everyday preoccupations too often leave unnoticed. Everybody has potentialities of art appreciation, but most have little opportunity to develop them. This is one reason the artist plays an important social role in his specialized profession, which is sometimes overlooked. He keeps alive one of the important faculties of man by cultivating it, and, by his work, continues to give objective proof day by day of the possibility of enjoyment of the form and color of our environment.

Bass Rocks expresses the great variety of interest which can be found in the shapes, color, sizes, and positions of a simple subject. By implication it shows the variety of this kind of interest which can be found in all aspects of nature. Anyone looking for stories, advice on domestic or political problems, economic council, or psychoanalytical instruction, will not find it in this picture.

Visa (1952) *Stuart Davis*

Mr. Barr said, in regard to this painting, that he wanted to know why these particular words were chosen and whether they had any special significance other than their compositional value. In regard to that I would say that I very often used words in my pictures, from the time I started in art school, because words were often a part of the urban subject matter that I used, so that the question of why words at all is answered by saying that they are part of my subject matter.

As to this particular painting, the big word in there, the word "champion," is clearly the subject matter of the painting and that was derived quite casually and spontaneously from a book of paper matches which has this word printed on it, and the design of this matchbook was singularly uninteresting and it was the challenge of the lack of interest in this case, rather than the direct stimulus of a subject, but nevertheless the matchbook was the source. Needless to say, the letters themselves in "champion" and the color and their arrangement have no identity with the source.

In the process of making this picture and the operational complex set

Statement for Alfred Barr, then Director of The Museum of Modern Art, New York, November 3, 1952.

Stuart Davis

up by the placement of this word "champion," a number of new ideas arose which were completely unconnected with the initial impulse. In painting, the work that is done each day becomes in itself a new subject matter on seeing it the next day. And in this painting, as in all my work, ideas are derived from sources both conscious and spontaneously given without preconception, which become of equal importance to the primary subject matter.

Now in the first painting that I did of this subject, which was called *Little Giant Still Life,* I had the idea while completing it of doing another one with certain modifications and additions. The modifications consisted primarily of changing the widths of the diagonal lines that cross the word "champion." The reason for this was not a sense that the original lines were inadequate but that these line arrangements could have in themselves a greater variety of work, which in turn affects all the other width relations in the picture.

Another modification is the extension in length of the rectangle at the top center, as well as a change in the width of the two vertical areas to the left of it. Additions not in the first painting consist of a loop at the extreme upper left, a vertical rectangle at the bottom, right of center, the word "else" (not "Elsie") and the phrase "the amazing continuity"; and, of course, the entire color sequence of the painting is completely different.

I have explained why I have used words at all in saying that they were a part of my continuing store of subject matter. And the use of the word "else" in this case was in harmony with my thought at the time that all subject matter is equal. The word "else" was not selected but was given, and since it did not obtrude by specific meanings ulterior to the general character of the picture, I used it. One could say that any four-letter word that filled that area would be as good as the one used, but this would not be the case because, while there could be any number of words which occupied the same space and performed the same color-space structural function, their specific meaning would have an importance that would divert the attention. There is no painting in which the subject matter, whether it be a series of straight lines or a recognizable object, is not identified by the spectator in some way in terms of his own experience. In this particular case if the word "Adlai" had been written instead of "else" it could have been made to function compositionally but the identification of its meaning as subject would have diverted attention from the picture into an area of ideas completely unrelated to it. The word "else," while having different associations to different people, nevertheless has a fundamental dynamic content which consists of the thought that something else being possible there is an immediate sense of motion as an integrant of that thought. Therefore the word "else" is in harmony with the dynamic color intervals of the painting as a whole.

Then in regard to the phrase "the amazing continuity," it can be said that I was moved to animate the area at the extreme right in which a large orange cross is drawn. This involved quite naturally the introduction of a new element, considered as a plane in its most general form, and as some words in its particular form. Which words were used follows the same authority as that in relation to the word "else." The word "amazing" was in my mind at that period as being appropriate to the kind of painting I wanted to look at. The word "continuity" was also in my thoughts for many years as a definition of the experience of seeing the same thing in many paintings of completely different subject matter and style. It has no further significance than that. The phrase "the amazing continuity" has a content of experience which defines that kind of percept which occurs when you see any painting of the type which we call art as distinct from other types. Therefore the content of this phrase is real, as real as any shape of a face or a tree, and this content has a constant character which does not divert the attention by some transient illustration.

On the question of my subject matter in general, I always start with something I have just seen, remembered music, or something that is immediately in front of me, or something I read. That is part of the subject matter, as is the mood I am in. Whether it is good or bad, I regard the mood I am in as part of the subject, and both as completely irrelevant to the piece of work which I plan to do. The doing of the work, regardless of mood or subject, is a completely new experience which does not transmit the character of either. This is a very good point, with reference to people saying they get a wonderful feeling from a painting, and so on. Making a painting is an architectural discipline from the purchase of the stretcher to the precise instruments used to execute it. The act of painting changes all idea and feeling precedent to it to the immediate experience of liking the painting itself, never disliking it. When it is understood that the painting is completely disassociated in content from the experience in subject matter and psychological attitude that preceded it, it becomes possible to talk about an absolute, universal art, an art in which there can be much or little indication of the time, place and personal situation of the artist. Never a standardized art or a pure art as a substitute for absolute art, but an art in which the amazing continuity of the obligatory dimension of free decision given in each percent-quantum is the exclusive authority and valid reason for its shape.

Stuart Davis

Something on the Eight Ball (1954)   *Stuart Davis*

My work in general is done in giving first importance to vivid and exciting reactions to the casual subject matter in everyday experience. It is never the intrinsic significance of the subject but the selective feeling of awareness itself that determines my attitude. Awareness includes the sense of innate power to accept or reject by an act of will among the diverse elements of subject matter which are the constant identity of awareness. Such an act of choice constitutes the direction of Reality and Truth in Art. It is the continuity of Free Choice as a right and obligation, in identification with the color-space idiom of painting, that gives art its unique shape and meaning. My painting *Something on the Eight Ball* is a product of this attitude, and its essential psychological content.

Its origin in subject matter was a simple and commonplace still life. The fact is irrelevant except as a matter of record. Any resemblance between the still life and the painting is purely nonexistent. The visual idiom used consists of clearly defined color-shapes and the complex relations which are set up by their different positions in space. There is nothing difficult or "abstract" about this color-space idiom, because ability to identify and respond to color and shape is universal. It becomes noncommunicative or occult only when approached with the presumption that these individual terms mean something beyond their normal content of meaning. They don't. Such a viewer seeing a green circle with the prejudgment that it must represent a tree will find it meaningless since he finds no tree. And along with this frustration he will debase his own lively sense of immediate recognition of the green circle to a category of no significance. The same viewer, however, will read at a glance the horror headline in his newspaper without demanding to know what the letter M means in murder.

This successful reader of headlines does so on the basis of certain minimum requirements of experience in the meaning and use of words. The same condition applies to the "reading" of pictures. All pictures are not alike. The terms and intentions of [the] art of the past have become more or less familiar and are widely accepted without challenge. The meaning of certain types of Modern Art are put in question by those who have not yet met the minimum conditions for their understanding. The meaning of a picture is in its total aspect, not in the individual terms which compose it.

In the case of my *Eight Ball,* for example, there is a tendency for some people to inquire what the words, "any," "it," "facilities," are in-

Memo to Henry Clifford, then Director of the Philadelphia Museum of Art, April 17, 1954.

tended to signify. I have used words in many of my pictures, and in all cases they are used in the same sense and feeling as the nonword shapes. Everyone knows what the word "any" or "it" means just as they know and recognize a rectangle, an irregular shape, or a color. Words in an infinite variety of visual forms are an important part of the subject matter of our daily experience. I can think of no good reason to exclude them where they present themselves spontaneously to my attention. I accept or reject their shape in the same way as any other shape. Whatever specific context of meaning they have is changed into their context of meaning as a part of the total meaning of the picture. Similarly, there is no shape, mark, or color which in itself is devoid of associations and analogies of meaning. A square is a square, but beyond that it has a great variety of significances for different groups and individuals. But its use as an element in the composition of a painting gives it an additional dimension of meaning as art not inherent in its other meanings. Art does not rob the square of its everyday meanings, it enlarges the scope of its usefulness in enriching our experience with common things. So with the word "any" and all the others which I have employed in my work.

In brief, my purpose in art is to make a pictorial image which maintains the spontaneous excitement and enjoyment that is received in momentary flashes from all kinds of things. Visual things, things heard, uncalculated free associations, calculated logical things, art, music, the dynamics of New York City, etc. I demand that the picture maintain this kind of continuity of mood throughout its manifold relations. When I feel that it does I regard it as complete.

As to the title, I select words or phrases in much the same way. I apply them to a painting for purposes of identification when they seem appropriate in sound, not for any descriptive reason. In the present case *Something on the Eight Ball* is a switch on the usual phrase "behind the eight ball." I used it without knowledge of hearing it before in a conversation with some jazz musicians [and] it got a laugh, causing me to remember it. Strangely enough, three days later a man I had not seen for twenty-five years phoned me long distance for advice on where to send a protégé of his to study art in New York. In describing the unusual talents of this boy he ended by saying, "I really think he's got something on the eight ball." I decided then and there that I had a good usable title for the picture I was working on.

Stuart Davis

Owh! In San Pão (1952)   *Stuart Davis*

My painting *Owh! in San Pão,* like my *Amazene* and *Rapt at Rappaport's,* [is a statement] in a visual-proprioceptive idiom as simple as a Tabloid headline. Anyone with enough coordination to decipher a traffic beacon, granted they accept the premise of its function, can handle their communicative potential with ease. There are no mathematics of Abstract or Naturalist Expressionistic Idealism to befuddle here, and the Department of Philosophical Displacement Relativisms is on the floor below. Emotion and Feeling, that crucial Emulsion, is a dimension at right angle to the plane of the canvas in these paintings. They appropriately offer only a modest common-sense image of a familiar object in the Shape of Color-Space Logic. Their content of Feeling occupies exactly the same place it did in the artist, that is to say, in the person facing the unfeeling canvas. Only a sadistic brute would demand simultaneous emphatic immersion in the artist's Feelings from a spectator already completely self-emulsified in contemplation of the Cool painting. There is such a thing as good manners in Art as well as in the other forms of decent good-will in social relations. I think it is primarily this regard for the privacy of others which accounts for the enormous prestige of Art, and gives it a universal currency rating exceeded only by Money. A recent resurgence of the trend to confuse the function of Art with things of the order of out-house utilities becomes all the more regrettable in this light, and exposes the absurdity of its Economics of Emulsion-behavior. A degree of sentimentality can be tolerated in people, but in painting the words bathetic and emetic are synonymous.

The title of my painting is reasonable in the same way as the image itself. It has been scientifically established that the acoustics of Idealism give off the Humanistic Sounds of Snoring, whereas Reality always says "Ouch!" Clearly then, when the realism has San Pão as its locale, a proper regard for the protocol of alliteration changes it to "Owh!"

Statement in *Contemporary Painting,* catalogue of an exhibition at the University of Illinois, Urbana, 1952, pp. 183–84.

V the place of abstract painting in america

The Place of Abstract Painting in America
(letter to Henry McBride) (1930)   *Stuart Davis*

Dear Mr. McBride:

I appreciate the good will shown in your review of the watercolors I showed at the Whitney Galleries. There is a point in it, however, on which I think it necessary to take issue with you. In the review you speak of your enthusiasm for my work and call me a "swell American painter." This attitude on your part I heartily approve, but you further state that my style is French and that if Picasso had never lived I would have had to think out a style of my own. Now is that nice, Mr. McBride? And if it is, does it mean anything? My own answer is that it does not, for reasons, some of which are furnished below.

In speaking of French art as opposed to American the assumption is made that there is an American art. Where is it and how does one recognize it? Has any American artist created a style which was unique in painting, completely divorced from European models? To soften this flock of hard questions I will answer the last, no, J. S. Copley was working in the style of the English portrait painters and to my taste doing better work than they did. Whistler's best work was directly inspired by the Japanese while he was housed and fed in England. Ryder's technique derives from Rembrandt by devious ways and Homer's style is no style at all but the natural method of a man who has seen a lot of photographic illustration and likes it. I have never heard the names of the European masters that Eakins particularly admired but from his work I should say that they included Rembrandt and Velázquez. These painters are now regarded as the best that America has produced. Suppose a selected show of the painting of Europe and America for the last four hundred years were held, would the American contribution stand isolated as a distinct point of view, unrelated to the European? Again the answer is, no.

Since this is obviously true, why should an American artist today be expected to be oblivious to European thought when Europe is a hundred times closer to us than it ever was before? If a Scotchman is working on television do similarly interested American inventors avoid all information as to his methods? Not if they can help it. If a Norwegian has the most interesting theory of atomic physics do American scientists make a bonfire of his works on the campus? Hardly. If Darwin says that the species evolved, do American educators try to keep one hundred per cent Americans from hearing it? Yes, they do in Tennessee.

Picasso, I suppose, is not a hundred per cent Spaniard otherwise he

From *Creative Art,* VI (February, 1930).

wouldn't disregard the home industries and live in Paris. But regardless of that fact he has been incomparably the dominant painter of the world for the last twenty years and there are very few of the young painters of any country who have not been influenced by him. The ones who were not, simply chose some other artist to be influenced by.

I did not spring into the world fully equipped to paint the kind of pictures I want to paint. It was therefore necessary to ask people for advice. This resulted in my attending the school of Robert Henri where I received encouragement and a vague idea of what it was all about. After leaving the direct influence of Mr. Henri I sought other sources of information and as the artists whose work I admired were not personally available I tried to find out what they were thinking about by looking at their pictures. Chief among those consulted were Aubrey Beardsley, Toulouse Lautrec, Fernand Léger and Picasso. This process of learning is from my observation identical with that followed by all artists. The only variation lies in the choice of work to be studied. If Picasso had been a practicing artist in Akron, Ohio, I would have admired his work just the same. I admit the study and the influence and regard it as all to the good. But why one should be penalized for a Picasso influence and not for a Rembrandt or a Renoir influence I can't understand.

I can't understand that any more than I can understand how one is supposed to be devoid of influence. I never heard of or saw anyone who was. Picasso himself has as many influences as Carter has pills, as Tad frequently said and I suppose this shows a Tad influence.

In view of all this I insist that I am as American as any other American painter. I was born here as were my parents and their parents before, which fact makes me an American whether I want to be or not. While I admit the foreign influence I strongly deny speaking their language. If my work were an imitation I am sure it couldn't arouse in you that enthusiasm from which, you state in your review, the bridles were almost removed. Over here we are racially English-American, Irish-American, German-American, French, Italian, Russian or Jewish-American and artistically we are Rembrandt-American, Renoir-American and Picasso-American. But since we live here and paint here we are first of all, American.

Sincerely,
(signed) Stuart Davis

Recent Painting in Oil and Watercolor (1931)
Stuart Davis

Although a painter's means of expression is paint, it is of value to have the painter himself translate his ideas into another medium. The following extracts from a series of letters addressed to The Downtown Gallery by Stuart Davis throw an interesting light on the artist's approach to his work:

These pictures are in part the result of the following ideas:

That a picture must tell a story.

This story can have pictorial existence only through the artist's concept of form. There are an infinite number of form concepts available.

My own is very simple and is based on the assumption that space is continuous, and that matter is discontinuous. In my formal concept the question of two or more dimensions does not enter. I never ask the question, "Does this picture have depth or is it flat?"

I consider such a question irrelevant. I conceive of form (matter) as existing in space, in terms of linear direction. It follows then that the forms of the subject are analyzed in terms of angular variation from successive bases of directional radiation.

The phenomena of color, size, shape and texture are the result of such angular variation.

I wish to make clear that I do not employ any system of angular proportion. The directions chosen and the resultant form of the picture are arbitrary.

I believe that all possible forms are valid and that limitations resulting from a set ratio or angle or area are not helpful in the production of forms other than themselves.

In other words, that the concept of a certain type of design which is good, opposed to another which is bad, is the wrong way to think about it. Any design which achieves variety is good.

If it achieves a known variety it does not interest us.

If it achieves a known but still unanalyzed variety, it has value.

In my conception, the idea of a picture which has good color and bad drawing is a meaningless one.

It can have meaning only from the standpoint of the spectator selecting a drawing made by the color in part, as opposed to the entire drawing of the artist.

Color must be thought of as texture which automatically allows one to visualize it in terms of space.

Aside from this, it has no meaning.

From catalogue of an exhibition at The Downtown Gallery, New York, 1931.

Abstract Painting in America (1935)   *Stuart Davis*

A short preface must by its space limitations be so broad in its view-point as to exclude the personalities of the movement. Only the large groups and masses can be dealt with. Personal feelings, egos and evaluations must be dealt with elsewhere. Questions such as who was the first American to paint in the abstract manner are not pertinent here any more than critical evaluations regarding relative individual artistic merit.

Therefore, I begin very, very broadly by saying that the American artist became conscious of abstract art by the impact of the Armory Show in 1913. Previous to this important event in the art education in the United States, there were several American artists working in Europe who were incorporating the abstract viewpoint in their canvases. But it was the Armory Show of 1913 with its huge panorama of the scene of art for the foregoing seventy-five years which brought to the American artist as a whole the realization of the existence of abstract art, along with its immediate artistic historical background. The abstract portion of the exhibition which consisted of works by European artists, with few exceptions, created a real sensation. Argumentation and dispute were constantly carried on in front of these canvases by laymen as well as artists. Friendships were broken and new friends made in the heat induced by these daily congresses of opinion. There was no American artist who saw this show but was forced to revalue his artistic concepts. The final charge was touched off in the foundations of the autocracy of the Academy in a blast which destroyed its strangle hold on critical art values forever. Henceforth the American artist realized his right to free expression and exercised that right. This was made very clear in the annual exhibitions of the Society of Independent Artists where all artists could show their works without submission to jury. Henceforth a more acute angularity was imparted to the divergence of approach of the different artist groups.

Among these groups the artists who followed the abstract attitude completely or in appreciable part were relatively small. Why this was so I do not know, I simply state it as a matter of fact for the record. But the function of this small group of abstract painters and sculptors continued to make more clear the special character of the aesthetic divergence, among American painters as a whole. They were the leaven implanted in the mass body of the American artists which continued the revolution of aesthetic opinion instigated in February, 1913, by the

Introduction to catalogue of an exhibition at the Whitney Museum of American Art, New York, February 12–March 22, 1935.

abstract section of the International Exhibition of Modern Art commonly called the Armory Show.

What is abstract art? The question will be answered differently by each artist to whom the question is put. This is so because the generative idea of abstract art is alive. It changes, moves and grows like any other living organism. However, from the various individual answers some basic concordance could doubtless be abstracted. This basic concordance of opinion would be very elementary and would probably run something like this. Art is not and never was a mirror reflection of nature. All efforts at imitation of nature are foredoomed to failure. Art is an understanding and interpretation of nature in various media. Therefore in our efforts to express our understanding of nature we will always bear in mind the limitations of our medium of expression. Our pictures will be expressions which are parallel to nature and parallel lines never meet. We will never try to copy the uncopyable but will seek to establish a material tangibility in our medium which will be a permanent record of an idea or emotion inspired by nature. This being so, we will never again ask the question of painting, "Is it a good likeness, does it look like the thing it is supposed to represent?" Instead we will ask the question, "Does this painting which is a defined two-dimensional surface convey to me a direct emotional or ideological stimulus?" Since we forego all efforts to reflect optical illusions and concentrate on the reality of our canvas, we will now study the material reality of our medium, paint on canvas or whatever it may be. The approach has become scientifically experimental. A painting for example is a two-dimensional plane surface and the process of making a painting is the act of defining two-dimensional space on that surface. Any analogy which is drawn from our two-dimensional expression to three-dimensional nature will only be forceful in the degree to which our painting has achieved a two-dimensional clarity and logic.

The above is my idea of the basic implications in the abstract concept and I think it is implicit in all the various explanations and viewpoints which have been advanced about abstract art. The American artists who from various angles have oriented themselves about the abstract idea have not in all cases been as wholeheartedly scientific as the above considerations would seem to call for. However, I believe that even in those cases where the artistic approach has been almost entirely emotional, the concept of the autonomous existence of the canvas as a reality which is parallel to nature has been recognized. It should also be noted that the ideas suggested above automatically explain the geometric character of many abstract works of art.

The period of greatest activity in abstract art in America was probably from about 1915 to 1927. This in no sense implies that abstract work was not done before and after the above dates nor does it even suggest that the best work in abstract form was done between those two dates. It merely indicates a rough calculation on my part to the effect that between those dates a greater number of American artists were in whole or in part following an abstract point of view in their work.

Abstract art in America as shown in this exhibition, although actively participated in by relatively few artists, has been a vital factor in the sharpening of issues. Its objective and real contributions will not be lost.

A Medium of 2 Dimensions (1935)   *Stuart Davis*

Mr. Weinstock finds contradictions in abstract art in his comments on the "Abstract Painting in America" exhibition at the Whitney Museum. There is nothing surprising in this as Mr. Weinstock is supposedly an advocate of the general theory of dialectical materialism, in which nature and society are perceived to be in a constant state of revolutionary movement through the struggle of the contradictions or opposites present in all unities.

I think that in searching for the contradictions he has overlooked some very apparent affirmations. One, that abstract painting actually does exist. Two, that a number of abstract paintings of the last twenty-five years clearly come within the field of first-rate art. Three, the revolutionary history of abstract painting.

In his first paragraph he admits having received distinct emotional pleasure on observing the pictures in this exhibition. In his next to last paragraph he denies the primary statement, proving I suppose further contradictions. In his desire to affirm the approaching revolutionary art of the international labor movement he is undialectical in his tendency to deny the reality of bourgeois origins and concomitants. For example, in the recent exhibitions of painting and sculpture at the Artists' Union, there were quite a few exhibits well within the category of abstract art, and no one could say that they were among the worst of the exhibits. True, these abstractions were not in general the expression of that class consciousness which a more lengthy participation in any union activities tends to produce. But these, and all abstractions, were the result of a revolutionary struggle relative to the bourgeois academic traditions of the immediate past and even the present. In the materialism of abstract art in general, is implicit a negation of many ideals dear to the bourgeois heart. Abstract art will in turn be negated along with its bourgeois associations, but in our awareness of this let us see the situation realis-

From *Art Front* (May, 1935).

Stuart Davis

tically and admit that abstract art is still in the picture. Does Mr. Weinstock pretend that the abstract tendencies in painting and the Fascist tendencies of the American Scene school of Benton, etc., are both alike because they are both within the bourgeois scheme? Such a view would not seem to be realistic.

In regard to Mr. Weinstock's criticism of my introduction to the catalogue of the Abstract Show at the Whitney Museum, I can well imagine that the introduction is open to criticism. However, I am not sure that the points selected by Mr. Weinstock are the weakest. My description of a painting as a two-dimensional space definition which is parallel to nature, and which is forceful to the degree of its logical clarity, he finds inadequate and undialectical. Perhaps it is, to one not too familiar with the subject, but with this theory I have gotten results which are admitted to be good relative to the time and place. The definition assumed that the artist was already in possession of an idea which was the result of his contact with nature, which idea was qualitatively different [from] the sum of the sources of its generation. Add conditioning by the mind material and the emergence of a new quality by its transference to a medium of two dimensions, the canvas. Maybe the use of the phrase "parallel to nature" is incorrect from the standpoint of philosophical usage. But the definition was meant to be a description of the material quality of a painting and did not by intention imply that because the painting was a quality distinct from its sources, it had no connection with them. Further, it did not by intention imply that the two-dimensional space definition was an act undirected by social purpose.

Finally, I wish to say that I was asked by the Whitney Museum to write a very short résumé of the abstract movement in America, and that considerations of space caused them to omit, among other items, the following extracts from my introduction as submitted to them.

"At about 1926 or 1927 three separate tendencies began to make themselves felt (in American art). They were, a desire to be wholly American and disassociate oneself from foreign ideas. Two, a following of the surrealist objectives as they were being developed in Paris, and three, a growing belief in the necessity of social content in art."

"This school (the American tendency) quite illogically stated in effect that an American artist could only be conscious of America and that foreign influences should like devils be cast out. They waved the flag. They denied progress and chose a parochial objective."

"The third tendency, the necessity of a social content in art, has a firmer base on which to stand. The adherents of this school argue that abstract art was divorced from reality, that it had no contact with the people. While admitting its technical contributions they deny it any cultural validity. Because fundamentally the concern of the abstract artist had been his own canvas and a select group of those interested in art. The abstract artist did not concern himself with the life problems of the people around him. Therefore, says the social-content school, he has betrayed his place of trust as cultural leader. He has not been realistic."

"But the abstract artist was realistic at least with regard to his materials."

"If the historical process is forcing the artist to relinquish his individualistic isolation and come into the arena of life problems, it may be the abstract artist who is best equipped to give vital artistic expression to such problems—because he has already learned to abandon the ivory tower in his objective approach to his materials."

Abstract Painting Today (1940)   *Stuart Davis*

The first comprehensive showing of abstract art in the United States was held in the Sixty-ninth Infantry Armory in New York City in February, 1913. The Association of American Painters and Sculptors, Inc., which promoted it, warned American artists, in the preface to the catalogue, not to pride themselves on freedom from European influence, because such purity might mean nothing more than isolation from the most progressive forces in art. It specifically called attention to the fact that the Association "is against cowardice even when it takes the form of amiable self satisfaction." But in spite of this inspired advice, the powerful propaganda carried on by some critics and artists today for the cultural isolation of the American artist proves that the battle of the Armory Show has not yet been won, and that there are many who are willing to exploit cultural provincialism at the expense of progress.

American artists were profoundly moved by this exhibit and showed it in their work. It was clearly evident that a genuine effort was being made to comprehend and incorporate these new forms and their meanings. But as time went by the intensity of this effort decreased, and although a lasting imprint has been left on American painting the progressive spirit increasingly waned and some of that "cowardice" in the form of "amiable self satisfaction" began to creep back into the cultural picture. Domestic naturalism, the chicken yard, the pussy cat, the farmer's wife, natural beauties of the home town, etc., became the order of the day in painting. And on the reverse side of the popular trend toward domestic naturalism was found the more trying aspect of man's struggle with nature and society, such as the picket line, the Dust Bowl, the home-relief office, the evicted family, etc. In mural paintings it was the same thing; on the one hand—American history-in-costume, cowboys

Unpublished article commissioned by Art for the Millions.

1. *The Poolroom,* 1911. Watercolor, 15″ x 11″. Collection of Mrs. Stuart Davis.

2. *Negro Dance Hall, ca.* 1912. Crayon and watercolor, 15″ x 11″. Collection of Mrs. Stuart Davis.

3. *Babe La Tour,* 1913. Watercolor, 15″ x 11″. Private collection.

4. Stuart Davis painting at Gloucester, Massachusetts, *ca.* 1918. Photograph courtesy of Mrs. Stuart Davis.

5. (opposite) *The President,* 1917. Oil, 36″ x 26¼″. Collection of the Munson-Williams-Proctor Institute, Utica, New York.

6. *Multiple Views,* 1918. Oil, 47" x 35". Collection of Mrs. Stuart Davis.

7. *Havana Landscape,* 1919. Watercolor, 17⅞" x 23⅝".
Collection of Mrs. Stuart Davis.

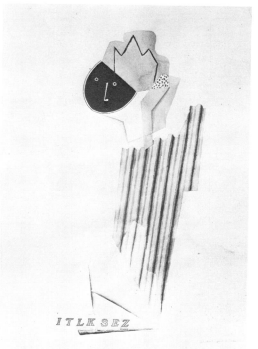

8. ITLKSEZ, 1921. Collage and watercolor, 22" x 16". The
Lane Collection.

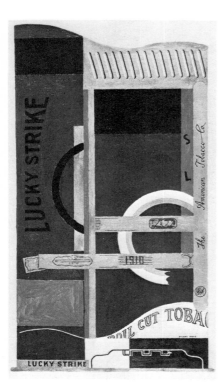

9. *Lucky Strike,* 1921. Oil, 33¼″ x 18″. Collection, The Museum of Modern Art, New York. Gift of The American Tobacco Company, Inc.

10. *New Mexican Landscape,* 1923. Oil, 22″ x 32″. Collection of Whitney Museum of American Art, New York.

11. *Still Life,* 1925. Oil, 26″ x 34″. Courtesy Wadsworth Atheneum, Hartford.

12. *Eggbeater Number 1,* 1927. Oil, 27″ x 38¼″. The Phillips Collection, Washington, D.C.

13. *Eggbeater Number 2,* 1927. Oil, 29⅛″ x 36″.
Collection of Whitney Museum of American
Art, New York.

14. *Rue Vercingetorix,* 1928. Oil, 18″ x 14¾″.
Collection of Mr. and Mrs. John Carney.

15. *Percolator,* 1927. Oil, 36″ x 29″. The Metropolitan Museum of Art, New York. Arthur H. Hearn Fund, 1956.

16. *Eggbeater V,* 1930. Oil, 50⅛″ x 32¼″. Collection, The Museum of Modern Art, New York. Abby Aldrich Rockefeller Fund.

17. Mural in Gar Sparks's Candy Store, Newark, New Jersey, *ca.* 1916 (destroyed). Photograph courtesy of Mrs. Stuart Davis.

18. Mural in the Men's Lounge, Radio City Music Hall, New York, 1932. Photography courtesy of Mrs. Stuart Davis.

19. *Swing Landscape,* mural at Indiana University, Bloomington, 1938. (Painted for the WPA Federal Art Project.)

20. Study for *History of Communications,* mural in the Hall of Communications, New York World's Fair, 1939 (destroyed). Ink, 15″ x 34″. Photograph courtesy of Mrs. Stuart Davis.

21. Mural for Studio B, WNYC Municipal Broadcasting Company, New York, 1939. (Painted for the WPA Federal Art Project.) Photograph courtesy of Mrs. Stuart Davis.

22. *Allée,* mural at Drake University, Des Moines, Iowa, 1955. Photograph courtesy of Mrs. Stuart Davis.

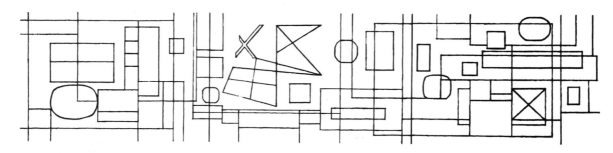

23. Scale drawing for *Allée,* 1954. Ink, 24″ x 34⅛″. Collection of Mrs. Stuart Davis.

24. Study for mural for Conference Room Number 3, the United Nations, New York, 1956. Oil, 28″ x 70″. The Lane Collection.

25. *Composition Concrete,* mural at the H. J. Heinz Research Center, Pittsburgh, 1957–61. Photograph courtesy of Mrs. Stuart Davis.

26. Study for *Composition Concrete,*
1957–60. Oil, 43″ x 20″. Contemporary Collection of The Cleveland
Museum of Art.

and Indians, frontier days; and on the other hand, Mexican muralism, the fetish of fresco, etc. American art was, and I wish to add, still is, right back with the Rogers Groups and J. G. Brown's ragged little shoeshine boys.

Taking the large exhibition of contemporary American art at the New York World's Fair, 1939, as a comprehensive cross section of our national art production, it is undeniable that a good deal of the expressive content of this representative exhibition consisted of an "amiable self satisfaction" with the most elementary aspects of the physical and cultural environment. The spirit of discovery, of new possibilities, of the dynamism of contemporary life, of the uniqueness of our time—these things are rare in the general content of exhibitions which show a real cross section of American art today. Instead we find extreme formal and tonal conservatism as a general characteristic. . . .

Heightened sensibility to reality, or aesthetic reaction, has always been regarded as a positive social value. The proof of this can be found in the art museums of the world. To affirm the necessity of aesthetics is not to say that man lives by art alone, any more than he lives by bread alone. To say that there must be an art of real order, which communicates directly, by the concrete example of its real order in the materials of art, the coordinating emotional message that it is possible to successfully control the environment, is not to say that no other forms of art must exist. Drawing and painting have always been used to communicate ideas which were not and didn't intend to be aesthetic. Various arts of illustration are valid at all times and convey political, educational, entertaining, or sentimental and romantic ideas. Academic art is a form of illustration. But the thing called "art" throughout history has been so called without reference to its illustration message, and independently of any particular objects or subject matter.

The quality called "art" has always been abstract and has had its material existence in a series of unique and real orders in the materials of art. Therefore when as today a popular sentiment is organized and promoted which sets up the arts of illustration and domestic naturalism as the inheritors of the social role of art, then an enormous perversion of values takes place which lowers the cultural level and destroys the sources of art production.

When I sit for two hours and a half in a concert hall listening to a piece of music written 200 years ago, which the composer never heard played in its entirety, and which was started in the form of a Protestant mass and ended up in the form of a Catholic mass, but was not really either one, and taking into account the fact that the composer knew there [were] no facilities in his time to perform the work and that he could never hear it, and considering that it is sung in Latin, a language which means nothing to me, the fact that I am able to sit with a concentrated interest for two hours and a half listening to Bach's B-minor mass, in a hall in which all seats have been sold out for weeks before the event, proves to me that abstract art existed long before abstract painting of today and that it fulfills a powerful human need.

In music no one disputes the fact or thinks it curious that there is music with a program or story, and also music which has no program. No one is disturbed by the fact that Alec Templeton plays the piano to tell musical anecdotes, and that on the other hand Earl Hines plays it to create pure musical structures. People going to a concert hall expect a program describing the meaning of the various themes and instruments in a Richard Strauss tone poem, but when they listen to Bach they do not require any explanation.

Certainly there are many examples from the arts of the past whose symbolic content, though meaningful to the persons for whom they were painted, has no meaning for the average person today, and yet despite this fact these works of art provide aesthetic pleasure for us. Very few of us know much about the lives of the saints which form the major subject matter of painting from Giotto through the Renaissance, and yet I believe the paintings of Giotto or Piero provide enormous aesthetic satisfaction for the modern man.

But if one asserts that a pure abstract art exists in painting, people become agitated and start to argue instead of accepting the simple fact at its face value. They move to the attack from two main bases. On the one hand, they agree that pure art exists, but they deny that modern abstract art is an example of it. They point to Greece and the Italian Renaissance as examples of what real art must be. They agree with Hitler that modern art is degenerate. On the other hand, there is the sociological school of art theory. Its exponents look at a work of art as they would a newspaper, to find out what is going on in current events. "Very interesting," they say on looking at a picture, "see how the artist has left his ivory tower and gone amongst the workers to paint their picket lines. This is a real progressive art." When these people look at modern art and can't find a social message somewhere in the picture, [and] it means nothing to them, they make common cause with Hitler and the academicians and pronounce modern art to be degenerate and an escape from reality.

From divergent origins these two viewpoints arrive at the same conclusion because of their inadequate conception of reality. Their conception is unrealistic because it sees art from the point of view of an observer who watches a process in which [he] is not involved. The academician sees art as a process going on in the remote past. He studies it from his remote point of vantage and tries to imitate its character. The configurations of art to the academician were eternally established long ago. He fails to understand art as a social expression, and the fact

Stuart Davis

that his interest in it consists precisely of the social message it conveys. Unaware of this, he fails to recognize his own responsibility to society through art, which is to make those crucial decisions about the order of relations in the materials of art which are exemplified in that art of the past which he admires. But seeing art as a pre-established order of relations, he rejects the idea that he has the power to change them. He underestimates the potentialities of man and sees modern art as degenerate because it is not a replica of the past.

The sociological idea of art which finds modern art degenerate is unrealistic for the same reason as the academic, namely, it sees art as a remote process in which the observer is not involved. Only instead of the quality called "art" [being regarded] as a process going on in the remote past, it is regarded as located in the remote future. But strangely enough, it conceives this art of the future to be identical in character with the academician's art of the past, a replica or mirror reflection of nature. The sociological theorist says that art is a social expression and changes as society changes, and so it does. But when it becomes clear what is meant by this statement, we see that it really doesn't visualize the possibility of change in art at all. It conceives [of] art as a social function changed and molded by the social forces in its environment merely in a passive way. The lack of reality in this viewpoint consists of its failure to include art as an active social force, not only acted upon by other social categories, but in turn reacting upon them. Seeing only that social forces move art and failing to visualize the concrete work of art which is acted upon, this viewpoint fails to see that the work of art itself changes the emotions and ideas of people. This failure to visualize the specific concrete work of art under discussion leads to a conception of art which is a mere logical product of social theory. But since art has not been included as an active social category in the theory, real, concrete contemporary art has not been visualized at all.

But it happens that there already exists an art which satisfies all the social and political requirements of the sociological theory of art, namely, the art of illustration. The theory logically demands an art that can be read like a newspaper, that mirrors the social and political events of the time, but which is not itself a new event. Therefore when [this theory] considers a modern picture and sees that it is not a record of a recent social event, and not having given any place to real art in its analysis of reality, [it dismisses] the work of art . . . as degenerate. But this is not all, because since this social theory does employ the word "art," and the future society which this theory predicts will have art in it, so it has the obligation to define the character of that art. But since it has mistaken contemporary illustration for real contemporary art, its historical survey of art starts with a false premise. Starting with contemporary illustration it goes back through the years picking out the illustrative social reportage in works of art. Where this element is not prominent the work is rejected. The theory is eventually applied to the Old Masters, the holy art of the academicians, who love it for its real order. The academician is satisfied to contemplate the real art process in the past. But the sociological art theorist is concerned about the art in his future society. He has observed that the real art of the past was vastly superior to what he thinks is the real art of the present. If contemporary art could develop to a point where it was as good as this art of the past he sees that it would be a great improvement. So he enthrones the art of the past in his system of the future society and moves forward confidently—in the wrong direction.

These sociological theorists think nothing of referring to the lack of ideas and the inadequate reflection of reality in a modern picture and then praising its powerful color and dynamic form. I have always found it extremely difficult to visualize a powerful color and dynamic form as disembodied spirit, which the above view seems to affirm.

But despite these idealistic theories there is a contemporary art of real order as well as the various arts of illustration. The best painting in the last seventy-five years, that work which has added something new to the development of art, has unquestionably been done in France. But this was valid not only for Frenchmen, because the qualities that made it great were real values of art structure. The greatness of modern art or any art is not a private affair that concerns only the artist who made it and the patron who bought it. A work of art is the artist's contribution to society and is the property of all who have the opportunity and ability to understand it. So when we say that great painting has been done in France, it is a matter of great concern to anyone interested in art. They must accept it or refute it and refutation must be accompanied by the proof of work done. You can't disprove the work of Seurat by bringing forward an anecdotal illustration to take its place.

The best work of the last seventy-five years is great because it is real contemporary art, which expresses in the materials of art the new lights, speeds, and spaces of our epoch. Modern chemistry, physics, electricity, petroleum, radio, have produced a world in which all the conceptions of Time and Space have been enormously expanded and modern and abstract art both reflect and are an active agent in this expansion.

When a Frenchman . . . invented the canning process over 100 years ago it wasn't just an interesting example of French ingenuity and talent. It was a real event which was studied and developed by men in other countries until it was improved and perfected. And when Frenchmen make great art it is not just an interesting example of French genius. It is a real event to be studied and developed by artists in other countries.

Stuart Davis

It is perfectly valid to paint the chicken yard in one's home town, the model in the studio, or a picket line, but if it is to have any cultural value it must be done in the light of the real discoveries of modern art, not in the light of calendar lithography of the last century.

America is the only place in the world at this moment of writing where art can develop in freedom of expression. American artists, museums, and collectors, government art projects, foundations that promote art projects, all these have at this time the right of free choice in their cultural orientation. This right of free choice is the crucial condition for the future of American art, and the other condition is whether the choice made is realistic or idealistic. Whether art is regarded as a passive or active social function.

Abstract art, in the most broad use of the term, is the actual progressive force in the art of our epoch. It has brought ideas into art which couldn't occur in art before because they didn't exist. These art ideas are not just sentiments and tastes, they are real things which must be learned and applied to the new problems of art, which social environment and art itself bring about.

Is There a Revolution in the Arts? (1940)
Stuart Davis

I wouldn't want to try to argue that there is no revolution in the arts. The only point of debate can be what kind of revolution is going on and whether it is good or bad. I am sure there is a revolution in the art of painting. I think it is good and will attempt to explain why I think so.

Now most people agree that art is one of the necessary forms of social expression, but they do not all agree on the way it functions socially. The person who said that art holds a mirror up to nature provided a monkey wrench which has been long used by provincialism to mangle the wheels of progress. Art does not hold a mirror up to nature and it does not reflect the social struggle, because a reflection is simply a copy. Art is conditioned by both, but it conditions both.

Social change can spring from a work of art as well as art from social change. It predicts as well as records. The revolution in art is an integral part of the revolution in society, not just a death mask of it. Painting has gone through a whole series of revolutions even in the last forty years. This has taken place chiefly in France, and is being carried on in America. The current exhibition at the Museum of Modern Art contrasts excellent examples of this period with works by Italian masters of

From *Bulletin of America's Town Meeting of the Air*, V, No. 19 (February, 1940).

the Renaissance. A great difference is clear and a great identity is clear in the works of the two periods. We prefer the modern works because they are closer to our daily experience. They were painted by men who lived, and who still live, in the revolutionary lights, speeds, and spaces of today, which science and art have made possible.

An artist who has traveled on a steam train, driven an automobile, or flown in an airplane doesn't feel the same way about form and space as one who has not. An artist who has used telegraph, telephone, and radio doesn't feel the same way about time and space as one who has not. And an artist who lives in a world of the motion picture, electricity, and synthetic chemistry doesn't feel the same way about light and color as one who has not. An artist who has lived in a democratic society has a different view of what a human being really is than one who has not. These new experiences, emotions, and ideas are reflected in modern art, but not as a copy of them. They are coordinated by the artist and established as a real order in the materials of art. Art changes the person who sees it, and these changes are reflected in other fields of social action. The Renaissance artist and the modern artist are alike in that they both organize their experience into a real and coherent order in the materials of art. But this order is always unique, acted upon by, and in turn reacting upon, the society of its time. The real order of art is not an ideal order, or system of beauty, because an ideal order would be timeless, and art exists in time.

The cultural heritage of the American artist today has its roots and is fed by the cultures of all times and races. Therefore—in view of this fact—some large and best-selling books on art, of the last few years, are a menace to American art, because these books preach a provincial brand of American totalitarianism in art which, if carried out, would be the equivalent of Fascism in American art. They would deprive American artists of their cultural heritage. But the great majority of American artists are not seduced by this totalitarian hillbilly aesthetics, with its vicious political and racial implications, for they have formed organizations like the Artists' Congress, An American Group, and the United American Artists, which are progressive and have a completely democratic orientation. The existence of these organizations is in itself proof that there is a revolution in art, because none having their social scope existed five years ago. These organizations and others are the vehicle through which American artists can think out their social and art problems and give them effective expression. The Federal support of art is another sign that there is a revolution in art, because, aside from its economic aspect, it has placed art in the category of essential Federal social services. This raises the cultural level, and I hope the American people don't let shortsighted politicians take this service away from them.

Yes, there is a revolution in the arts, there always was a revolution in the arts, and I think it is a darn good thing.

Cubism is one of the forms of art which have reflected the artists' sensitivity to the environment that we live in. It shows the possibility of having a number of experiences in a very short space of time; of being in many parts of the city, in many parts of the country; of hearing sounds on records which have been made a long time before, and so forth. It simply reflects the possibility that the relations which are real in nature are diverse, that experiences one has had five minutes ago, or ten years ago, or that will be in process of being at the moment, are capable of coordinated expression; that they can be ordered, just as in synthetic chemistry new orders that never existed in nature before can be made. As for what use it can be to America—an example of coordination in thought or action is of use anywhere, whether it is America or not.

The abstract art is a reassertion of a feeling that certain artists have, that real order is the expression which art communicates. It doesn't exclude literary art. There are all kinds of art. The materials of art are used for political art, for an art of preserving the orders of the past, for an art of scholarship, for an art of naturalism. All those arts are valid. Abstract art affirms an art of real order.

Abstract Art in the American Scene (1941)
Stuart Davis

The term "abstract art" has no single meaning. It changes with the intellectual scope of the person who uses it, but this does not mean that it is exclusively a subjective term. To a majority of that part of the public which has even heard it used, it is synonymous with the word "puzzle." They give vocal expression to this conviction by repeating the phrase "What does it mean?" over and over again when confronted with an "abstract" painting. To a smaller group of those who include aesthetic slang in their vocabulary it denotes certain contemporary styles of painting, such as Cubism and its various offshoots. To another group it signifies the artist's flight from subject matter and reality as the result of historically determined forces in the development of society. To a still smaller and somewhat esoteric group it denotes an impure and earthbound art, a sort of distressing hurdle on the road to "non-objective" art, or "art without an object," as one of its exponents has quaintly phrased it.

Now all of these definitions are true, at least relatively so, because

From *Parnassus,* XIII, No. 3 (March, 1941).

there is no question that abstract art IS a puzzle to people who don't understand it, just as persons who have never learned to read are puzzled by the printed page. And there is no doubt that Cubism is an abstract art, developed in Paris in the first decade of the century. Also I think most people will agree that society does evolve, and that it imposes certain limiting factors on the freedom of expression of the artist. If the sewer backs up in his studio, for example, the artist's muse may well be affronted, and if he continues work on his masterpiece, "Myopic Vista," in spite of this, it is no doubt true that in a sense he is "fleeing from reality." Finally, there is no question whatever that "abstract art" is impure and earthbound, because its forms are tainted with references to the world around us, such as the red of the neon sign, the spatial intervals of the forest trees, and the ideological arabesques of the skywriter, to name a few.

The foregoing truths may prompt one to ask, as many have, whether the "abstract" artist has a leg to stand on. If his art is unintelligible to the public; if it is just something that was appropriate to the Parisian environment of twenty or thirty years ago; if it is a social anachronism; if it is aesthetically polluted, like typhoid in the reservoir; is it not true then that the "abstract" artist is merely playing hooky from a well-deserved assignment in a concentration camp? I do not believe so, because I do not accept the popular or official estimates I have summarized as important truths.

In conceding at once that my understanding of art is somewhat short of the absolute, I do not admit it to be predominantly subjective, because I have found many persons who buy my pictures and hang them on their walls. I draw the conclusion from this that my aesthetic observations of nature are understood and shared by others, and hence have a legitimate social role. This fact is a determining factor in the formulation of my theory and philosophy of art.

Informed people use the word "art," as applied to painting, to mean a varied but coherent organization of form and color. They do not mean that the painting is art because the subject represents a scene of great social moment, a patriotic sentiment, or a mystical thesis. They apply the word "art" to a painting of a plate of apples or a purely geometric composition (irrespective of style or manner of treatment) as freely as they do to a great figure composition or a Renaissance saint or duke. This informed usage of the word "art" refers to nothing else but the artist's abstraction of the color-space of a subject, entirely separate from its political, economic, or domestic meaning and utility; and his reconstruction of that abstraction in the materials of his art. Thus all real art has always been and will always be essentially abstract, regardless of changes in subject matter, material, and technique.

It is very essential to realize that this abstract form which is the essence of art does not consist of shapes and colors which are free from political, psychological, or utilitarian associations, because no such forms exist. When one makes coffee in a pot the action is directed toward making a refreshing drink. But when one uses the coffee pot as a still-life subject the action is directed toward an assimilation of its color-space reality. The coffee pot still remains a utilitarian object in the field of nutrition, but the abstract painting of it does not express this utility, because if it did it would not be art, but an illustration having a commercial, educational, or propaganda purpose. A genuine work of art having a coffee pot as a subject would express the artist's general sense of the three-dimensional color-space of the real world, concretely applied to the contemplation of a simple object. The source of the artist's awareness of the color-space of the real world is available to all because it consists of his optical experience, his experience of the physical motions of his body in moving about, and his knowledge of similar experiences by other people gained through conversation, reading, and by looking at other works of art. The aesthetic quality of his art expression consists of the heightened awareness he has achieved in successfully unifying these experiences in relation to a concrete event. The only proof we need of the objective truth and social value of the artist's expression is given when other people look at his work and find in it a verification of their own experience and imagination.

This brings up the question of absolute and relative values. If values are only relative then the aesthetic opinions of any person, or even a barbaric society, are as objectively true and humanly valuable as any other. Hitler's pronouncement, for example, that modern art is degenerate is doubtless true relative to his own political program, but it is certainly not true in relation to the great traditions of art, and therefore we judge it to be barbaric. Similarly, the general American anesthesia to modern art, which arises from different reasons, must be judged as cultural retrogression. A recent but typical example of this is the outburst by the Detroit city budget director, David Victor Addy, against modern art, which he is said to have compared to the testing equipment of the psychiatric clinic. If aesthetic values are merely relative, then Mr. Addy's views are as worthy of consideration as the informed opinions of Dr. William Valentiner, director of the Detroit Institute of Arts, who defended modern art in this instance. There is, however, an absolute value for art, which is a living and changing thing, but which nevertheless retains its qualitative distinctness throughout human history. If we accept the pure relativism of the values assigned to it as a mere political weapon by the dictatorships, or as a commercial or sentimental illustration in the United States, then art will cease to exist. The "Sunday-painter" theory of art is still baloney, no matter how thin you slice it.

Modern art differs from art of the past not in its abstractness but in its new and contemporary concept of color-space, or form. Modern art has not changed the social function of art but has kept it alive by using as its subject matter the new and interesting relations of form and color which are everywhere apparent in our environment. A radio is the product of an extremely complex set of abstract generalizations, but no one calls it "an abstraction" or "an escape from reality" because the loudspeaker is not equipped with a set of false teeth. In view of these considerations it is needlessly confusing to isolate modern art and call it "abstraction." Some of the more "slangy" in the office force of art have gotten into the habit of referring to a modern painting as "an abstract," in the same spirit as a clerk would shout, "toss me that little $2.98 number in brown." Terms like "Impressionism," "Pointillism," "Cubism," often had their origin among artists as wisecracks or satirical jibes, but writers on art have given them a dogmatic and almost legal authority which reacts unfavorably on the direct appreciation of the works to which they have been applied. I have often been forced to use the term "abstract" in referring to my own work in order to be understood, although I have opposed it for fifteen years. I have the conviction that modern art is definitely abstract, but, more significantly, that in the past and in the present it has produced splendid examples which carry on the best tradition of art. When its opponents can say as much for the work they uphold, their claims may seem more plausible.

The materials of art can legitimately be used, and usually are, for many other purposes than recording concepts of color-space. Raincoats can be made of canvas, linseed oil, and pigment, for example. Similarly, most drawings and paintings are not art in the proper usage of the term, because they were not intended to be. Instead, the designer's purpose was to convey information, such as political, sentimental, literary, or scholarly ideas, through visual and ideological symbols. The wonderful development of color photography has already greatly enriched the expressive means in this field and has outmoded hand drawing in many cases. The distinction between real art and an illustrative art is never a matter of manual skill, or even of inventive ingenuity and fine sensibility as such; it is always a matter of the expressive purpose of the artist. The validity of a work of art stands in no proportionate relation whatever to the cogency of its ideological content, and vice versa. If any care to call this viewpoint "art for art's sake," let them make the most of it. I call it art for society's sake. A society which cannot afford such an art is poor indeed.

An enormous amount of defeatism is current today in regard to art. This takes various forms (aside from outright suppression under the dictatorships), such as propaganda for "social-comment" in art; using the aesthetic limitations of the postmasters throughout the country as an apology for the art criterion of a certain well-known government department; ballyhoo for Americanism in art; attacks on "abstract" art as un-American; etc. I call these manifestations defeatism because they are all in basic agreement in denying the independent social role of art, and in proclaiming its illustrative or propaganda function as its real value. This anti-cultural torrent has gained cloud-burst proportions and is the most immediate menace to the development, the understanding, and the social assimilation of real art in the United States. I do not mean that all the work produced under these various trends is devoid of merit as art, my objection is to the theoretical formulations and not the individual works which might be classified under them.

Most informed people agree that the most vital art of the last one hundred years was developed in France. This was done neither because of nor in conformity with governmental and academic edicts, nor in compliance with historically determined cultural forces, but in spite of them. Such art had no official standing during the lives of most of its producers, but there were a few who understood it or bought it. Today it has the prestige of a market listing and has acquired a niche in the catacombs of the art historians, but its popular and official rating as a genuine social value is as low today as at the time of its production. It is "degenerate" in Germany, "the formal and hedonistic art of a former epoch of bourgeois capitalism" in Russia, and "un-American" in the United States. This all adds up to the conclusion that the best art of our most recent past has never gained official recognition as a living and contemporary social value. In spite of the fact that American collectors and institutions often pay huge prices for works by the best modern French masters, in their patronage of American art they predominantly favor the illustrative and the anecdotal. I cite this merely to demonstrate their unwillingness to support those same qualities, which made French art great, when they appear in American art. If the objective and universal formal values of modern abstract art are to be preserved and developed, the burden rests entirely on our artists, and they will have to be less ready than now seems to be the case in conforming with the official and popular trends toward an American art of political or sentimental illustration.

Modern art was first shown in its full scope in America at the Armory Show in New York City in 1913. It is extremely important to note that this exhibition was organized exclusively by artists, who proclaimed in the catalogue their opposition to the isolationist spirit of many American artists, and further declared that they were against "cowardice even when it takes the form of amiable self-satisfaction." If this pronouncement were warranted at that time, it goes septuple today; but if our artists have proven themselves unworthy of the challenge of the Armory Show, the patronage mentioned above is even more culpable. This patronage which in its entirety consists of the government art projects, the cultural foundations, the museums, the private collectors, art societies of laymen, art schools, art dealers, lecturers and writers of books on art, and art editors and reviewers. It would be an extremely interesting and valuable project for some qualified person to systematically chart the chief activities of these groups during the last twenty-five years, and to evaluate their cultural contribution in its main trends. Whatever the findings might show, I feel sure that the words, "provincial conservatism," "academic scholasticism," "commercial exploitation," and "social snobism" would have a prominent place in the summing-up. Instead of calling on the talent of American artists for a genuine art of the color-space of our epoch, this group has demanded, "Regionalism in art"; "Americana in art"; "The New Deal in art"; "Social-content in art"; and "Sanity in art." To have a strong art in America the patronage will have to develop a little of that talent and discrimination which is automatically expected of the artist.

Since it was our artists who made modern art an integral part of the American Scene by introducing it here twenty-eight years ago, we must look to them today for the preservation and development of its values. But if they achieve this obligation their attitude will have to be much more purposeful and positive than is generally now the case. Whatever organizational form this effort may take, it will include two main points of strategy. One, to develop in the artist an understanding and belief in the social utility and necessity of genuine art, and two, to gain a voice in the councils of the art patronage to the end that it may be directed in support of a genuine art. Only when this has been achieved will art become a truly progressive factor in our cultural life.

The Cube Root (1943) *Stuart Davis*

Having received the rare privilege of writing something about my own work, at the invitation of *Art News,* it is my desire to speak as objectively as possible, and to answer some of the questions that append themselves to those elegant cultural queries, "What is it?" and "What does it mean?"

My pictures fall into the category commonly called Modern Art, and more specifically into a pigeonhole which the professors have labeled Abstract Art. I have long opposed this "typing" for reasons that seem sensible to me, although time has shown that my arguments do not impress the professors. When I get a part, it is always as an abstract artist. But nevertheless modern art is a real entity despite the Surreal nature

From *Art News* (February 1, 1943).

Stuart Davis

of many of the things said about it by professors and artists alike. It consists of a body of work produced in the last six or seven decades by men whose names are sufficiently known to preclude the need for particularization.

It would be an error to omit mention that Paris was the geographical center of this movement, because while unimportant in itself, this place of origin has been used as the basis for various attacks on the validity of the movement as a whole. In America, for example, it has often been asserted that virtue in our artists could only be found by complete repudiation of the School of Paris, as they called it. The results of these campaigns have not been beneficial for American art, to give it the maximum understatement. But it is the simple truth that the modern art movement was, and in its influence remains, the only objective proof that free expression of the human spirit in art is possible in our epoch.

In my own case, I first saw a comprehensive showing of these pictures at the Armory Show in New York City in 1913. My enthusiasm was aroused by what they had to say, and the fact that they were European in origin in no way inhibited it. I found nothing incompatible between this art and the things I had seen and felt in my own environment. On the contrary, I found an elucidation of those things and an enlarging of my understanding of them.

To many people, a picture is a replica of a thing, or a story about some kind of a situation. To an artist, on the other hand, it is an object which has been formed by an individual in response to emotional and intellectual needs. His purpose is never to counterfeit a subject but to develop a new subject. His purpose is also to live in giving importance to certain qualities in himself, which everyone presumably possesses, but which relatively few cultivate. Art is a denial of the utilitarian considerations of everyday activity. It does not give directives or convey information. Other people, usually at a much later date, extol it as a marvelous achievement, presumably because it is.

Of course, the artist doesn't dream his work into existence, he has the often arduous task of transposing his dream into the dimensional materials of painting. Thus he not only cultivates his soul, as the saying goes, but wrestles with the obstinate physical laws of three-dimensional Color-Space Design on a two-dimensional surface. Necessary theorization on these laws may come under the heading of abstract thought, but the artist does not paint his theories. His picture is shaped by his desire and there is nothing abstract about that. Proof: direct emotional response to it by people who have no knowledge or interest in his theories.

What the people respond to is the new subject the artist has found—his picture. And if the question be asked why they should be interested in that, it is because they find here a new example of the kind of things that have delighted them many times before, in nature and in art. It must be admitted that it generally takes new people to respond to new subjects. But at any rate let's have done with the academic term "abstraction" and call my pictures by the titles I give them as a means of identification. And if a generic term still be called for, just say Color-Space Composition, which they are. What they really are, of course, should only be seen and not heard.

Modern art rediscovered humanity in painting, an essential social service unrestricted by racial or national boundaries. I refer to the discovery that an artist had the power to see the world with a fresh eye. Whether he painted people, still-life, landscape, or invented subjects, every picture was an objective proof of that power to see beyond the traditional. Man's senses were restored to him. It is natural, of course, that people who had forgotten they owned any found no reflection of themselves in these pictures. They attacked them as the vicious jokes of dissolute bohemians.

It has been often said, even by proponents of those pictures known in aesthetic slang as Cubist and Abstract, that they have no subject matter. Such a statement is equivalent to saying that life has no subject matter. On the contrary, modern pictures deal with contemporary subject matter in terms of art. The artist does not exercise his freedom in a nonmaterial world. Science has created a new environment, in which new forms, lights, speeds, and spaces, are a reality. The perspectives and chiaroscuro of the Renaissance are no longer physically with us, even though their ghosts linger in many of the best modern work.

In my own case, I have enjoyed the dynamic American scene for many years past, and all of my pictures (including the ones I painted in Paris) are referential to it. They all have their originating impulse in the impact of the contemporary American environment. And it is certainly a fact that the relevant art, literature, and music of other times and places are among the most cherished realities of that environment. I mention this last point only because there is a continuing trend by strong groups in American art who, in this way or that, have sought to deny it.

Some of the things which have made me want to paint, outside of other paintings, are: American wood and iron work of the past; Civil War and skyscraper architecture; the brilliant colors on gasoline stations; chain-store fronts, and taxi-cabs; the music of Bach; synthetic chemistry; the poetry of Rimbeau; fast travel by train, auto, and aeroplane which brought new and multiple perspectives; electric signs; the landscape and boats of Gloucester, Mass.; 5 & 10 cent store kitchen utensils; movies and radio; Earl Hines hot piano and Negro jazz music in general, etc. In one way or another the quality of these things plays a role in determining the character of my paintings. Not in the sense

Stuart Davis

of describing them in graphic images, but by predetermining an analogous dynamics in the design, which becomes a new part of the American environment. Paris School, Abstraction, Escapism? Nope, just Color-Space Compositions celebrating the resolution in art of stresses set up by some aspects of the American scene.

The development of modern art in Europe is probably at an end. Indeed, its strength seems to have been sapped for some years past. During its regime it broke down traditional concepts of composition unsuited to contemporary expression. It brought new light, color, and perspectives to art, suited to its new subject matter. It clarified the prevalent confusion which identified a graphic image with the word "art." It proved once [and] for all that art is a dimensional language, and that its subject matter moves us in terms of an objective dimensional coherence. But enormous changes are taking place which demand new forms, and it is up to artists living in America to find them. New environments present themselves. As far as creating art is concerned, it is no solution to represent them in illustration. If new forms are found it will be by artists who believe in their right to find them, and in that belief have the courage to look.

What About Modern Art and Democracy?
With Special Reference to George Biddle's
Proposals (1943)* *Stuart Davis*

I

A great increase in the production and distribution of art has taken place in the United States during the past ten years. Political, economic, and technological events have resulted in the establishment of a number of agencies which sponsor and disseminate art in various ways and for various reasons. An ever-widening public awareness of and participation in art have been the logical result of this process, which many have characterized as the beginning of a great American renaissance in art. However retarded by the war, it is certain to be accelerated with the coming of peace. A vast machinery for popularization of art is now available, and we face the question: who controls it and to what ends?

As we must define our political and social objectives as we prosecute the war against Fascist reaction, so it is appropriate to discuss our cultural direction in relation to them. George Biddle has already covered

* Mr. Biddle had written a spirited defense of the Works Progress Administration's Federal Art Project ("Art Under Five Years of Federal Patronage," *The American Scholar*, IX, No. 3 [Summer, 1940], 327–38).
From *Harper's* (December, 1943).

this subject in *Harper's*. In two articles entitled "The Victory and Defeat of Modernism" and "The Government and the Arts" he has discussed the subject in its aesthetic, social, and economic aspects. Knowing that a great many artists and other interested persons have reached conclusions different from Mr. Biddle's, I believe that some of these should be formulated to round out the discussion.

In particular, his conclusion that the Modern movement has run its course involves arguments that go far beyond any mere quibble about styles in painting. Taken as a premise, it colors his attitude toward all the other aspects of the matter, involving the whole question of the artist's role in society. In brief, his thesis is that Modernism in art eventuates in Ivory Towerism, an escape from life [which is] incapable of meeting the challenge of contemporary reality; that "the most momentous event in the world of art since the Italian Renaissance" is now under way; that we have developed agencies and media for mass art distribution which make an "art for the masses" possible and necessary, and that this art must speak a common language; that in totalitarian countries this apparatus will be used to convert the "masses to sadism and fear"; but that in a democracy the artist "has the uncensored privilege of expressing a social faith."

These are very definite conclusions. It is chiefly on four points that I differ with Mr. Biddle. These are (1) his estimate of Modern Art; (2) his claim as to a contemporary renaissance in American art; (3) his argument that art must speak a common language; and (4) his confidence on the question of censorship.

In the first place, it seems to me that the term "Ivory Tower" is inappropriately applied to an art movement that has had repercussions in all parts of the civilized world on aesthetic perception and industrial design. In the second place, anyone who predicts a renaissance because the apparatus for broad art activity is now available should be reminded that power can be used to subvert as well as to implement human welfare. In the third place, anyone who discusses the question of "an art for the masses" which must speak "a common language" should bear in mind the fact that Modern Art does speak a common language to thousands who have had the opportunity and the will to cultivate it. It will become part of the common art language of the masses as opportunity for participation in authentic art experience is made available to them. But that language cannot be formulated in terms of their relative illiteracy in art and the prejudices resulting from it. Opportunity will bring new terms to clarify and extend the scope of their present understanding. Increased understanding must certainly involve ultimate knowledge of the most advanced forms of contemporary Modernism as well as the art forms of past epochs. To assume incapacity on the part of the masses for the fullest cultural growth is incompatible with belief in the democratic principle. Finally, Mr. Biddle's belief that the artist in a democracy is free from censorship or coercion requires certain reservations if it is to check with the facts.

Between the artist and the public there are the agencies of sponsorship and distribution, in whose policies the artist has little or no voice. These policies, which both reflect and create public opinion, react directly on the economic status of the artist and on his aesthetic orientation. Mr. Biddle perceives that in totalitarian countries the artist is coerced into "converting the masses to sadism and fear," but apparently he does not see the possibility of coercion here. While examples of outright suppression or destruction of art in the United States are infrequent, there have been a number of them. The most spectacular was the complete destruction of Rivera's mural in Rockefeller Center by the management in 1933. In this instance Mr. Rivera, whose work Mr. Biddle admires and who definitely had a "social faith," discovered that a very active censorship could operate in a democracy. (The adjacent murals by Sert, expressing the social faith in international Academism, were not destroyed.) But overt suppression is only the cruder form of censorship; the preferred instruments of coercion are propaganda and economic attrition. I share Mr. Biddle's hope that a great renaissance in art is at hand, but am less ready than he to change it to a prediction.

II

To discuss the matter further we must first of all try to define what kind of art we are talking about. The field of art is broad and includes many valuable activities other than the painting of easel and mural pictures, or the creation of sculpture. But our interest in folk arts and crafts, commercial art, political and literary illustration, applied design, etc. does not preclude us from wishing to create works which have no such immediate utilitarian function, works which proceed from and satisfy spiritual needs. It is this order of work which is commonly meant by the word "art." Today the word connotes a certain level of emotional and intellectual values which have been sought and realized by men at different times and in different historical environments. Art is not a mere reflection of reality, but rather a revelation of subjective values as integral with all its aspects. It is expressed through a dimensional structure—art form—which is always different from the natural forms that inspired it. Art is not in the subject matter but in the artist, and communicates his personal realization directly through its form. Art is not the recording of the impact of natural forms on the retina; it is the synthesis of all the perceptive faculties in emotional equilibrium, objectified in a language of form. Emotional response to nature does not create art except when it is integrated with an interest in imaginative construction for its own sake. The act of painting is not a duplication of experience, but the extension of experience on the plane of formal invention.

Such an activity takes time and space for its realization, and is not an automatic by-product of other activities. He is an artist who not only is inspired by reality but extends its scope by creating a new reality shaped by his imagination. We perceive this personal spiritual realization in art works of the past and cherish them for that reason without regard to the limitations of their subject matter. Modern art brings to its subject matter the new spatial concepts of our epoch that are being realized in all the forms of accelerated communication. There is no innate barrier between public understanding of modern social and technological concepts and their spiritual equation in the advanced forms of Modern Art. It is on the basis of the considerations noted above that questions of art must be discussed today if we wish our art facilities to be used creatively.

Although the "formalist" concept of art and the concept of "an art of ideas" are at opposite poles, it is obvious that whatever the "ideas" may be they must be visualized in terms of "form" to exist as art. It is also clear that verisimilitude to natural form and appearance does not make a work of art. A flesh-colored cast of the human head is not art, although it may express a number of physiological and psychological ideas. Norman Rockwell has all his facts straight but his work remains in the category of illustration. It is agreed by both theories that art must have form; even those people who currently demand an art of cogent political and social directives agree to this. But if it is the story that makes art vital, why bother about the form of its telling? Mr. Rockwell's illustrations certainly have their own kind of form, even though it is not art form. Even if he changed his subject-matter from middle-class anecdotes to cogent ideas, would his work become vital art? In such a case it would express vital ideas through form. But we know very well that it would remain illustration, because his style shows more concern with imitation than invention of form and thus is barren of the creative formal realization which characterizes art. It should be clear from this that the quality of art does not depend on subject matter or story. And there is no existing principle of design which merely awaits an overlay of important ideas to materialize into art. Art design, art form, is precisely the "important idea" which we get from a work of art, and the real importance of a work of art stands in no direct ratio to the importance of its subject matter or ideological references.

But painting, we are still told, must in its very nature tell a story, and where it becomes "abstract" it is said to be "craft" art. Mr. Biddle supports this view, and says that the philosophy of abstract art asserts that "meaning in a work of art detracts from its beauty." I have spoken with a great many abstract artists but have never heard them put it that way. On the contrary I have received the impression that they eagerly sought "meaning," even though they refused to limit "meaning" to a literary connotation. The fact that ponderous Wagnerian operas exist does not somehow deprive Bach's "Art of the Fugue" of meaning. Nor do Rivera's more identifiable images preclude meaning in the more creative forms of Picasso's "Guernica."

But while Mr. Biddle argues that the philosophy of Modern Art is unsuited to American needs, and is dead of its own sterility, he doesn't leave the matter there. He finds that it still lives on as "a school of design" in the works of "our best artists." There is a seeming, and possibly actual, contradiction here. It involves the rather difficult maneuver of separating design from subject matter, form from content. It suggests that the skeleton of Modern Art is still alive even though the body is dead. It implies that the emotional content of art lies in the recognition of natural objects which tell a cogent story, but that underneath or behind this story lies an inert structural device called "design." This must be what Mr. Biddle means, because he finds the design of those modern pictures, which he says are lacking in meaning or content, as an active principle in the work of "our best artists." This can only mean that something new in the way of subject matter has been added to give American work that art content which is lacking in the work of modern artists in Europe. It suggests that it is only European Modern Art that is dead, and only American artists who are modern.

I cannot accept this view for two reasons. First, because my concept of "design," as integral with content, makes it impossible to borrow the "design" of a work which you pronounce empty of content and get something which will not in its turn be empty of content; and second, because you cannot borrow the "design" of a work of Modern European Art without contracting its philosophy as well. I know of course that certain mechanical structural principles of design, innate in the nature of the materials, are common to all graphic expression. These are necessarily transferable. But Mr. Biddle's use of the word refers to an emotional design even though his argument seems to contradict the idea by placing emotion in the subject matter. His argument, although I am sure not by intention, would in effect allow the enemies of Modern Art to clothe their nakedness with its prestige.

III

Mr. Biddle's implication that only European Modernism is defunct has suggestive connotations. I am reminded that there are currently living and working in the United States a great many exponents of this same "defunct" Modernism. In addition to the Americans there are a number of Europeans who are direct products of that philosophy which Mr. Biddle's analysis finds frustrated in the face of contemporary reality.

Are these artists to be regarded as essentially un-American, and remote from the possibility of inclusion in the category of "our best artists?" The logic of Mr. Biddle's argument suggests that possibility, in which case I should find it hard to distinguish his view from isolationist views in general. If the different approaches to the art problem evidenced in the work of artists such as Milton Avery, Paul Burlin, Byron Browne, Balcomb Greene, Carl Holty, Jacob Laurence, Jan Matulka, George L. K. Morris, Walter Quirt, Abe Rattner, Niles Spencer, Joseph Stella, and other American modernists—not to mention such European artists now in the United States as Jean Hélion, Fernand Léger, André Masson, Piet Mondrian, and Hans Richter—can play no part in our renaissance, except in its application to "craft design," we might do well to make the decision now. It would eliminate any confusion as to their proper status in the activities of Mr. Biddle's proposed national Bureau of Fine Arts in case it is set up. It would prevent artists, innately craft-designers but holding delusions of grandeur, from wasting the time of the Bureau's functionaries with misguided demands.

Democracy in culture is dependent on the free exchange of ideas, which isolationism seeks to frustrate by constantly working to perpetuate local racial, national, and cultural prejudices. In America there is a tendency to look with suspicion on "abstract" ideas or creative innovations when they occur outside the field of technology or commerce. Although we live in an industrial society built on abstract ideas, "professors" in politics and "abstractionists" in art are generally held to be crackpots. We do not call the radio an "abstraction," and we do not put bird feathers on the wings of our airplanes or artificial dentures in the radio loudspeaker. We regard synthetic quinine and sulfa drugs as very real and desirable despite their foreign origin and "unnaturalness." But where art is concerned the Currier and Ives model is held to be adequate. In science the word "abstract" is identified with progress; in social philosophy and art, with the Ivory Tower.

This fallacy could be cleared up in a week by the advertising agencies of big business, granted an extremely hypothetical motive. Instead, business puts its weight behind glorifying an art, supposedly founded on sound American traditions, which exploits the American Scene in terms of traditional and provincial ideology. This cultivated cultural backwardness of the public is reflected directly in any large cross-section of contemporary American art, and deprives its forms of any real contemporary quality. The familiar, the literal, or the "folksy" is reiterated to the exclusion of new vision and new synthesis. The public hears much of creative business executives of vision, but it seems to want its artists' vision in traditional form. Creative bathrooms and kitchens are eagerly desired, and we are told that it will soon be possible to bring home the dehydrated soup from the A & P in a helicopter; but in cultural matters, nostalgia for the old frontiers tends to dim out the new frontiers already in view. Any desire to realize the real spiritual values of contemporary industrial society is frustrated because we look for them in the wrong direction.

But this cultural situation, while historically determined in one sense, has been created, cultivated, and exploited as a matter of policy in a more important sense. In much the same way that Mr. Biddle extracts the skeletal design of Modern Art to clothe it with ideological meaning, so the authors of these policies find a way to separate form from content. They also want not only "ideas" but "art form" as well. So they sponsor artists with gallery and museum reputation—that supplies the "art design." This design is then clothed with a "meaning" of commercial import, or, for other purposes, with middle-class psychological palliatives. As examples, take the series of "genuine oil paintings" in the Lucky Strike advertisements, or the International Business Machines art collection and exhibitions. In the last analysis, much of the activity in Mr. Biddle's predicted renaissance will be financed by big business. Through cultural endowments, direct commercial investment, and advertising subsidy of publications, the interests of business are already reflected in the field of art. In these and other ways are established numerous agencies for the dissemination of art which are directly or remotely affected by the political, social and financial interests of business enterprise. From the evidence at hand one must judge that the general character of this influence is notable for uncreative literalism on one hand and nostalgia for past formulations of spiritual values on the other. The latter constitutes the American business man's surrealism.

Art has a good reputation even among those who cannot discriminate in it, and the draping of large enterprise in robes of art creates a good impression. But if in creating the good impression "dangerous thoughts" were generated in the public, a wrong impression would have been created. Business approves of art, yes, but an art of the status quo to soothe the public mind and keep it on the beam. An art of the glorified familiar and spiritual nostalgia in reverse. And by all means a one hundred per cent American art purged of the dangerous thoughts of foreign "isms," an isolationist art singing the American Way of Life.

But outside of its cultural interests business is not always isolationist; in many cases it is very cosmopolitan and cultivates an international language when seeking commercial purposes. But it fears that a public fed too rich a diet of creative art might develop creative ideas of its own, and might find that "creative" business has failed to create the best of all possible worlds. Modern Art is not useful to this program because it contains the "dangerous" thought that isolationist culture is historically outdated.

I do not mean to suggest that there is a totalitarian conspiracy by big business to control and subvert American art. But that there is among business-minded people an increasing concern about matters cultural there can be no doubt, however unformulated it may be and however variously idealistic, naïve, opportunistic, or conscious. Any cross-section of American art today reflects it in impoverishment of spirit. Recent acts of Congress reflect it in the expulsion of "professors" from government posts as suspected of "dangerous un-American thoughts," and their replacement by business and advertising men. It is reflected in the fact that the advertising agencies of big business now determine the character of our war posters and the cultural standards of the National Association of Manufacturers hold sway. Congress took away the funds from the Graphics Division of the Domestic Branch of the OWI, which had idealistically hoped to produce posters with some artistic merit as part of their effectiveness. Similarly, Mr. Biddle's own sponsor in painting war-front pictures, the War Department Art Advisory Committee, has been shot out from under him by Congress. The magazine *Life* now pays his expenses. I assume that Peyton Boswell, Jr., expresses the general attitude of *Life* toward art in his book, *American Art Today*. Its illustrations consist of a collection of *Life*'s art color plates, with elucidating text by Mr. Boswell. He says, "Because of our Anglo-Saxon heritage American art is a literal three-dimensional art. There is little room in its pattern for such aesthetic detours as cubism or non-objective painting." From this I gather that artists with other racial origins or those tainted with foreign "isms" have to get in the Anglo-Saxon groove if they want to be American.

IV

Mr. Biddle does not seem to fear that the flowering of our renaissance in art might be obstructed by censorship or diverted by other pressures. His freedom from fear is apparently based on his faith in the inexorable workings of a certain cultural law. After noting that "frequent surveys made by hard-headed editors of various magazines . . . establish the amazing fact that the people prefer the best," he formulates this law. It states that "when good art and less good art are indiscriminately offered in large quantities to a large audience there is an ever-increasing demand for the best." He sees this law quietly delivering the goods through the apparently "indiscriminate" activity of such agencies as *Life, Esquire, Fortune,* International Business Machines, N. W. Ayer & Son, Associated American Artists, the now defunct government Art Projects, and others.

I am willing to grant Mr. Biddle his law, with the reservation that other counter-laws may, in certain situations, inhibit its flawless operation. Granted an aesthetically uncoerced public and a group of benign and "indiscriminate" cultural donors, possibly his law might work if given plenty of time. But the exploitation of art through mass media does not now offer the scientific conditions essential for such an experiment. One of the reasons it does not, in addition to those indicated above, is that a number of people feel that such a test is unnecessary and have jumped the gun by revealing the secret that the American Scene is "the best" and that the search is over.

Sentiment for an isolationist culture has been rallied round the slogan of "The American Scene." Through institutional and individual propaganda a school of illustrative painting has been created and patronized and has attained an almost official status. An appropriate slogan for it would be, "The Academy is dead, long live the Academy!" In opposition to the democratic international spirit of Modern Art, this "official art" fosters regional and provincial concepts and flatters public prejudice. Isolationist culture is reactionary and undemocratic in character in that it seeks to suppress that free exchange of ideas which alone can develop an authentic modern American Art. It exercises a censorship in our channels of art communication which Mr. Biddle apparently does not detect. It is not that the American artist is prevented from painting any way he chooses, but that he faces a public preconditioned to look with suspicion on anything beyond the literal, the sentimental, or the academic. He is not coerced into leading the masses to "sadism and fear"; he is coerced into leading them to complacency. The American Scene philosophy parallels political isolationism in its desire to preserve the status quo of the American Way of Life.

For many years past such men as Thomas Craven, Peyton Boswell, Jr., editor of *Art Digest,* Forbes Watson, and many others have been propagating their versions of the American Scene idea. Through books, magazines, newspapers, and lectures they reach a vast audience which is told that Modern Art is un-American and devoid of content. The Modern artist is outlawed and deprived of cultural citizenship, and the idea of democracy in culture goes down the drain. The relations between art and politics are devious, and often obscure, but they exist. The American Scene ideology has in it germs which the Fascist-minded among us may find it profitable to cultivate.

V

When the New Deal was new, Federal subsidy of art became a reality. The WPA Art Project, organized and directed by Holger Cahill, and the Section of Fine Arts, headed by Edward Bruce, employed between them many thousands of artists. The WPA employed them on a broad basis of abilities and skills and produced much valuable work. In general, there was a fair approximation to democratic procedure, and the artists gained considerable voice in the determination of the Art Project's policies, up to the point of its political decline. The Section of Fine Arts, on the other hand, was conducted on different principles, inherent in its original purpose, which was to employ "the best artists" to embellish government buildings. In both cases a great number of the artists employed had already been softened up by American Scene propaganda, which determined the general character of the output. But under the WPA some modern art was produced, in mural and easel form, without undue censorship. Sincere efforts were made to allocate and give it social currency. The policy of the Section of Fine Arts, by contrast, effectively censored such work with few exceptions, as a survey of their several hundred murals will show. In the eyes of the Section, Modernism was not a matter for concern by "our best artists," which its competitions were designed to lure from obscurity.

However this may be denied by pointing to "open competitions" and juries of artist judges, the facts as to the works chosen support my statement. The participation of artists in the policy of the Section's program, on the basis of its results, suggests the possibly unconscious presence of the "divide and rule" principle and the "company union" idea. Whatever causes lay behind this situation, it is not irrelevant to note that the late Mr. Bruce held both Modern Art and the more democratic artists' organizations of the period in low regard. Another contributing factor may have been the presence of Forbes Watson, writer on art and proponent of his own version of the American Scene, as an active member of the staff in publicizing its policies and activities. Nor does it seem out of place to recall, in view of his recent frank expression of beliefs, that Mr. Biddle himself was closely associated with the activities of the Section from its origin.

The idea that our government should be concerned with the cultural welfare of the citizens it represents seems self-evident. And that efforts to revive its now-withdrawn support of art should be vigorously pursued is beyond question. What remains to be decided is the form that such support should take and how it should be organized. Mr. Biddle's proposal for a national Bureau of Fine Arts is extremely valuable in bringing the whole question before the public. The practical question of how this Bureau is to be integrated in the hierarchies of governmental bureaus is beyond my scope. Also its internal structure and the scope of its activities are matters requiring much fuller discussion by all those whose interests are most directly involved. But Mr. Biddle's proposal that the director of the national Bureau of Fine Arts be chosen by presidential appointment seems to me highly debatable.

Such a bureau will be of no service to our cultural advancement unless guarantees for a broad policy in its functions are written into its administrative program. Such guarantees can be made real only by direct artist representation in its continuing policies as they develop.

That the idea of a direct artists' voice in government affairs is not new is

Stuart Davis

evidenced by Report No. 198 to the 35th Congress, dated March 3, 1859—over eighty-four years ago. Addressed to the Senate and House, this document began:

"The memorial of the artists of the United States, in convention assembled, respectfully represents:

"That your memorialists appear before your honorable bodies to solicit for American Art that consideration and encouragement to which they conceive it to be entitled at the hand of the general government." Their purpose was the establishment of an Art Commission which should function to "the great end proposed," namely, "the advancement of art in the United States." This Commission, they went on to say, should be "composed of those designated by the United Voice of American artists as competent to the office. . . ." The report was signed by 115 important artists of the time, from many different States, headed by Rembrandt Peale of Philadelphia. The Commission was duly established by Congress in 1910, but the "United Voice" idea was changed in the Act, as passed, to "the President." It was the President who had the power to appoint the seven members and to fill all vacancies. The scope of the Commission was limited chiefly to an advisory function and in no sense fulfilled the intention of the memorialists' proposal.

Since an ultimate concern of man is man, there must be an enormous spiritual potential in our epoch. It must find its objectification in political, social, and cultural forms, or the spiritual equilibrium essential to civilized progress will be destroyed. In the field of art, freedom for creative realization must be established and maintained. Currently the narrow views of isolationism are inadequate to create such freedom.

In contrast to them I want to end by quoting from another statement made by American Artists, thirty years ago. Although much has happened in the interval, I think the ideas it contained are still a sound ideological antidote for the American Scene concept.

Organized exclusively by artists, the International Exhibition of Modern Art was held in the Sixty-ninth Infantry Armory in New York City in 1913, and subsequently in Chicago (where students of the Art Institute burned a Matisse painting in effigy), and later in Boston. They formed the Association of American Painters and Sculptors, Inc., and gave their reason in the preface to the catalogue:

The American artists exhibiting here consider the exhibition as of equal importance for themselves as for the public. The less they find their work showing signs of the development indicated in the Europeans, the more reason they will have to consider whether or not painters and sculptors here have fallen behind, through escaping the incidence through distance, and for other reasons, of the forces that have manifested themselves on the other side of the Atlantic. Art is a sign of life. And to be afraid of life is to be afraid of truth, and to be a champion of superstition. This exhibition is an indication that the Association of American Painters and Sculptors is against cowardice even when it takes the form of amiable self-satisfaction.

The "United Voice of American artists" of 1859 became a whisper, but the 1913 version of that "Voice" has a more clarion note, and can still be heard through the more nasal sounds of the American Scene. But is it not enough for the "Voice" to be heard. What it says must be translated into action by our modern painters, who through their work keep the channels of cultural communication free, and constitute the promise that "the most momentous event in the world of art since the Italian Renaissance" may yet realize its potentialities.

What Abstract Art Means to Me (1951)
Stuart Davis

I think of Abstract Art in the same way I think of all Art, Past and Present. I see it as divided into two Major categories, Objective and Subjective. Objective Art is Absolute Art. Subjective Art is Illustration, or communication by Symbols, Replicas, and Oblique Emotional Passes. They are both Art, but their Content has no Identity. Their difference cannot be defined as a difference of Idiom, because all Paintings have the Laws of Design as a common denominator. Design exists as an Idiom of Color-Space Logic, and it also exists in an Idiom of Representational Likenesses. Objective Art and Subjective Art exist in both Idioms. Their difference can only be defined in terms of what the Artist thinks his Purpose means—its Content as a Design Image.

Objective Art sees the Percept of the Real World as an Immediate Given Event, without any Abstract Term in it. But there is Consciousness of Change, of Motion, in it. The Real Object, its Image in the Idiom of Idea, and the external Image of Idea as Design, are experienced as a simultaneous event in Consciousness. These three distinct realities are Perceived as a single Object; a Headline on the Display-Surface of Common Sense. The consciousness of change experienced in these separate identifications is understood as the Total Form of this Object. To know this is the experience of its Free Accomplishment; an act amenable to Volition. This is the Total Appearance, hence Total Content of Objective Art, Absolute Art. Its Universal Principle is the Sense of Freedom.

Subjective Art is a "Horse of Another Color," to use the current

From "What Abstract Art Means to Me," *Bulletin* of The Museum of Modern Art, XVIII, No. 3 (Spring, 1951), and reprinted by the permission of the publisher.

Bop phrase; as it refers to shots of "Horse," or Heroin, which come in different colors to suit the Esthetic Taste and Poetic Mood of the client. Taste and Mood are well-known attributes of Subjective Art, inherent in its concept of Reality. Unlike Objective Art it sees the Change between the Real Object, the Idea Object, and Real Design, as an Abyss, a Chasm, a Void. These terms appear frequently in its literature, and often as Holes in the Paintings. Its concept of Universal Principle has no Objective continuity. Spanning the Gaps in it is accomplished in an emotional Context of Anxiety, Fear, and Awe. That is how Subjective Art was born. Its Universal Principle has more the character of a Universal Bellyache.

The Security Image of Objective Art is in the Familiar Likeness of Change as a Topical Subject. But the Security Image of Subjective Art has a hypothetical location somewhere in Tibet. As a result it has become the greatest builder of Arachnoid Bridges in the world. Like the Laminated Iconography of the Scholars, it has a Perverse Passion for the Detour. It Eschews Route 66, and has a million broken bones to the mile. Over thirty years ago, Learned Proponents for Expressionism variously identified its Content as a "Psychic Discharge"; "Soul-Substance"; and a "Belch from the Unconscious," communicating the Distress of the Suffering Artist, as a sort of Moral Cathartic.

My interest in Art does not arise from this kind of Distraction, which still has a number of Fans. Art is not a Subjective Expression to me, whether it be called Dadaism, Surrealism, Non-Objectivism, Abstractionism, or Intra-Subjectivism. But when paintings live up to these Advance Agent Press Releases, I turn on the Ball Game.

Fortunately any similarity between the Painting and the Publicity is purely coincidental in many cases. In such a number of cases, in fact, that Modern Art as a whole is not more subjectively expressionistic in character than the most Durable Remains of Past Art. So-called Abstract Art to me is an Idiom of Color-Space Logic as the Design of a Topical Subject, understood as the Universal Free Subject. In that understanding there is No Abstract term. My intention is to keep it that way.

The Place of Painting in Contemporary Culture: The Easel Is a Cool Spot at an Arena of Hot Events (1957)   *Stuart Davis*

The scope of Subject Matter indicated by the title of this essay could be taken as formidable and even alarming, but as a Scholar without

From *Art News* (June, 1957).

Scholarship, I find it more convenient to take a Do-It-Yourself attitude and simply follow the Instructions on the package of my own experience.

In line with that decision, I feel able to make the categorical statement that The Place of Painting in Contemporary Culture consists entirely of what each artist emergently makes it. In my understanding the word Culture means a Subject Matter for art, as opposed to the notion of it as an Historical Imperative which makes the Rules, and then Scoops the Artist before the Algebra of his Dream has become a real Event. The Predictions of Cultural Determinism might allow the Artist to read his own Obituary in the Morning Paper, so to speak, but at the same time it would rob the Artist of his Birthright of the Enjoyment of it. But when culture is understood to be simply a splendid Environment of Events with no questions asked, the role of Painting seems much less Macabre, and can even be considered quite attractive. By the foregoing I think I have succeeded in changing the title of this occasion to one more suited to my ability in dealing with it. It now reads, "The Place of Culture in Contemporary Painting."

Contemporary Culture as a Subject includes the Past in the form of the Past and Present Individual Formulations of it. These exist on the same plane of our Awareness with what is Uniquely Immediate to the Twentieth Century. The latter includes New Lights, Speeds, Sounds, Communications and Jazz in general, as the Ornaments of daily Experience. Their continuous presentation to the Front Page of our Common Sense constitutes a Montage Perspective—a Short-Cut to the necessary Implementation for Knowing you are Alive. It holds the promise of an Automation Psychology suited to the Know-How for a Pre-Fabricated Humanism. It suggests a Button for the Correct determination of Obligatory Moral Categories.

And then of course there is Modern Art with its Natural Giants of Painting in the last fifty years. That, too, is a laminated Fact in the Cultural Subject Matter for Today's Artist with a normal Appetite for the Air-Conditioned Now. The Continuity of Culture exists as a Sequence of Unconsidered and Unlicensed Choices and Identifications by Artists. They reserve their Faculty of Consideration and Comparison for the Mathematics of Tangibility which gives to Choice its forms as Public Currency. The Painting itself is the Responsible Social Act of the Artist, and is one of the surest, most direct forms of Communication known to man.

At one time or another, including the present, this question of Communication has been Viewed with Alarm by Scholars, Critics and others occupying a position Tangent to the Main Point. They are fond of saying that the Content of much of Modern Art is Perversely Cryptic, disassociated from the interests and observations of the Citizens, and that its Visual Idiom is impossible to Translate. In effect they demand of Art an Audit and Notarized Itemization of its Contents. I regard this as the Wrong Approach. It is not the Property Assets of the Painting's Subject which are the Measure of its Civic function, but rather the Un-solicited Blueprint of the picture's Shape-Identity—a Photostat of the Individual's Deed of Ownership to the Enjoyment of his own Senses.

There is nothing more Universal in Experience than Enjoyment, but Art is simply *one* of the Techniques for its Social Communication and Use. To propose that the worth of Art stands in Direct Ratio to the Universality of its Appeal is a fairly meaningless Proposition. It represents basically an un-Democratic impulse to coerce not only the Artist but the Audience as well. In effect it would deprive the Individual of his Right to Free Choice of Technique in Creative Social Communication. It is necessary that the Right to Hate Art as well as to love it be preserved and that the current Popularity of the Aptitude Test be respected. In brief, since Modern Art is very well understood by Millions who are impelled to concern themselves with it—why quibble?

My personal guess as to the Meaning and Enormous Popularity of Modern Painting goes somewhat as follows:—I see the Artist as a Cool Spectator-Reporter at an Arena of Hot Events. Its continuing appeal to me since the Armory Show of 1913 is due, I believe, to its American Dynamics, even though the best Reporters then were Europeans operating in terms of European Identifications. Fortunately, we have our own share of Aces today. In his Professional Capacity the Modern Artist regards the subject of Subjective Feelings as a Casualty and never confuses them with the Splendor of the Continuity of Process, the Event itself. I see the Paintings as being made by Competent Workmen outside the self—not as a Signed Convulsion communicating an Enormous Capacity for Frustration with the Outside. I am aware that a number of excellent Artists today might seem to fall into the latter category and would regard my remark as offensive. But Offense is no part of my intention which is entirely one of Notation. I believe that there is a vast Audience which, like myself, is more interested in the Scenery than the Familiar Furnished Room of their own Short-Circuited Emotional Wiring.

I think that if the Contemporary Artist, with a reasonable amount of Taste for the Excitement and Impact of contemporary Culture in the sense I have indicated, will make his Report to the very Hip People—then both Art and Culture will do all right.

Interview (1957)   *Stuart Davis*

I think that a painting is a logical process from the time you buy the stretcher. You buy one that is rectilinear, because, while it is possible to make other kinds of stretchers (you can have them leaning over, or round, or in all kinds of geometrical shapes), a rectilinear shape fits in with the kind of houses we live in, it fits in with our being able to stand up straight, and it is not disturbing. Whatever feeling there is about making a rectilinear canvas as the base on which we paint, the selection was made long ago and we don't feel it any more. You just use it as a matter of common sense. So from that point on your composition, your design, your painting are implicitly conditioned by the original selection of a rectilinear area. It's a geometrical decision.

The older type of painting, which was valid for its time, was one wherein things were seen in a slower-living atmosphere. The speeds of moving from place to place were very much slower; the communication of ideas was thousands, literally thousands, of times slower than it is today. Today the visualization of an image which would express the content of an artist's thought about what things are, what the visual character of the subject matter of his thoughts was at any time, is a multifaceted affair. We have information about events all the world over practically instantaneously with their happening. We have it by the written word, by ear, and even visually, at almost the time of the event itself.

These events and incidents, which are the subject matter of our interest in living today, follow one another in rapid succession. And it doesn't stop on Sundays or holidays—it's a continuous thing. So in order to establish any sense of balance in this multiple impact of life, we use what I suppose you would call abstract generalizations, which can stand for a whole group of things. We maintain our balance under the impact of this multiple series of events, but we also have the capacity, in maintaining our balance, to group them. Since in drawing and painting we are concerned with what is essentially a geometric event, we are able to use the limitations of this geometrical medium. We are able to control it in subtle ways, and the limitations are, in effect, no limitation to developing a complete correspondence to our subjective feelings and our thoughts, which are not geometrical but which are spontaneously given and logically carried out. These are not geometrical things; but we are able, through a geometrical medium, to make them a continuous part of our awareness.

In order to make a visual image you have to have something going

Excerpt from an Interview published in *Stuart Davis,* catalogue of an exhibition at the Walker Art Center, Minneapolis, Minn., 1957, pp. 44–45.

on, and as soon as you have two things instead of one, an event is taking place. I regard an event as some kind of action. That's how we are aware of it. If it were a complete, undifferentiated unity, you wouldn't know you were alive, so to speak. So I consider my drawing, my painting, as a progressive and continuous event or activity, and the direction and character of it are determined by my obligation to make choices in what is presented to me as subject matter. I may be watching a prize fight while I have a painting in progress, and some sort of action in the fight, or some sort of decision in it, may create an emotional attitude which gives me an idea for the painting. I don't mean in any sense of imitating the motion of the fighters, etc., but one which gives me an impulse to do something else in the painting. . . .

My pictures are developed without preconception as to the way they will be finished. They start with a simple impulse to make something, which is always specific, something outside myself. It could be a box of matches on the table, it could be a news report, it could be a recording of the pianola rolls that Fats Waller made when he was twenty years old, it could be a political event. It could be anything that would be the initiation of an impulse to draw something. The emotional energy, so to speak, would be brought about by some external event. I don't regard the significance of the event itself as important to the specific content of the picture. What is important is that one has the impulse to do it. I proceed in developing an idea in what is to me a very logical way. I think of a shape as a drawn shape, as a thing in itself, not as a replica of the thing that gave me the impulse to draw it. I don't in any sense preclude the use of specific shapes, that is to say, that would be specific to the appearance of a particular person or landscape or object. I don't hold the notion that I would never draw such a shape, even though currently I don't do it. But in no case do I identify the shape of the thing or the person that gave me the impulse to draw with what I have drawn.

27. *Salt Shaker,* 1931. Oil, 49⅞″ x 32″. Collection, The Museum of Modern Art, New York. Gift of Mrs. Edith Gregor Halpert.

28. *Mandolin and Saw,* 1930. Oil, 26″ x 34″. The Phillips Collection, Washington, D.C.

29. *New York–Paris, Number 1,* 1931. Oil, 35⅝″ x 51¾″. School of Art Gallery, University of Iowa, Iowa City.

30. *Sixth Avenue El,* 1932. Lithograph, 11⅞″ x 17⅞″. Photograph courtesy of Mrs. Stuart Davis.

31. *Hot Still Scape for Six Colors,* 1940. Oil, 36″ x 45″. Collection of The Downtown Gallery, New York.

32. Stuart Davis working on *Hot Still Scape for Six Colors,* 1940. Photograph courtesy of Mrs. Stuart Davis.

33. *Report from Rockport,* 1940. Oil, 24″ x 30″. Collection of Mr. and Mrs. Milton Lowenthal.

34. *Owh! In San Pão,* 1951. Oil, 52¼″ x 41¾″. Collection of Whitney Museum of American Art, New York.

35. *Rapt at Rappaport's,* 1952. Oil, 52″ x 40″. The Joseph H. Hirshhorn Foundation, New York.

36. *Visa,* 1951. Oil, 40″ x 52″. Collection, The Museum of Modern Art, New York. Gift of Mrs. Gertrud A. Mellon.

37. Study for *Windshield Mirror, ca.* 1952. Oil, 54″ x 76″. Collection of Mrs. Stuart Davis. Photograph courtesy of the Lawrence Rubin Gallery.

38. *Nu,* 1953. Oil, 8″ x 6″. Collection of Mr. Ira Herbert.

39. *Colonial Cubism,* 1954. Oil, 45″ x 60″. Walker Art Center, Minneapolis.

40. *Semé,* 1953. Oil, 52″ x 40″. The Metropolitan Museum of Art, New York.
George A. Hearn Fund, 1953.

41. *Tournos,* 1954. Oil, 35⅞″ x 28″. Collection of the Munson-Williams-Proctor
Institute, Utica, New York.

42. *Cliché,* 1955. Oil, 56¼" x 42". The Solomon R. Guggenheim Museum, New York.

43. *Stele,* 1956. Oil, 52" x 40". Milwaukee Art Center Collection. Gift of Mr. and Mrs. Harry Lynde Bradley.

44. *Tropes de Teens,* 1956. Oil, 45″ x 60″. The Joseph H. Hirshhorn Foundation, New York.

45. Preparatory drawing for *Tropes de Teens,* 1956. (Photograph taken before completion of the painting.)

46. *Premiere,* 1957. Oil, 58″ x 50″. Los Angeles County Museum of Art. Art
Museum Council Purchase.

47. *The Paris Bit,* 1959. Oil, 46″ x 60″. Collection of Whitney Museum of American Art, New York. Gift of the Friends of the Whitney Museum of American Art.

48. Preparatory drawing for *The Paris Bit,* 1959. (Photograph taken before completion of the painting.)

49. *Letter and His Ecol, ca.* 1963. Oil, 24″ x 30″. Courtesy of the Pennsylvania Academy of the Fine Arts, Philadelphia.

50. *Blips and Ifs,* 1963–64. Oil, 71″ x 53″. Courtesy Amon Carter Museum, Fort Worth, Texas.

51, 52. Notebook drawings for last painting, 1963–64. Collection of Mrs. Stuart Davis.

VI the artist, government, and society

From Our Friends (1934)* *Stuart Davis*

The project of the Artists' Committee of Action has potentialities of tremendous importance to all the artists of New York City in particular, and to all the artists of the United States in general. This project, the Municipal Art Gallery and Center, implies in its achievement a new and necessary orientation of the artist to his audience.

That audience in the past, primarily composed of a very small class of society with large incomes, left much to be desired. This economically enfranchised class automatically dictated, through their patronage, the art taste of their time. No artist could be free from their vulgar domination.

The private art dealer, who, of necessity, flattered the taste of the buyer, was the only outlet for the artist who had to live by his work. The art dealer demanded work he could sell to the money dilettante, and the aesthetic connoisseur.

The Municipal Art Gallery and Center, administered by artists, will be the realization by the artists of New York of the necessity of putting an end to this intolerable condition. Through the Municipal Art Gallery and Center, which will be guided in its policy by directors elected from the rank and file of the artists, a cultural impetus will be established in the community which will make possible a powerful art expression, having its roots in the masses of the American people.

A Municipal Art Center in New York City will be followed by the establishment of similar centers in cities throughout the country, with a consequent realization of social solidarity on the part of the American artists.

The New York American Scene in Art (1935)†
Stuart Davis

In the above article ["The U.S. Scene in Art," *Time Magazine,* Dec. 24, 1934], the magazine *Time* gives a short résumé of the life and work of Thomas Benton, Reginald Marsh, Charles Burchfield, John Steuart Curry, Grant Wood and others. These artists are reported to have in common, first—a passion for local Americana, and second—a contempt for the foreign artist and his influence. They have the "my country right or wrong" attitude and are suspicious of strangers. New-fangled ideas in art are not for them, and they would probably support

* From *Art Front* (November, 1934).
† From *Art Front* (February, 1935), Reviews, February, 1935.

a movement to prove that Artemus Ward or Josh Billings had more on the ball than René Clair. They demand that the artist paint the American scene, although their works suggest that what they really mean is Hearst's *New York American* scene. They paint burlesque shows, Civil War architecture, the wonderful meals that farm help receives under the New Deal, Mother Nature acting tough in Kansas, and caricatures of Negroes and farmers done in a style which is an amazing filly out of EARLY PUCK AND JUDGE by REPRODUCTION OF MICHAEL ANGELO.

This is the work of the men who, to quote *Time,* "are destined to turn the tide of artistic taste in the United States." They offer us, says *Time,* "direct representation in place of introspective abstractions." Is the well-fed farmhand under the New Deal, as painted by Grant Wood, a direct representation or is it an introspective abstraction?

Are the gross caricatures of Negroes by Benton to be passed off as "direct representation"? The only thing they directly represent is a third-rate vaudeville character cliché with the humor omitted. Had they a little more wit, they would automatically take their place in the body of propaganda which is constantly being utilized to disfranchise the Negro politically, socially and economically. The same can be said of all people he paints including the portrait of himself which is reproduced on the cover of *Time.* We must at least give him credit for not making any exceptions in his general underestimation of the human race.

Benton, according to *Time* was saved by the U.S. Navy and he wants to do something big in return. So he has fired off a big gun in salute to America which was loaded with a commodity not listed in the *Consumer's Weekly.*

The U.S. scene in art and direct representation, as opposed to introspective abstraction—this is the program of these artists, a program so general and undefined as to be valueless. In the absence of theory we must judge them solely by their works.

By John Steuart Curry we have a series of rural subjects, cheaply dramatic and executed without the slightest regard for the valuable, practical and technical contributions to painting which have been carried on in the last fifty years. How can a man who paints as though no laboratory work had ever been done in painting, who willfully or through ignorance ignores the discoveries of Monet, Seurat, Cézanne and Picasso and proceeds as though painting were a jolly lark for amateurs, to be exhibited in county fairs, how can a man with this mental attitude be considered an assset to the development of American painting? The people of Kansas who are glorified in Curry's pictures do not buy his paintings, *Time* reports. Mr. Curry explains why this is so. "They have Kansas. They hardly need paintings of it," says Mr. Curry. Apparently the people of Kansas have some discrimination as to what kind of "direct representation" they want. Apparently they resent the insult to their intelligence implied in these works, which always present the obvious and stop. I think it is self-evident that Curry's pictures are technically and ideologically negative. How then are we supposed to benefit from his self-imposed isolation from the French school which, if nothing else, has important and advanced technical knowledge that is available to all artists. The Soviet Union, which rejects our political and economic systems, nevertheless admits our superior industrial technical equipment and seeks by study and advice to avail itself of it.

Painting the American scene is not a new manifestation. George Bellows, John Sloan, Glenn Coleman, John Marin are a few who have done so from their various viewpoints. A list of the artists who have concerned themselves with the American scene would require research which is unnecessary for the purposes of this article. All of these artists without exception were deeply influenced by foreign art and most of them studied in Europe. There were some among them, however, who boasted that they had never been in Europe and seemed to regard it as a distinct advantage to themselves as American artists. Nevertheless, their library shelves were well stocked with books containing reproduction of the works of European painters of the past and present. In other words, they traveled by proxy. With all respect for their great individual talent, the ideological content of the work of these painters was in a very general sense provincial, melodramatic and sentimental. Their direct representations were much the same in substance as the group referred to in the article in *Time*. The earlier group, however, had the advantage of not being burdened by the vicious and windy chauvinistic ballyhoo carried on in their defense by a writer like Thomas Craven whose critical values may possibly be clouded by a lively sense of commercial expediency. His efforts to bring art values to the plane of a Rotarian luncheon are a particularly repellent form of petty opportunism and should be so understood and explained whenever one has the misfortune to slip on them. Craven's ideas are unimportant, but the currency given to them through the medium of the Hearst press means that we must not underestimate their soggy impact. Artists are warned not to be complacent in the face of these insults.

"Well-bred people are no fun to paint," says Reginald Marsh. A proletarian orientation might be suspected in this statement. An examination of his work, however, quickly dispels this illusion. We find merely that he means exactly what he says, namely, that painting is fun, and that excursions to the Bowery and the burlesque show to make sketches constitute his artistic horizon—the psychology of the bourgeois art school taken seriously and carried through life as a handicap. His paintings are made of a lot of these sketches put together on a surface and submitted to a series of glazings and tonings to give them a superficial correspondence to an equally superficial concept of what a Renaissance painting is. Can this be called "direct representation"? I think not. In his attitude toward his subject matter and in his attitude toward the technique of painting, Marsh reflects no objectivity. Would it be flattery to apply the term "introspective abstractionist" to him?

The slight burp which this school of the U.S. scene in art has made, may not indicate the stomach ulcer of Fascism. I am not a political doctor, but I have heard the burp and as a fellow artist I would advise those concerned to submit themselves to a qualified diagnostician, other than witch doctor Craven, just to be on the safe side.

Some Chance (1935)   *Stuart Davis*

Forbes Watson is the publicity director and editor of the Bulletin of the Section of Painting and Sculpture, of the Procurement Division of the Treasury Department of the U.S. Government. We assume that he is responsible to that Section for his public statements regarding artists and their relation to the government art projects. This being so, his article in the August, 1935, issue of the *American Magazine of Art,* "The Chance in a Thousand," has significance in that it reflects the "official" attitude toward the artists in general.

On the basis of Watson's expositions this "official attitude" must be regarded as unrealistic and, because of that, irresponsible. The article clearly indicates that the functionaries of the Section of Painting and Sculpture are ideologically unequipped to deal with the problem before them. Their idealistic orientation betrays them into alignments which they, to give them the benefit of the doubt, certainly would not consciously accept. There are many statements in Watson's article which are identical in content with the expressions of those two Hearst reporters, Fred McCormick and Thomas Craven. (It is perhaps superfluous to add that it is the constant purpose of Hearst's employees to discredit the present administration and its relief and "social security" program.) For example, in a previous article in the *New York Times,* July 28, 1935, Watson says that the administration must not be too uncritical in extending relief to "that heterogeneous mob, the members of which all insist that they are artists." In the same article he says, "What we need in this country . . . is fewer and better artists," . . . and that out of 3,000 works examined by him on the WPA, only 500 could be said to have been done by artists, without using quotation marks on

From *Art Front* (November, 1935).

the word artist. In the article in the *American Magazine of Art,* referred to above, he speaks of "the romantic appeal which the professions of art have for countless young ladies and gentlemen who are not fore-ordained to be artists." In another place in the same article he refers to "the mildly intelligent dreamers and predestined amateurs who constitute the immense army of art's hangers-on." Compare these estimates with the statement of Thomas Craven in the *New York American,* June 11, 1935, that "New York is pestilent with artists . . . who can neither make art nor leave it." The too-numerous-to-quote statements of Fred McCormick in Hearst's Sunday *Mirror* of September 1, 8 and 15 support Watson's estimates in much more direct and vulgar terminology. "Hobohemian Chiselers and Squawkers who bite the hand (of Uncle Sam) that feeds them," is a fair sample of the *Mirror's* estimate of the artists on government projects. The above quotations are basically all of a piece. Translated into terms of living conditions, they mean reclassification and sub-subsistence wage levels for artists.

Such an estimate is to be expected from the antilabor and Fascist Hearst and his employees, but it seems a trifle out of key coming from a spokesman of the Section of Painting and Sculpture, especially when the same spokesman has said in the *New York Times* of July 28, 1935, "The present administration has proved its faith in art." Watson's confusion is indicated in the same article when he refers to the government's "first good deed toward the artist" and "that first federal good deed toward our art." According to this concept the art projects are benevolences to be extended and withdrawn at will by a kindly father, the government. The grateful artist may some day be able to make a pilgrimage to kiss the hand of the father who has granted him the right to work at a smashed trade-union wage scale.

Mr. Watson speaks with some pride of the success of the P.W.A.P., which came into being on December 11, 1933, and ceased to exist on June 30, 1934, with nearly $100,000 of its allotment unexpended. It is pointed out that 3,749 artists were employed at craftsmen's wages. Without going into a discussion of what kind of craftsmen's wages were paid, the statement in itself is misleading. $1,184,748.32 was paid as wages to 3,749 artists who produced a total of 15,663 works of art over a period of approximately six and one-half months. A little arithmetic shows that the average sum received by these 3,749 artists for six and one-half months' work was about $316.00, or about $48.00 per month. This is surely not a sum that could be honestly referred to as "craftsmen's wages." If you pay one man $38.00 a week for six and one-half months and another man $38.00 for one week, this does not mean that two men received "craftsmen's wages" for six and one-half months. Mr. Watson was not speaking of the success of the artists in receiving craftsmen's wages. He referred, rather, to the good quality of the work received. This successful quality he attributes to "the fact that many more artists were in need than the number which the Treasury set out to employ." But even this selective employment undertaking could produce only 500 works out of the 15,663 total, which could be said to be the work of artists, without using quotation marks on the word artist, according to Watson. It seems to be clear that Mr. Watson holds a rather low opinion of the artists in general, and, since we must assume that he speaks for the Section of Painting and Sculpture, the artists who are awake will surely think twice before they accept on its face value the statement that the Section is giving to artists "the best chance that they have ever had."

How is this "best chance" to be established? First by reclassification; by setting up regional committees of nonartists who will eliminate from the competitions those "countless young ladies and gentlemen who are not foreordained to be artists." These regional committees composed of museum directors, art collectors, business men, etc., will read your fortune, fellow artists, and tell you what you are foreordained to be, at least as far as the Section of Printing and Sculpture is concerned. If they find that you are not foreordained to be an artist, you can at least feel that you are helping your more successful fellows along the path toward getting the best chance he ever had. A second step in the establishment of this "best chance" is the impartial selection of the victor in any given competition. Watson says, "All competitors submit unsigned numbered sketches, and the envelopes containing their names are not opened until the victor has been chosen." Further on he says, "What gives the work of the Section its health is the fact that it is holding fair competitions in which the works submitted are considered solely on their merits and no name is known until after the winner is decided." This sounds good, but Superintendent Rowan naïvely lets the cat out of the bag when he says, among other enlightening remarks, in Bulletin No. 4, put out by the Section, "Looking over the work . . . on internal evidence (the envelopes attached to the sketches were still unopened), I could see that the leading painters of Chicago had submitted their wares." Are we to assume that the other functionaries of the Section are less adroit than Superintendent Rowan in detecting the superficial characteristics of an artist's style? After being filtered through Chairmen, Regional Committees, Section functionaries, etc., the "unknown artist" has one more hurdle to take in this "best chance" he has ever had. This hurdle takes the form of an Advisory Jury of Painters and Sculptors. In a way this is a break for the artist because his course so far, as I understand it, has been directed by persons who write about art, talk about art, buy and sell art—but do not make art. Therefore, there is no reason to quarrel with the fact that a jury of artists is sitting in judgment in this case. However, it must be pointed out that this jury is not representative of

Stuart Davis

the breadth of aesthetic practice in America. Without mentioning the names—they are published in Bulletin No. 2—it is possible to say without fear of contradiction that this jury represents exclusively the academic approach to aesthetic opinion or, in one or two cases, opinion closely allied to the academic. Would this best competitive chance that the artist has ever had not be made a better chance if a "modern" artist, an "abstract" artist and a proletarian artist were included on this committee of judgment?

Watson is resourceful in finding various angles from which to show his scorn of the artists as a class. In his article, "The Chance in a Thousand," he berates the artist for being a poor sap, with no head for business. He praises the honesty and efficiency of the advertising campaigns of the man of business. He points to the far-seeing character of many advertising campaigns and says that their seeming extravagance is disproved by the results in dollars and cents that they bring in. If the poor dope of an artist had only sense enough to follow this example, Watson concludes, he wouldn't be in the economic jam he finds himself in. The artist tastes the dregs of senseless competition because of the "irritation which these romantic souls, who will never know the joys of first-rate craftsmanship, naturally feel toward the mere thought of associating so romantic a quality as efficiency with the creations of their incorruptible egos." One feels prompted to ask why the efficiency of business did not forestall the Depression, or maybe Mr. Watson didn't know there was a Depression in business. He further castigates the artist class by pointing to the professions and saying, "Youths who decide to be doctors, lawyers, teachers . . . are likely to make an investigation to find out if the profession is overcrowded." It logically follows, therefore, according to Watson, that there is no Depression among doctors, lawyers, teachers, engineers, chemists, etc. I heard differently. When all trains are overcrowded, Mr. Watson, we get on board anyhow, because we have no private cars.

The functionaries of the Section of Painting and Sculpture are very idealistic in mood. The economic aspect of the project finds little place in their statements. It should be noted in passing that none of the selected competitors in these competitions are paid for their work. Only the victor takes the prize. Edward Bruce, consulting expert to the Section, in his statement in Bulletin No. 3, idealistically conceives the function of the project to be a means of preventing revolution. "Conditions like those existing today breed the kind of spirit that revolutions are made of," says Mr. Bruce. His statement is too long to quote, but the central idea is that the growth of our national wealth is over, our physical frontiers are gone, that with the decrease of working hours, idleness will breed boredom and discontent; but that, if the Section brings art to the people, a sufficient distraction from the irritation of material deficiencies

The Artist, Government, and Society   157 will be effected to offset possible protests of an annoying character—something like hypnotizing a cobra with a simple tune on a flute. Superintendent Rowan leaves all worldly cares behind when he says of the work of the Section that, "One superb masterpiece in this whole program would justify it." Not to be outdone by his fellows in flights of fantasy, Mr. Watson, very materialistic in his admiration for the advertising methods of big business, takes time off to remark, "The market for works of art has its foundation in the intangible demands of the imagination and the vision of the passionate few."

The bulletins are full of these inspired musings. I have quoted only a few. I advise all artists to read their bulletins carefully, and, if after doing so, they do not feel impelled to join the Artists' Union, then maybe what Mr. Watson says about them is true.

I want to quote one more passage from Mr. Watson's article in the August issue of *Art*. Speaking of the advertising methods of the artist, he comments on the character of the foreword, usually found in the catalogue of a one-man show, "Its purpose is to puff the artist, not to estimate him." The aim is to "boost his sales." "Less than frank, the bought-and-paid-for introduction . . . would avail more if it were given its right name—a blurb." Could it be possible that in this inspired denunciation, Mr. Watson has found the proper designation for his own numerous bought-and-paid-for introductions to the Section of Painting and Sculpture?

Why an Artists' Congress?
Stuart Davis, Secretary

The American Artists' Congress is unique in the history of American art. That it takes place now is no accident. For it is the response of artists to a situation facing them today. How can we describe this situation?

Its immediate background is a Depression unparalleled in the history of this country. The cracks and strains in the general social fabric resulting from the economic crisis inevitably reached the world of art, shaking those psychological and aesthetic certainties which had once given force and direction to the work of artists.

In order to withstand the severe shock of the crisis, artists have had to seek a new grip on reality. Around the pros and cons of "social content," a dominant issue in discussions of present day American art, we are witnessing determined efforts by artists to find a meaningful direc-

First American Artists' Congress, New York City (1936).

tion. Increasing expression of social problems of the day in the new American art makes it clear that in times such as we are living in, few artists can honestly remain aloof, wrapt up in studio problems.

But the artist has not simply looked out the window; he has had to step into the street. He has done things that would have been scarcely conceivable a few years back.

Nearly two years ago prominent New York artists started a campaign through the Artists' Committee of Action for a Municipal Art Gallery to provide a badly needed outlet for the artists of this city.

When the city administration finally took up the idea, without recognition of the Artists' Committee of Action, it opened a gallery in a remodeled private house early in 1936, on a basis of discrimination against noncitizens and censorship of art disapproved by the administration. Such reactionary ideas could never have been introduced under a truly democratic management of the Municipal Gallery by the artists themselves, which the Artists' Committee of Action had repeatedly called for.

What's more, leading New York artists, together with the Artists' Union, showed that they would not stand for such practices by making a prompt and emphatic protest. The result was an immediate victory! Both citizenship and censorship clauses were speedily withdrawn.

Sharp necessity likewise drove the most hard-pressed artists into organized efforts for federal government support. Their opportunity had come through the initiation of a limited government art project in December, 1933. This project was no more than a liberal gesture, employing a select few, and ignoring the dire distress of the great majority of American artists.

But that move of the liberal New Deal government awakened artists to the realization that they had every right to go to the Government when all other resources and prospects had been exhausted, to demand support for their continued functioning as creative workers.

Artists at last discovered that, like other workers, they could only protect their basic interests through powerful organizations. The great mass of artists left out of the project found it possible to win demands from the administration only by joint and militant demonstrations. Their efforts led naturally to the building of the Artists' Union.

The relatively greater scope of the present art projects is due, in large measure, to the militant stand of the various artists' unions, on behalf of all unemployed artists.

The unions have also gone a long way toward showing that the best American art cannot be developed by merely encouraging a hand-picked few. Their insistence on a democratic extension of government support to young and unknown artists has brought out a vast variety of talent completely ignored by private patronage and commercial galleries.

For the young generation of American artists there is no visible hope except continuation and expansion of Government art projects.

Growing economic insecurity cannot be ignored by even the most firmly established American artists, those who contribute regularly to the big museum exhibitions. Now they are organizing to gain at least a minimum compensation for their important contributions through the loan of contemporary art to museums. They are requesting that the museums pay a small rental fee for the use of their work.

The hostility of most museum officials, and their boards of trustees, to the proposals of the American Society of Painters, Sculptors and Gravers is indicative of their indifference to the needs of artists.

In the struggle around the rental policy, the American Society has found its campaign can only be advanced through the active cooperation of other artists' societies and the Artists' Unions. Here is a concrete instance of how great numbers of American artists are drawing together on an ever widening front for mutual support against exploitation.

But we can give no adequate picture of the extreme urgency for concerted group action of all progressive American artists, an urgency which is tangibly demonstrated by the gathering of representative artists from all sections of the United States, from Mexico, Cuba and even from South America, here in this Congress, unless we portray realistically the possibilities contained actually within the situation in the United States and throughout the world today.

The increasingly open drive of arch reactionaries like William Randolph Hearst and the American Liberty League to promote so-called recovery at the expense of the living standards and freedom of expression of the great masses of American people is a direct menace to the whole body of American artists.

It is Hearst's *Daily Mirror* that launches the most vicious attack against the artists on government projects, calling them "Hobohemian chiselers" and "ingrates ready to bite the hand that feeds them."

It is probably no accident that a prominent art critic, associated with the Hearst press, writes of his disgust with the work produced on the projects. He advises the young artists to disperse, return home, admit they were not intended to be artists, and take up pursuits more suited to their abilities.

Hearst, today the spearhead of the sharpest attacks upon intellectual freedom in this country, focuses his drive against the artists at just that point where they have made their only real advance toward economic security, namely, the government projects.

This attack is part of a general drive by powerful vested interests to perpetuate exploitation by smashing the efforts of the underprivileged American masses to gain security and a decent living standard. The goal

Stuart Davis

of intrenched interests is a regime founded on suppression of all those liberties which Americans fought to establish and are today struggling to maintain. This goal is shrewdly screened with such slogans as "Back to the Constitution" and "Save America for Democracy," and hypocritical appeal to Americanism and love of country.

The examples of the so-called national resurgence that were accompanied by the most brutal destruction of the economic and cultural standards of the masses of people in Italy and Germany through the introduction of Fascism should warn us of the real threats that lie behind the rabidly nationalistic movements in this country.

There is a real danger of Fascism in America.

How Fascism is plunging headlong toward a devastating new World War is evident to every reader of the daily press. Fascists have no other solution for the crying needs of their people than an outburst of war.

To carry out their program of death and destruction they would enlist the services of even the artists. Here is how Mussolini employs an artist, F. T. Marinetti.

"We, Futurist poets and artists," Marinetti says, "have recognized for twenty-seven years that war is the only world hygiene. War is beautiful because it creates new architectures, as the heavy tank. It creates the flying geometries of the aeroplane, the spiral smoke of burning villages. War is beautiful because it completes the beauty of a flowery meadow with the passionate orchids of machine-gun fire. War is beautiful because it serves the greatness of great Fascist Italy."

That is the way a Fascist artist speaks.

The talents of many American artists were employed to whip up the war psychology essential to win over the mass of Americans to support participation of the United States in the last World War.

It is because artists do not want their creative talents perverted and used to mask a barbaric war that they have signed the Call for an American Artists' Congress and come together here to show their solidarity. And this struggle against war cannot be divorced from the struggle against every manifestation of war-mongering reaction.

The members of this Congress who have come together to discuss their problems in the light of the pressing social issues of the day are representative of the most progressive forces in American art today. The applicants for membership were accepted on the basis of their representative power, which simply means that they had already achieved a degree of recognition and esteem as artists in the spheres in which they function.

We, members of the Congress, have recognized that we are not alone in this fight. We recognize that our basic interests are not remote from those who do the work of the world. And with this recognition comes the realization that if we are to be serious, we can only attack even the most highly specialized problems that confront us, in relation to our main objective, which is to build a bulwark for the defense of intellectual freedom, for economic security.

Even if we were to rally all the American artists to our cause, we would achieve little working as an isolated group. But we have faith in our potential effectiveness precisely because our direction naturally parallels that of the great body of productive workers in American industrial, agricultural and professional life.

The Congress will enable us to focus our objectives.

To realize them, we plan to form a permanent organization on a national scale.

It will not be affiliated with any political group or clique of sectarian opinion.

It will be an organization of artists which will be alert to take action on all issues vital to the continued free functioning of the artist.

It will be alert to ways and means for extending this freedom and for making contact with a broader audience.

It will be a strengthening element to the whole field of progressive organization against War and Fascism.

It will be another obstacle to the reactionary forces which would rob us of our liberties.

I call on all artists of standing to join the permanent organization which will carry out the program planned by the succeeding sessions of the Congress.

Federal Art Project and the Social Education of the Artist (*ca.* 1938) *Stuart Davis*

The unrealistic idealism of American artist painters in the immediate past has caused them to strive for extreme individualism in both the content and form of their work, even though few achieved it. They have been unconscious but ardent supporters of the code of rugged individualism. They have fought and plotted shamelessly among themselves for the favor of the private patron and museum prize. This attitude has been very destructive to artistic progress as well as to the economic stability of the artist stratum, because their individualistic theory has left them wide open to commercial exploitation of the lowest and most wasteful order.

Those with the least ethical and artistic integrity were the first to willingly prostitute their talent to speculating dealers, museums and collectors, and those who were least capable artistically often became the

Unpublished essay.

accepted standard of excellence for the speculator-controlled art market. Even the most talented artists were infected with the disease of insincerity and vulgarity which was bred by its social and ethical anarchy.

The world-wide economic Depression, which threatened the very lives of millions, hit the individualistic artist with a force of unmistakable authority. His social and artistic idealism was cracked and crunched, and he tottered from the pieces of his celluloid ivory tower to find himself, where, as a matter of fact, he had always been, surrounded by suffering millions who were as badly off as himself. His prized illusion of the immunity of some art value, which he believed was above political and economic reality, was stripped from him. Thousands of artists found themselves in the relief offices where they waited their turn shoulder to shoulder with manual laborer, skilled and professional worker, for the chance to prove the humiliation of pauperism. The more fortunate who still retained some degree of security were deeply disturbed in their former self-assurance of economic freedom and social prestige.

The establishment of the Federal Art Project as part of the general work relief program of the New Deal administration saved contemporary American art from practical destruction. Numerous exhibitions of work done on the Federal Art Project bear testimony to the truth of the statement of Holger Cahill, national director, when he says, "The organization of the project has proceeded on the principal that it is not the solitary genius but a sound general movement which maintains art as a vital, functioning part of any cultural scheme. . . . In a genuine art movement a great reservoir of art is created in many forms both major and minor."

The bitter experience of the Depression as well as the experience of working for a single employer, the federal government, have given the American artist a degree of social consciousness which has found expression in the formation of two national organizations, the Artists' Unions, and the American Artists' Congress. The members of these organizations, which include many of the most prominent artists of our country, are keenly aware of the direct dependence of cultural and artistic progress on the preservation of democratic processes in government and industry. Since their formation these organizations have been on the side of democracy against Fascism and war, and those economic royalists who continuously seek to suppress democracy in government, industry, and culture.

The American artists today express their social consciousness directly, through special exhibitions against war and Fascism, through symposia in which the relationship between art and society is discussed from various angles, and through united struggle to establish a permanent Bureau of Fine Arts, based on the present Federal Art Projects, in the United States government. A bill, known as H. R. 8239, to accomplish this has already been introduced in Congress by Representative Coffee of Washington. It should have the whole-hearted support of everyone interested in artistic progress in America. Private patronage will not and cannot support a vital American art.

The effect of the social consciousness of the artist and the Federal support of art is already clearly manifested in painting itself. This can be seen in the greatly increased number of pictures which have a specific social meaning that reflects the artists' awareness of the social phenomena of our time. In place of the still-life or reclining nude we now very often find industrial landscapes, industrial workers or farmers, drought, picket lines and strikes, or war, taken as subject matter. At the same time we find a newly awakened interest in abstract art of various tendencies. This results directly from the minimum security given young artists by the Federal Art Project which enables them to develop partially free from the scramble for favor in the cutthroat chaos of irresponsible private patronage.

Some critics have sought to place abstract art in contradiction to art with social content. Such a thesis is superficial and incorrect. Abstract art has specific social content. That it does not have a subject matter which describes certain specific social relations does not mean that it is without important social content. For example, it would be vain to argue that the great Daumier had social content and Seurat had not, because the first painted the daily life of the workers and the other painted the leisure enjoyments of the bourgeoisie. The matter is not so simple. Seurat's subjects from the standpoint of meaningful social relations were passive, Daumier's were active and progressive in meaning. But Seurat's conception of the form and spatial relations through which his subject exists was revolutionary. The objective and social formal concept of which Seurat's pictures are the record, is a vital part of the cultural inheritance of all the people. To argue that it is not is to argue that the people are unworthy of the fruits of their own greatest talents.

Does this contradict the importance of the development of a content of specific social relations in art? It does not.

The social consciousness of the young artist today will be reflected in his art. But in the meantime the development of broader social vision in the artist will include a respect for the historical and technological development of the art of painting, and in that development abstract art continues to play an important role.

The Federal Art Project, which in a sense has sponsored this new development in abstract art just as it has the art of social realism, has performed another very important function. By the establishment of art galleries and centers, where exhibitions, lectures and instruction are given, throughout those sections of the country where these facilities were nonexistent, it has made a positive contribution toward democratization of artistic culture. Through these art centers, numerous exhibitions in the big cities, as well as hundreds of murals placed in public buildings, including the abstract murals in Newark Airport and the Williamsburg Housing Project, a vast education in art is being made available to the American people.

The artists employed on the Federal Art Project have repaid many times over the cost of the project through their enormous contribution to American culture, and the indication their work has given of a renaissance in art if federal patronage continues.

There are forces at work today who would sacrifice the art project in their drive to balance the financial budget at the expense of the human budget. All those who are interested in artistic progress must actively oppose this threat and work for a permanent Bureau of Fine Arts in the government which will continue to provide a support which is adequate to preserve and develop the artistic genius of our country.

The American Artist Now (1941) *Stuart Davis*

From one point of view the artist's job has been made easy today, as a result of the many agencies in the fields of politics and culture which are ready to do his thinking for him. He has but to choose the one he likes and from then on his social outlook, subject matter, and even his technique, cease to be problems of major concern. After he has torn the big red letters off the box and mailed them to the central office, he has only to follow the printed instructions which are sent to him absolutely free. But in some cases, the artist may hesitate to adopt this streamlined road to art, because of a persistent and old-fashioned belief that real art and freedom of expression are interdependent factors. He may hold the curious opinion that art needs no "good-housekeeping" stamp of approval to guarantee its quality, and in some cases he may even question the integrity, or competence, of those who would sell him "protection." Some very stubborn artists may like to believe that art is not the proper tool for fixing things that are out of order on the political or economic level, and they may oppose its use for such purposes, fearing art itself will be destroyed in the bungling attempt. They may "idealistically" conceive art to be an independent and special form of social action, in which the solutions made do not exactly coincide in time with solutions in other fields. Genuine art may be produced in a very chaotic society, and it may be the most important organizing force for progress at such a period. It may be the only concrete symbol of the possibility of order when every joint in the social plumbing is aleak.

From *Now,* I, No. 1 (August, 1941).

But in any epoch, including our own, there are powerful individuals and agencies who would deny an independent role to art, and from various motives, political, academic, social snobbery, or plain stupidity, they strive to hitch the artistic wagon to their star. In accordance with this effort, theories are advanced which attempt to locate the origin of art in "social forces," in academic scholarship, Americana, government, or the Aryan race. From divergent premises they all succeed in converging on the opinion that, where art is concerned, the artist has very little to do with it. They gladly release him of responsibility to society for the preservation and development of art.

Such views are widely held today, not only in totalitarian Europe, but in the field of art itself right here in the United States. While we give big-hearted welcome to the artist and writer refugee victims of totalitarian "culture," our own monopoly in culture keeps its blueprints up to date for proper direction of Americanism in art. And while our artists themselves are not guiltless of a fifth-column-like free surrender of their own rights, it is the monopoly who are the real aggressors. Its existence is not a recent manifestation, and it is composed of that vast hierarchy which makes its living, saves its taxes, or develops its prestige, on the artists' work. Whatever internal strife, jealousies, or back-stabbing may exist between its components, the monopoly stands as one man when the question arises of where authority lies for the proper conduct of art. It lies with them, in spite of the fact that their nomination and election was achieved without recourse to cumbersome democratic methods. The nomination may have been made by a patent-medicine in one case, a shirt sweat-shop in another, or possibly a diploma from the "right" school was sometimes sufficient, and in general, a great big wad of dough was sure-fire. After nomination, one vote was necessary for election, and this was supplied quite effortlessly by the nominee himself. Thus, that great representative body, our monopoly in culture, was born, to make authoritative decision and give public direction to art.

This usurpation of power and inversion of values by the monopoly would be unimportant except for one thing. They own and control the channels of art distribution, both economic and cultural, and through this control, form public opinion in their own image. It is often said that the artist today has freedom of expression through his work, but this is an empty sophistry. The artist not only paints, he works for a public, and when he has no voice in the administration of the channels of contact, his art expression is automatically distorted and weakened. In a country where the right of collective bargaining is guaranteed by federal law, the artist is denied this right. And the fact that "company-union" tactics are a federal offense does not prevent our monopoly in culture from using them, when the usual outright autocratic method is abandoned, in their relations with artists.

Stuart Davis

This is the situation in American art today, and without recognition of the fact, nothing worth saying about our art can be thought of. Our great annual cross-section exhibitions are generally agreed, by artists, critics, and monopolist usurpers alike, to be too dreary and too dull. Those who deny it in public, for this reason or that, ardently announce it in private. The general character of the work in these shows does not represent the potentialities of our creative talent. It represents the uncreative character of our monopoly in culture and even they don't like the work, except as a symbol of their own power over it. All the concentrated propaganda carried on by them about the great renaissance in American art has not produced one. It has merely produced greater commercial exploitation of artists, and more subtle and ingenious methods for suppressing their freedom of expression. And although I have often been accused of being an "abstract" artist, these statements are not the product of abstract thought. They are the result of firsthand observation of considerable breadth, extending over a number of years, and detailed documentation of them would be an easy, if boring, task.

When we read that Picasso is in a concentration camp, everyone cries "Fascism," even the latent-Fascists in our field of art. The art and freedom of expression, for which Picasso stands, have been in the concentration camps of our monopoly in culture for many years past. It is not at all fantastic to predict that those of our artists who continue to demand freedom may soon occupy them in person. Thus, our monopoly dictator has sponsored and developed an American art, which, in its general aspect, gives hardly a hint that vital and inspiring art has ever existed, much less in our recent past.

If I felt that the situation were hopeless I would not bother to describe it. But I believe that it can be changed, because we have the potential power to make the change. This power rests nowhere except in the artists themselves. Not in all the artists, certainly, because many by their very nature don't want a change, and they eagerly support the dictatorship by their servile work. But there are many others who, in spite of the general reactionary trend toward illustration and academism, have maintained some semblance of freedom of expression in their art. Their morale has stood up against the impact of such slogans as, "The American Scene in Art," "Sanity in Art," "Social Content in Art," and "Life Magazine in Art," to name a few out of many. Although manifesting occasional jitters, they have managed at least a sort of Dunkerque victory, and can still consolidate their forces before artistic Fascism can bring up more barbed wire. Their first weapon of defense is their work, and this must be supplemented by the development of free channels of public contact. The action must take place where it counts most, in the field of art. Fascism on the political and economic level can only be stopped by political and military action. Genuine art is ineffective there, and in that fight the artist acts in whatever capacity he may as a citizen. But if a political victory be gained over Fascism and the artist returns to find American art completely and finally hog-tied, he may well begin to question the value of that victory, as it refers to him.

No, the fight for free art must be made now, precisely at this time, when, completely suppressed in Europe, it is threatened with final suppression in the United States. Don't be fooled by the mountainous transactions in art and culture that are going on, into believing that they represent artistic growth. Just ask the question as to what voice the artist has had in promoting these developments, and it should be clear that he has had little. His only voice is in his work, and too often that is no voice at all, but a mere echo of a record played by the monopoly in culture. Through museum policy; through Federal Art Projects; through dealers; through critics, lecturers, teachers, book writers, and artists subsidized by jobs and scholarships; through national magazines and radio, the tune from the monopoly's record is piped for all to hear. Oh, they occasionally play other records, too, having a profound humanitarian content, but that is only the come-on. The record they're actually plugging and selling is a neat little number stolen from "America, I love you," with lyrics, also stolen and patched together, from every maudlin ballad ever written. Here and there is a militant touch, serving as a sort of synthetic vitamin B1, such as "Postmasters on Parade" or "John Brown's Body," just so the boys won't get too anaemic. The monopoly's record department doesn't plug anything American which has artistic authenticity, and you'll never hear our great Negro artists, such as Father Earl Hines, or Louis Armstrong. When it comes to that department, you'll hear Manny DeKay and his Dribbling Rhythm.

But leaving allegory aside, the monopoly specifically repudiates Modern Art, the only recent proof that freedom of expression through art is possible. They buy it all right, and are proud of it, but that's because it's worth money, and they can own it and control its influence through subversion of its meaning. If you want to know what Modern Art means, don't think, go to one of their art historians, and they will pigeon-hole it for you. It is nothing that should directly concern you, really. You can look, of course, and admire, but you mustn't touch. Your concern as an artist must be something truly American, something to do with "corn." But the only corn-fed art I know of was pre-Columbian, and that was a long time ago.

The greatest living exponent of Modern Art is now in a concentration camp in France, but fortunately for us the art itself was made an integral part of American culture twenty-eight years ago by the Armory Show. The works of Modern Art, and its meaning, are still available to us here, for those who have the courage to consult it. But the Armory Show was

Stuart Davis

organized exclusively by artists, and its spirit was free from commercialism, or academic snobbery. It is in that spirit that our artists must consolidate their resources today if they would regain their freedom and take leadership in their own affairs.

The artistic problems which were tackled in Modern Art were undertaken in a hostile environment, but one which was more nearly allied to our own, in its physical aspects, than the art of epochs more remote. Van Gogh painted railroad bridges made of concrete, and electric lights, as well as subjects of more traditional European character. And while the sun has been available to artists of all times, his interpretation of it could only have been made by a man living in the new lights, speeds, and spaces of our machine civilization. The dots of Seurat have direct reference to modern physics, although he did not use them to illustrate a treatise on the subject. Cézanne, and Picasso's Cubism, whatever else, reflect a contemporary sense of prefabricated structure. But all of these men, and the rest, used their imagination and intellect in the service of a free art, and not to propagandize a chamber-of-commerce campaign or a political party. Whatever action, if any, our artists may take in defense of their freedom, they can look, for their staunchest support, to the spirit and the practice of the men who made Modern Art.

VII writings on other artists

A Painter of City Streets
(Glenn Coleman) (1923) *Stuart Davis*

(An analysis of the work of Glenn Coleman, whose canvases are unique in their vivid portrayal of the human aspects of street life)

In Paris, in the Luxembourg Gallery, hangs a painting of a little street down in Greenwich Village called Minetta Lane. In passing thru the galleries you are attracted by the vivid reality of this picture, and are likely to give it more than the usual amount of attention. It shows a short, narrow street lined with old three- and four-story buildings. The street is covered with snow, on which the lights from the windows of small shops throw angular patterns. In the foreground of the picture, the dark figure of a woman with a shawl over her head is crossing the street, while farther back another woman is sweeping snow from the sidewalk, and a man without an overcoat hurries along with his hands in his pockets. At the end of the street, against the red of a building made brilliant by an arc-light, the silhouetted figures of children are seen, playing a game.

All of these facts are indicated in the most simple and direct manner imaginable. There is no elaboration of detail; in fact, 90 per cent of the ordinary features of the scene are left out, and yet when you look at the picture a mood is created that makes you feel that the place is one with which you are very familiar. This power is the result of instinctive selection of the essentials that make up the character of the scene.

In a whole row of buildings the artist may only paint a dozen windows, but each one of these windows will have been selected because of some distinguishing characteristic that makes it a thing of importance in creating the mood of the scene, and as a result you forget all about the windows that are left out because of your interest in the ones that are there. It may be the way that a shutter hangs on one window that calls to your mind similar windows you have noticed, or it may be the color of the light that comes from it that stimulates your memory into recognition.

A red sign protrudes from over the doorway of a shop, with the words *Hop Sing, Laundry* on it; a group of children play in the street, a woman is leaning out of a window calling to them; a beggar is holding his palm extended for money; through the window of a butcher-shop the proprietor is going over an assortment of sausages with a customer; a large wooden horseshoe painted yellow announces the presence of the blacksmith; an arc-light throws its concentric circles of light on the

From *Shadowland*, VIII, No. 6 (August, 1923), pp. 11, 75.

street . . . and as a result the spectator feels himself transported to the scene itself.

This picture was painted by Glenn Coleman, a New York artist, who is primarily a painter of the manifold aspects of the city streets. His work is notable for a personal viewpoint that is always interesting because of its humanity. He is never the technical experimenter, never the abstract interpreter of light, but always an artist with a keen sensitivity to the essential human character of the scene. With the most simple of technical procedures he has painted many canvases that are unique in their vivid portrayal of certain aspects of New York street life. His earlier works are records of a life that has already passed away. The old Chinatown, Coney Island, and the burlesque theaters of the same period, the Bowery, Atlantic Garden, the Haymarket can now be seen only in Coleman's works.

His artistic derivation is not obvious, in fact it is difficult to think of any American painter who is less influenced by the styles and tendencies of the art world. He is not a conscious artist, but a man of great sensibility, who finds life interesting and is able to express himself in paint in a direct and vivid manner.

Glenn Coleman was born in Ohio but spent his boyhood in Indianapolis, Indiana, where he attended high school and later worked in the art department of a newspaper. He conceived the idea of coming to New York to study art, and made the trip in the capacity of attendant to cattle which were bound for the same place for a different purpose. On arrival, he took up his residence with two other art students in a tenement-house on the West Side, and doubtless this actual contact with the life he chose to depict is responsible to some extent for the vivid reality of his work.

He studied in the classes of William Chase and Robert Henri, and after a year had developed sufficiently to make that remarkable series of street scenes and interiors that were reproduced in portfolio form in a private edition called *Scenes from the Lives of the People.* The small edition was quickly sold out to artists and a few friends who appreciated the quality of his work. Later on the originals were exhibited and met with similar success. However, efforts to get his work in magazines and books were all but unavailing, although much of it was admirably suited to that purpose. The one exception was a book called *Types from City Streets,* by Hutchins Hapgood, for which Coleman made the illustrations.

His inability to get his black and white work used in this field led him to devote his energies to painting in color. These products of his brush were notable for their color harmonies and the same intense appreciation of character that was in the drawings, but were even less successful from a financial point of view. He turned his attention to more lucrative occupations, and a period of artistic unproductivity followed. Circumstances again made it possible for him to paint, and a trip to Cuba in 1919 was the inspiration for some paintings that have all the qualities of his previous things, with the addition of a greater color range and more decorative treatment.

Coleman's picture, *Minetta Lane,* which hangs in the Luxembourg Gallery, was purchased for that collection by the French Government. An American artist of reputation who is familiar with Coleman's work and also the Luxembourg collection, said, when he heard of the sale: "They are looking up over there."

Paintings by Salvador Dali, Julien Levy Gallery (1935) *Stuart Davis*

The paintings of Salvador Dali are completely successful. His expression is achieved to a degree which demands comparison with artists who are regarded as the leaders in the different epochs. His native skill in the reproduction of common optical effects is unique relative to artists of the day. Manual and muscular sensitivity are apparent in the execution of his paintings. His observations of visual aspects imply a man who is not nervous in the contemporary sense. His sense of time belongs to another century. His paintings are robust and have in them that sense of security in familiar associations which are common to people whose psychological environment is undisturbed. The paintings of Dali are so concrete in their expression that the spectator cannot help but feel the earth beneath his feet. Here is an artist who includes in his subject matter not alone the human model, the still life and the landscape, but also all those immaterial and equally real mental associations which are a part of the conscious life of the human being. His ability to isolate and give concrete form to the associational aspects of a subject is unparalleled. The intensity of curiosity displayed in these paintings is astounding. Dali shows himself to be a human being of admirable vitality, incorporating dignity, humor, tenderness, cruelty, etc.

The work of Dali is in no sense revolutionary. His extreme concern with the commonplace aspect of his subjects precludes any intention of change or movement. To Dali, a sky is blue, a rock hard, water wet, and a human figure is the well-known shape and color. His primitive realization of these facts constitutes his strength and his conservatism. To Dali, that which is real is the established. His visualizations of the immaterial are as commonplace as a calendar picture and as casual in their acceptance of the conventionally beautiful. Dali paints together the lion and

From *Art Front* (January, 1935).

the lamb, it is true, but there is no sense of the revolutionary structure. He paints only that which has been painted, but his energy in gathering the conventions of the past is phenomenal.

His fantastic visual juxtapositions are the property of all. He expresses with great clarity and precise discrimination the uncoordinated in human emotions and thought. To these careful visual symbols of the immaterial he assigns the most commonplace materiality. There is no form of painting of Dali with which we are not familiar. We contemplate a desert of the familiar bric-a-brac of human hopes and realities and through them a man wanders with a dust cloth and a moth spray. In these scenes one looks only backward and the sun is setting. Artists who intend to continue will have to change cars.

Guernica—Picasso (1947) *Stuart Davis*

Painting and the Graphic Arts are legitimately used for all kinds of purposes other than to make Art, as that term is generally meant. But a quality of experience called Art exists, and is chiefly evident today as an individual realization. Not a private realization, but a Personal one which becomes Public property through the communication of the work of Art. To paint, is in itself a Social act. Apocalyptic revelation is not essential to Art to insure its Social Use and Function. A more modest approach to Truth can deserve certain Medals. Why should the painter be looked to for answers to Political and Moral problems that the strongest forces in the world today cannot answer. This point is raised because questions of this kind have centered around Picasso's *Guernica* since its inception. It has been repudiated as arrogant egotism on one hand, and lamented over as failing to fulfill its promise on the other. It is Degenerate Bourgeoise Art to some, and a sad proof of the failure of an Epic Hero to emerge to others. I look at it in a different way. In fact, I just look at it in the same way I look at any other painting, and do not inquire into its origins nor the intellectual and prophetic scope of the artist.

I am probably the only one on the platform who has not had the privilege of meeting Picasso. I do not know what he intended to do in this painting, or how he rationalized its Meaning. I only know what he Did, and all I see there is that Picasso the Artist emerged. I do not consider that *Guernica* is necessarily his best work, but it is certainly not his worst. The concept of the composition from the first sketches is not unusual. The assemblage of Allegorical personnel does not seem especially brilliant in itself to me. The arbitrary limitation of the Color range

Written for a symposium on *Guernica* at The Museum of Modern Art, New York, November 25, 1947.

Stuart Davis

does not call for cheers. If these were the dominant meanings present, the thing might be a turkey. The fact that several styles from his past work are brought together in this case seems of little importance to me. What is important, is what he did with all this material, which in itself could have been assembled by others. The point I want to make is that the Subject Matter, while various, is not a condition for *Guernica*'s importance, anymore than the Subjects of his other works constitute their significance as Art. Whether the Bull or the Horse represent the People is a matter that interests me less than a Crossword Puzzle. Or whether the Piercing Lance signifies an attempted alliance with Voodoo Art is certainly not a Headline Item. One can rummage in any well stocked Attic and come up with many curiosities not necessarily Atomic in implication.

In my view, the role of Subject in Art is the business of the Artist. And Freedom of Choice in Subject is a Condition for Art. The Artist deals with the same Subject Matter as everyone else, and reacts to it fundamentally in the same way. He is concerned with all kinds of Meanings in Subject outside of Art. His concern with Subject does not constitute Art. Only a purpose to *apprehend* and realize those Meanings on a certain level of awareness constitutes the Decision of the Artist. Art is not a Catharsis, a Purge, or a Purification. It is an active use of Faculties to meet the impact of Reality on a day-to-day basis, and to understand it in the Sense of those Faculties. To do this a Method is required (and where the Dimensional Means of Painting are the chosen medium) that Understanding is had within the Terms and Limitations of Dimensional Logic. When those Means are submitted to the personal Sense of Equilibrium in Space, the result is a Physical Equilibrium in the work of Art. Certainly no Logical Equilibrium, but one Intuitively determined, and directly communicated by the painting. Art knocks you out on a physical level, without showing you its Passport. The impact of *Guernica* rests on that basis. The emotional and intellectual concern of Picasso for his Subject are there. That is to say their Dynamics are there, felt by him as a personal Spatial Balance among Subject Elements in which that Personal Sense naturally did not exist. It is the Morale of his Victory as Artist that is communicated and constitutes *Guernica*'s Social and Moral legitimacy. If it were the Defeat of Human Integrity that it communicates, one might question such a contribution at this particular time, when Defeats are a dime a dozen.

I think it is very important at this time to avoid a Confusion of Values, in which Art along with everything else is being Raided and its papers called in Question. Actually, it can not be Raided, but it can surely be Suppressed, through denying the validity of its assumption of Freedom. Such Raids come from Right and Left alike, but for different reasons, and are accompanied by a propaganda planned to subvert

Public Opinion. Everybody who can't, or doesn't, take the trouble to create or give Value to Art can tell you what is wrong with Modern Art. If you ask them to give a sign that they are an authorized Messenger of Truth, they will show you a questionable Old Master, among other things, or an example of Social Realism, in the style that was regarded as the real thing in the Salons of 1870. These Signs are unconvincing, a suspicion of Forgery seems to leak through somehow. One suspects that there are Five Aces in the Deck, or maybe Six. And what is that Bulge under the Messenger's armpit. No, I cannot accept these slanders on Art as Ivory Tower, by Agents who would not complain at all if the Artist occupied a Cell to which they held the Key.

In brief, my thesis is that the Method of Art as a Form of Knowledge needs no apology. The fact that it does not subsume all knowledge is in its favor. It makes the matter simpler that way, and the achievement more real.

Arshile Gorky in the 1930's:
A Personal Recollection (1951)   *Stuart Davis*

I remember knowing Arshile Gorky in 1929 after I came back from Europe, but have no recollection before that. I may have met him in Romany Marie's through Paul Gaulois or John Graham. In any case we became close friends and saw each other often. Being artists, we had nothing trivial to do and were thus available at all hours of the day or night for loitering around places to beat our gums. In that way there was ample time to gain complete familiarity with each other's ideas. He had quick intelligence, a strong sense of humor and a playful temperament, and we did not bring each other down.

He lived in a fairly decent artistic-type studio on the edge of the slums near Washington Square on Sullivan Street. It was equipped with the paraphernalia popularly believed to be the appropriate sign of the true artist. A massive easel of foreign make, great quantities of canvases of large size, hundreds of tubes of the most expensive colors, dozens of palettes covered with huge piles of paint, forests of fine brushes, bolts of linen for paint rags, and carboys of oil and turpentine. This is not an exaggeration, as other witnesses of the epoch can testify. I also recall that there were a few plaster casts around, and a stringed musical instrument of some kind to complete the setting. Outside of an art store, I had never seen anything like this collection of properties in one place before —nor since, for that matter. The question of how he acquired this truly impressive stockpile and kept it replenished was raised from time to time, but no really clear picture of the feat was ever arrived at.

From *Magazine of Art,* XLIV (February, 1951).

178   Stuart Davis

Gorky himself provided the punch-line to this dramatic impact. Nature had provided him with a tall, dark and impressive aspect easily identifiable with the "artist-type" by persons who had taken the trouble to inform themselves on these matters. He brought this asset to its maximum intensity by the adoption of a black velour hat pulled low over the eyes, and a black overcoat buttoned tight under the chin and extending to the ankles. The effect of this powerful disguise was excellently demonstrated by the terror it inspired in children when first confronted with it. A large quantity of dirty hoodlum urchins from the reeking tenements nearby had the habit of playing and maiming each other in the street in front of Gorky's studio. No ordinary external presence could penetrate the complete subjectivity of the fanaticism with which they pursued their aimless frenzies. But Gorky's presence was felt and reacted to with animal cries, followed by a barrage of filthy missiles hastily improvised from materials immediately available. He counterattacked and routed the little beasts, but this did not deter them from returning each day to re-create their epileptic orgies. Now forewarned, they were vigilant at all times to meet him coming and going. They organized derisive chants and drew large satirical and obscene images on the walls of his building. This war continued for some time, but eventually they tired of it and returned to their habit of morbid introspection. Gorky had a fondness for children, and as matters quieted down he fraternized with them and gave them lessons in street drawing. This state of amity continued, so that then they later became aware of a large, black and impressive beard he had quickly grown, their reaction was merely one of amusement. "Take 'em off Murphy, we know ya!" was the shout with which they greeted him. Gorky was very pleased with this and told it repeatedly with much laughter.

In addition to the costume, he expressed himself verbally in a complex personal jive that was extremely remote from accepted English usage. It was no mere matter of a simple foreign accent, although that was present, but an earthquake-like effect on sentence structure and a savagely perverse use of words to mean something they didn't. He was completely conscious of this bizarre linguistic collation, and on occasion messed it up still more in company where he thought it would be effective strategy. I do not imply here any lack of ability to express himself; on the contrary, he was very good at it. He was intensely interested in ideas and talked enthusiastically about them. He recited tales of his various exploits with florid embellishments and boastings that held the attention of his listeners, because a good deal of the objectivity of humor was included. The studio, the costume and the talk added up to a dramatization of his natural gifts which made him an unforgettable personality.

He had a continuous complaint about poverty, which was real enough, and sought to liquidate any vestige of doubt in an already long-convinced audience by displaying holes, patches and rags in the garments which he wore under the overcoat. This poverty was intensified by his method of painting. He would squeeze out a half-dozen tubes of each color he used in great piles on several palettes. These were left standing around for a certain number of days to acquire a viscous consistency. When ready to paint, he transferred this small fortune in pigment to one or more canvases with palette knives in a heat of creative excitement. But as his percentage of hits and misses was no better than average, he would often scrape it all off the next day and start again with a new batch of colors. Where the initial painting escaped this fate and was continued day by day to completion, the weight of the canvas increased proportionately. The finished product had an astounding weight. Persons uninformed about this would innocently approach a canvas to heft it at his invitation. Members of the weaker sex and anemic men would retreat from the dangerous experience with minor but none the less painful sprains and bruises. A standing joke around the Gorky studio, this never failed to get a laugh.

Gorky himself was very strong and was not reluctant to divulge the fact. On one occasion he was in my tenement room on lower Second Avenue when this topic came to the fore. Another person was present who also fancied his physique and liked to brag about it. Rendered silent by Gorky's voluble and lengthy rebuttal in disparagement of the fellow's claims to unusual potency and vigor, the guy finally erupted in challenge to a wrestling bout then and there. I was appointed as referee to call a halt to foul tactics. They stripped to the waist and fell to. As the bout progressed, with much panting, cigarette coughing and B.O., my commands to cease and disengage were respected several times. But the next time no heed was given, and I foolishly grappled with the perspiring contestants, who by this time had lost all sense of objectivity. I became entangled in the writhing mass and blundered into a head-lock that was very alarming. Fortunately they shortly realized that too many arms and legs were involved and allowed me to fall free onto the filthy floor. That terminated the contest, and while I was in no condition to render a decision, Gorky was definitely the fresher of the two and would have gone on to win. At another time I needed hastily to vacate an attic where I lived. The broken-down furniture, paintings and so forth were removed without comment by the truckmen, but a large and weighty trunk was rejected by them. They just wouldn't carry it out, and their minds were closed to reason or pity. The situation was solved by Gorky, who put it on his back and carried it down four flights of stairs to the sidewalk.

Gorky was ubiquitous and moved in several circles other than the one

Stuart Davis

I frequented. He was also nonalcoholic, which was all to the good with my friends. This was certainly not because of any anti-alcoholic sentiment among them, but because of the particular effect which a few drinks had upon him. On the comparatively infrequent occasions when he got loaded on the emetic wines of the period, he would go into a routine derived from the song and folk-dances of his native land. This performance took up a lot of room and the accompanying vocalizations drowned out all competitive conversations. This idiosyncrasy was frowned on by us, who would not tolerate musical deviations of any kind from our profoundly hip devotion to American Jazz. Gorky became aware of this ban very fast, and respected it after being properly indoctrinated in its rationale. He reserved his routine for other circles where it was appreciated and continued to go over big.

In 1931 the magazine *Creative Art* proposed to print a feature article on my work to appear in its September issue. The editor told me to write a statement to accompany the reproductions and allowed me to choose another person, who was to be paid, to write a critical appraisal. I chose Gorky, which indicated how sure I was of his friendship and sincere liking for my work. Having a free hand in the matter, I was not out to take any chances knowing that he was not a glib man with the pen. I explained the matter to him and asked if he could and would do it. He said he would be glad to do it and brushed aside my doubts about his getting the English put together right with "you'll see." During several weeks that followed I asked how it was coming along, to which he always replied that it was almost done. But my demands to see it were refused, and I never did see it until it appeared in the magazine. He had stuck to the specifications all right and laid it on thick—at that time it seemed too thick. The phrase "mountainlike" as applied to me was particularly embarrassing, and various persons of my acquaintance in Cafeteria Society lost no time in making the most of it. I knew he had never written the article in the form in which it appeared, although its general tone was faintly recognizable as his way of thinking. We kidded about it a lot, but he always stoutly maintained that he wrote it. Had he let me edit his preliminary drafts, his thoughts would have remained but the style would have remained his too. I'm sorry it didn't come out that way.

During the period that I knew him, Gorky's work was strongly influenced by certain styles of Picasso. This was apparent to everybody, and there was a tendency to criticize him as a naïve imitator. I took a different view and defended his work at all times. Admitting the influence, I would challenge the artist-critic on his own imitation of corny ideas about the old masters, Cézanne or some appeasement splinter-group of modernism, instead of the real thing. I told these carpers that their own work was so loaded with bad interpretations and imitation that they were the last ones who had a right to speak. I told them that what they were really bellyaching about was the directness and boldness of Gorky's ideas, regardless of source, which made their timid eclecticism look sick.

It must be remembered that at that remote period the exponents of modern art were much less numerous than they are today, and they needed to maintain a solid front against the Squares of every ilk who were always out to subvert it. The same thing goes on today because the Squares are always with us, but the ratio of strengths has changed. Under those conditions I would automatically have supported Gorky's work and kept questions of disagreement inside the family circle. But I had no equivocal opinions about it. I took it for what it was—the work of a talented artist in the process of development, and one who had the intelligence and energy to orient himself in the direction of the most dynamic ideas of the time.

During this period he visited me for a week at my home in Gloucester, Massachusetts. When he left I drove him to Boston and we called on some relatives of his in the deadly commuter-like suburbs. At this place a large number of his art-school period drawings were on file. These were done in the orthodox life- and portrait-class style. But his genuine talent was clearly expressed within the framework of ideas required in such studies, and I found them stimulating and distinguished.

Toward the latter part of our friendship, landlord trouble required him to hunt about for another place to live. In some way he discovered an enormous room in a moldering rookery on Union Square East and established himself there. Landlord trouble moved in with him. The dangerous stairs to this vault was ventilated by the aromas of a grease kitchen on the ground floor and a Civil-War-type dentist's parlor to the left. The room itself was pitch black at high noon, in spite of a sizable side-light let into the one wall which allowed it to be called a studio. Like all such skylight affairs, it was heavily sanded and etched by filth on the outside, and the few quantums of light that survived the struggle to penetrate it reeled to the floor one meter inside. Before adequate artificial light was introduced later on, it was unsafe to walk about in this cavern without a flashlight. But what it lacked in light was compensated for in acreage, and Gorky enjoyed this freedom of space very much. He painted it and scrubbed it, and was able to manipulate his large canvases and projects without let or hindrance.

In the early part of 1934 the economic situation for artists became so bad that they were forced to look around for ways and means to save themselves. They were shoved together by mutual distress, and artist organizations of one kind or another began to form as a natural result. I was in these things from the beginning and so was Gorky. I took the business as seriously as the serious situation demanded and devoted

182   Stuart Davis

much time to the organizational work. Gorky was less intense about it and still wanted to play. In the nature of the situation, our interests began to diverge and finally ceased to coincide altogether. Our friendship terminated and was never resumed.

I had one final contact with Gorky's work several years later. He had made some murals for the Federal Art Project which were allocated and temporarily installed in an airport in Newark, New Jersey. A local committee who had to approve them was hemming and hawing, and trying to find some valid excuse to reject them. It became necessary to smash this pesky rebellion, and the New York Project organized a delegation of overpowering authority to invade this benighted suburb and put the locals in their place. I was the artist member of the committee. We drove over the swamps in a determined mood and shortly met the stubborn and ill-armed locals face to face. There was nothing to it after the first broadside fired by our oratorical Professors, Doctors and Experts. One of the locals quickly joined our side, and the rout was complete. But their unhorsed chairman made a final convulsive effort by whistling for an ace air pilot who charged into the room. "Tell these Yankees what you think of these so-called modernistic murals," the chairman gasped. The ace surveyed the huge pieces of canvas. They hung in drapery-like folds on the walls, owing to some slip-up in the secret formula of the adhesive which was guaranteed to last forever. We all surveyed them; in spite of their unorthodox hanging, they were unmistakably done in an approved modernistic style. But the chairman's ace-in-the-hole blasted his last hope by saying that he didn't know nothin' about art but thought they were right pretty. He said he was reminded of wonderful things he had seen, and began to recite recollections of beautiful cloud formations observed on his numerous flights. He was warming up to give dates, locations and the particular hour of day of these events when the chairman silenced him. An official surrender was signed, and our cavalcade sped back victorious to the taverns of New York to celebrate. Whatever happened to the murals, I don't know.

Memo on Mondrian (1961)   *Stuart Davis*

Since the sluice gates have been opened up on Art, putting new life and fire into the old slogan "Run for the hills, boys, the dam has bust," it becomes increasingly difficult to focus on some individual of the past. Particularly so when the activities of the subject of inquiry are dated earlier than the previous month. Imagine then the problem of recall in

From *Arts Magazine Yearbook,* 1961.

the case of Mondrian, where more than fifteen years have elapsed since his death. In the past it was a normal perspective of memory to use certain individuals and events as coordinate locations in developing an idea without regard for Time differentials. It was implicit in this attitude that a certain continuity of Values existed. An interval of a decade, or perhaps a century or two here and there, was not an obstacle to the notion of unity. Today, of course, the linear-progression idea is unusable as a defense against uncertainty. As it is now generally accepted that the individual is a genetic tape in coded alphabet, a playback of the appropriate time-dubbings on your tape might be thought feasible. Clearly it is not, because your coded electronic-friend has long since been erased for reasons of economy and space under the frenetic impact of new releases and labels. Actually my contacts with Mondrian were few, and thus I am able to recall several of them by means of old-fashioned techniques.

Of course I had known about Mondrian for a number of years as a leader in the modern movement. The aspect he represented didn't interest me very much, although I had a decent respect for it. However, I saw him in Paris in 1928 or 1929 on a rather bizarre and amusing occasion. It was at the Place de la Contrescarpe, where I had been taken at three o'clock in the morning by my friend Elliot Paul, editor of *Transition,* to witness a test or drill of the Night-Soil Workers of Paris. He explained to me that a number of nasty incidents had recently occurred, involving faulty hoses, pipes, gauges and the like. The citizen victims of these frightening episodes had raised a hue and cry. Sabotage, or graft in the purchase of supplies, was suspected. Demand for immediate measures to stop the sinister menace had resulted in this gathering. Beyond that, Elliot said, there was growing suspicion that youth was losing its respect for traditional crafts and skills. A lack of devotion to the meticulous techniques of their fathers had made the streets unsafe for late strollers.

As we selected our table at the cafe, which remained open for the occasion, Elliot pointed out a man on the crowded curb diagonally across the Place from our position. "That's Mondrian, the great modern artist," he said. That was my first and last glimpse of him for over a decade. He seemed attentive to the array of medieval engines, tanks, hoses and other equipment gathered at this spot, famous for the richness of its historical material in vats, cisterns and other mysterious underground devices. The workers lined up, neatly accoutered in the armor of their touchy trade, and after a brief lecture by the superintendent, trotted to their stations in the adjacent streets and alleys. The well-oiled engines chugged along as each in turn was given the signal to start pumping. The engineers went about in an ordinary manner checking their meters and gauges. By this time the standees at the curbs were contentedly munching on some light snacks brought along to round out

Stuart Davis

their early-morning wine diet. Then without warning came a ghastly explosion from one of the contraptions, engulfing the crowd in the exact area where Mondrian had been standing. The blast had a high decibel rating but was slightly flatulent in tone. Taking note of how the wind of events was blowing, Elliot and I left the Arrondissement at once, stifling all natural curiosity about cause and effect. I feel sure that Mondrian must have left the scene before the fact. Had it been otherwise it is clear that the normal development schedule of Pure Plastic Art would have been retarded by a matter of months, or possibly even a year or two.

Early in the Modern Art script, through some syntactical quirk of his genetic code, Mondrian arrived at the preposterous notion that you could get rid of all the paraphernalia of pictural usage and still have a satisfactory painting left. It was a far-out idea, and still is. Of course there were immediate environmental factors going for him which gave support to his decision, but in my view it remains a personal choice. His intuitive literacy in translating his pre-recorded tape into usable prophetic idiom, for a relatively small but hip group, indicates the power of his personality. Who made the original copy of the original copy, etc., of his tape is a question I leave to professional experts and scholars of annularism. It is possible that some mutative Thing had tapped his wire and injected certain stern novelties making the illusion of free choice possible. At any rate all that concerns us for purposes of these remarks is that he set off a bomb.

Under the impact of its shock waves the rigorous and splendid images of Cubism seemed to take on the appearance of an uncured yak-hide rug for the time being. A hard-sell campaign developed in which the key words, "Pure" and "Plastic" were stressed. The Scotch Tape division of the Minnesota Mining Co. called in experts to trace an enormous but unexplainable increase in sales. I passed through these events without becoming too deeply involved, due to a slight touch of Rococo in the code of my genetic alphabet.

Some of my friends, and competitors in the field of Art were more directly involved. It was through them that I met Mondrian in person, not a recording, shortly after he came to New York around 1940. He was greatly interested in jazz and had been told of my high regard for it. On this basis we spent a friendly evening talking about that subject. I played a number of records which today could probably be found only in an abandoned crate in a suburb of Petersburg, Virginia. The summation of these conversations and entertainments was that Mondrian pronounced certain examples of boogie-woogie to be "Pure," or "The True Jazz"; as for the rest, it was worthy, provided an inferior status be granted. I found him to be a most amiable and sympathetic man, despite certain minor semantic oppositions in the designation of our enthusiasms. His preference for the term "Abstract" left me unmoved, but there seemed to be mutual unstated agreement that Nature was a great thing provided you didn't get mixed up with it.

There is no question that Mondrian was stimulated by the New York environment and developed new snapshot angles in the contemplation of his idea-monument. The breaking up of his Black-Line Areas into an extensive internal series reflected the impact of this new sense of Freedom.

In this connection I recall a conversation with him wherein he expressed the belief that the absence of clear-cut Academic Art standards in the United States was a liberating situation for the student, a great advantage over the European attitude. I maintained the opposite view in saying that the absence of relatively stable norms of procedure left the environs a bit drafty and devoid of stimuli to react against. Of course, since the sluice has already been unbolted, the whole question has become academic.

I recall one more meeting with Mondrian. It was at an exhibition of my paintings in 1943 at Mrs. Edith Halpert's Downtown Gallery on East 51st. Thanks to some kind of good will that was going around, a lot of people showed up for this private opening, Mondrian among them. It was a great honor to have the presence of an internationally famous European artist. At that remote time American artists had a strictly Class B rating on the international board, regardless of individual merit. The scene was enlivened, apart from the scenes on the wall, by the performance of a number of Grade A jazz musicians. Included among others were W. C. Handy, Mildred Bailey, Red Norvo, George Wettling, Duke Ellington and Pete Johnson, king of boogie-woogie pianists. The situation was much enjoyed by Mondrian, and he took time out to compliment me on my work, pointing out that in the latest examples I was approaching Pure Plastic Art. Using the terminology of his own doctrine, he explained to me in some detail how I was gradually getting the stuff in back up to the front.

So much for my meager but fond recollections of Mondrian. I prefer to think of him as one of the half-dozen top individual artists of the twentieth century rather than the symbol of an art movement.

Stuart Davis

VIII writing and criticism about stuart davis

Stuart Davis, American Painter (1928)
Elliot Paul

There are many creative artists whose vigor is concentrated upon their form of expression, whose best energy and continual thought are devoted to their conceptions. Such men see things in a large way and state them clearly. Performance is always painful to them, but they drive themselves to it with more zeal than those who delight in handiwork, because their inspiration springs from deeper sources and humanity's inertia and stupidity press upon them always. Rossini was so lazy that if, in the course of composing, a sheet of music slid from the bed to the floor he would compose another, sometimes quite different, rather than exert himself to pick up the first.

Stuart Davis, under any other circumstances, would have been a lazy man. Had there been one of his countrymen painting in a way that satisfied him, he would have been content, perhaps, to watch him and to approve. Such was not the case. While he was in his teens, the repercussions of the amazing upheavals which the artistic world in Europe had undergone at the hands of Cézanne and the young Picasso reached New York faintly and were met with the same smug imbecility which European picture merchants had exhibited twenty years before and had had time to repent bitterly. Davis had tried one or two art schools and had been thoroughly disgusted. He had heard the art students and professors chatter like magpies at East Gloucester each summer and exhibit their salable product in a setting which reeked of pretension and insincerity. As a boy, he cut himself off from all that and began, painstakingly, to learn to paint, drawing his inspiration from the genuine modern masters rejected by all his associates.

His development has been utterly natural and unimpeded for, while he has had no encouragement, he has not suffered from the advice of the kid-glove critic nor dealer who would like to be daring, like an old-maid, but does not know how. In the beginning, he did caricatures, adjusting the lines and planes of human or inanimate subjects in order to comment upon them. His early works are very much like Daumier and Toulouse-Lautrec in intent and execution, but in varying outlines and shapes for literary reasons he learned to do so for aesthetic purposes and before he had reached voting age had transcended the stage in which he was a glorified cartoonist. Unaided he passed that simple barrier which has stopped more than nine-tenths of the artists of promise in any age. He came upon the simple truth that forms are interdependent, that planes have inside and outside surfaces whether in nature

From *Transition* No. 14 (1928).

there is air or cream of wheat between them, that lines bend forward and backward as well as to the left and right.

Artists who are supersensitive to visual impressions, for whom the subtle relationships of colors and textures are intense experiences, tend always to simplification. Davis worked with landscapes in about the way Juan Gris studied still life, arriving at placid, harmonious results and identifying the objects which fathered the shapes he used as a sort of concession to the feeble spectator. Like Gris and Picasso, Davis resorted to all kinds of materials in order to produce the effects he desired. He glued pieces of tin or sewed buttons upon his canvases and used the letters of the alphabet and numerals in all sizes when their lines supplied whatever he required to occupy a given space. But like the other discerning painters abroad he dropped that line or procedure and studied the more difficult and effective art of mixing paint.

Davis' paintings are all logical and as his logic has improved, his painting has progressed. His work is no more haphazard than a Bach fugue. As soon as he had learned to paint landscapes which did not look as if they had been painted on the inside of a box and in which no foreground was interposed like a moat in front of the actual subject, he placed an interesting object like, for instance, a gasoline pump, in a given space and carried outward into the air and inward through solid material the implied surfaces and planes. In this he gained freedom, for in painting grass, trees, ships and sky it required years to rid himself of the bad start the accidental color relationships in nature always gave him. He painted egg-beaters and percolators, radiators and pumps, avoiding always the obvious. The exhibitions went on around him, with thousands of little daubs rolled out like dough into an ugly and uniform texture, entitled *Rocks and Water* or of Venetian canals varnished with moonlight.

His paintings are beautiful as objects. Their significance is beautiful. They are abstract in the sense that their origin lies in undiluted aesthetic impulses. He often borrows the form of an object without its irrelevant characteristics. He is the only American who has shown the simple common sense to be influenced by his important contemporaries rather than by his second-rate predecessors. He has been strong enough to withstand all the neglect, nonsense and misunderstanding which has fallen to his lot. He represents the age.

It is time now to salute him. He will be able to bear up under a little approval after all these years. A very few painters have learned from his example. Several young men gathered around him in the beginning and one by one have reverted to magazine cover decoration or three cheers for the soviets.

Stuart Davis' spirit is still intact. He has lost none of his good humor.

He will go on, in the direction all great artists have indicated, and, like those estimable men, will have to travel his way alone.

Downtown Gallery's Exhibition of His Work Proves a Lively One (1931)   *Henry McBride*

Stuart Davis is a good scout. I believe I mean this literally. You know what a scout is, of course? A good scout gets up in the middle of the night and goes far off into the enemy country and returns with useful information. Stuart Davis has been doing this for years. Sometimes he does it in the daytime, too, but always he returns with what you want to know.

When abstract art was invented in France, Stuart Davis was immediately on the job. Before anybody else in America he knew what it was all about. He was young enough then for it not to seem surprising to him. Like a child that is born in China and finds it easy to speak Chinese, Stuart Davis found it easy to think in terms of abstract art. Lots of people at the present day who come suddenly and in an unprepared moment upon the abstract think the whole thing is some kind of insanity or some kind of imposture, and they would be very much surprised if they knew how simple and natural the whole thing is to Stuart Davis.

The only thing wrong about Stuart Davis is that he picked the language up when out scouting. I love scouts and approve of scouting, but somehow—deep down in my heart—I should have preferred Stuart Davis to have invented the kind of talk he now hands out. But we can't have everything, and, next to the invention of a language, there is the speaking it nicely—and that Stuart Davis surely does. He speaks it better than any other American I know of. That is a distinction in itself.

His Best Showing

Furthermore, the exhibition he has just opened in the Downtown Galleries is the best he has ever given. Everybody who came to the opening day exercises smiled with pleasure as they entered the room much as people smile who enter pretty gardens, for the gay effect of the walls was a sufficient promise of the joys that could be, and were, extracted from the individual pictures. Somehow, these initiated people who also speak Chinese, were not puzzled by the pictures, which seemed quite

From "Stuart Davis Comes to Town," *New York Sun* (April 4, 1931).

clear and complete as pictures, and, in addition, had the new kind of elegance that is typical of the times we live in.

The pictures whether scoutwork or nonscout work, are certainly Stuart Davisy. In spite of all the Braques, Légers and Juan Grises, that loom formidably in the No-Man's Land of Mount Parnassus, the Stuart Davis work is always easy to distinguish. One thing that distinguishes it for me is the humor, for there is a sense of fun in the Davis concoctions that is unusual. It is healthy, wholesome and typically American fun. Braque and Picasso, the great leaders of the abstract movement, never make jokes; Miro's impulse is toward the fantastic and slightly macabre; Jean Hugo's is witty and drawingroomish, but also decadent. Stuart Davis is alone in giving you the hearty laughter of outdoors.

By Way of Explanation

Stuart Davis, however, is not so funny when he starts to explain his art. Few artists are. Here are some explanations he has been inveigled into giving and which appear in the catalogue to the show:

> I believe that all possible forms are valid and that limitations resulting from a set ratio of angle or area are not helpful in the production of forms other than themselves. In other words, that the concept of a certain type of design which is good, opposed to another which is bad, is the wrong way to think about it. Any design which achieves variety is good. . . . Color must be thought of as texture which automatically allows one to visualize it in terms of space. Aside from this it has no meaning.

Do you get it?

Stuart Davis (1931)   *Arshile Gorky*

. . . Yet the silent consequences of Stuart Davis move us to the cool and intellectual world where all human emotions are disciplined upon rectangular proportions. Here these relations take us to the scientific world where all dreams evaporate and logic plays its greatest victory, where the physical world triumphs over all tortures, where all the clumsiness dies, and leaves only the elements of virtue, where the aesthetic world takes new impulse for new consequences. Oh, what a glorious prospect! This man, this American, this pioneer, this modest painter, who never disarranges his age, who works to perfect his motives, who renders—clear, more definite, more and more decided—new forms and new objects. He chooses new rules to discipline his emotions. He gives

From *Creative Art,* IX (September, 1931), pp. 213, 217.

new shape to his experiences with new sequences—orange, red, yellow, green, brown and chalk-like white, metallic grays and dull blacks, profound spaces with sky-like blues, stabilized upon rectangular directions. He takes a new position upon the visible world. This artist, whether he paints egg-beaters, streets, or pure geometrical organizations, expresses his constructive attitude toward his successive experiences. He gives us symbols of tangible spaces, with gravity and physical laws. He, above his contemporaries, rises high—mountain-like! Oh, what clarity! One he is, and one of but few, who realizes his canvas as a rectangular shape with two-dimensional surface plane. Therefore he forbids himself to poke bumps and holes upon that potential surface. This man, Stuart Davis, works upon that platform where are working the giant painters of the century—Picasso, Léger, Kandinsky, Juan Gris—bringing to us new utility, new aspects, as does the art of Uccello. They take us to the supernatural world behind reality where once the great centuries danced.

Yet there are large numbers of critics, artists, and public suspended like vultures, waiting in the air for the death of the distinctive art of this century, the art of Léger, Picasso, Miró, Kandinsky, Stuart Davis. They forget that while the artist never works outside his time yet his art will go on to be merged gradually into the new art of a new age. There will be no short stop. We shall not, contrary to the expectation of these people, hear of the sudden death of Cubism, abstraction, so-called modern art. These critics, these artists, these spectators who wait for a sudden fall are doomed to disappointment. They have merely not understood the spiritual movement and the law of direct energy of the centuries, and they can never have understood the spiritual meaning of any form of art. If they could but realize that energy is a spiritual movement and that they must conceive of working under a law of universal aesthetic progress, as we do in science, in mathematics, in physics.

The twentieth century—what intensity, what activity, what restless nervous energy! Has there in six centuries been better art than Cubism? No. Centuries will go past—artists of gigantic stature will draw positive elements from Cubism.

Clumsy painters take a measurable space, a clear definite shape, a rectangle, a vertical or horizontal direction, and they call it blank canvas, while every time one stretches canvas he is drawing a new space. How could they ever have understood Cubism or the art of the twentieth century? How could they accept tranquility and expansion as elements of feeling in painting?

No painter in America has ever made such [a] definite and developed statement of his thoughts as Stuart Davis at his exhibition a few months ago. He made his vision clear.

"My concept of form is very simple and is based on the assumption that space is continuous and that matter is discontinuous. In my formal concept the question of two or more dimensions does not enter. I never ask the question 'Does this picture have depth or is it flat?'

"I consider such a question irrelevant. I conceive of form (matter) as existing in space, in terms of linear direction. It follows then that the forms of the subject are analyzed in terms of angular variation from bases of directional radiation.

"Color must be thought of as texture which automatically allows one to visualize it in terms of space. Aside from this it has no meaning."

Because Stuart Davis realizes the invisible relations and phenomena of this modern time he is the visible point to the progressive mind in his country.

When Cobblers Turn from the Last: Issues in the Debate Between Leading Exponents of "Abstract" and "Nationalist" Tendencies—Mr. Benton's Recent Painting (1935)
Edward Alden Jewell

If only artists would resist the temptation to wrangle and would stick instead to their paint, there would be less general befuddlement and there might also be more progress in art itself.

Often what an artist says in words is both pertinent and illuminating. But I think you could count upon your fingers the good artists who are as qualified to write as they are to paint.

In any event, it is difficult indeed to see what good can possibly come of this sometimes frenetic and sometimes heavy-footed bombardment that has been going on in the columns of *The Art Front* and reported from issue to issue in *The Art Digest*. The debate began with Stuart Davis's attack on "nationalism" in American art. This attack involved, among other artists, Thomas Benton. We learn that when Mr. Benton was invited to defend himself he declined, but agreed to answer any ten questions the editors of *The Art Front* cared to put. The questions were duly forthcoming, and Mr. Benton kept his word, after which Mr. Davis replied. There the issue rests at the moment, but like the Long-Coughlin-Johnson exchange, this art debate will probably continue until the reading public is too sick of the whole mess to read another line.

Points are undoubtedly scored on both sides. But the result of my reading to date is a sense of sadness over so much wasted time and the generation of so much hindering animosity.

As artists, when glancingly we compare their respective styles, their

From *The New York Times* (April 7, 1935).

194   Stuart Davis

divergent methods of dealing with a theme, Mr. Benton and Mr. Davis might, on first thought, be esteemed poles apart. But is the cleavage actually so formidable? Both artists, in so far as their art really counts, appear to be interested fundamentally in the aesthetic side. Both men are fundamentally interested in the creation of works of art rather than in the mere exploitation of subject.

Stuart Davis, if he chose, may call his abstraction "New York," just as he used to call the products of a now famous abstract series "Egg Beater No. 1," "Egg Beater No. 2," and so forth. Mr. Benton may elect as his "realistic" theme a lurid tale out of Buffalo Bill and the nickel novels, or a slice of modern cabaret life. In both cases it is the picture, ponderable strictly as a work of art, that counts, not the "abstraction" or the "realism"—no, nor the "nationalism" or its opposite—made use of in objectifying for us whatever the theme may be.

If Mr. Davis were wholly intent upon browsing among abstract theories that had their origin in Paris ateliers earlier in our century, and if Mr. Benton were wholly engrossed in American history and the contemporary American scene, neither would be worth bothering about as artists. Both of these men, on the other hand, are seriously preoccupied with the task of trying to paint pictures that shall meet the requirements of good art or great art. You might never guess it to hear them talk.

I do not propose to go into the involutions and convolutions of this fruitless debate, this largely befogging and frequently very dull display of verbal charge and counter-charge. As Alexander Woollcott said in his (one hopes but temporary) farewell on the radio last Sunday night, we all talk too much. Everybody talks too much. It is an international vice. Creative artists, however, would seem, when they deserve the epithet, more blameworthy than the rest. Their job is painting. Their job is to say all that they have to say in the form of created art. And if they do this to the very best of their ability, they will have said enough. A great work of art should tell the public all it needs to know. The rest may well be silence.

As for the American scene—with which both these artists, if we are to credit their titles, are concerned—that can be significantly communicated only in terms of art that is rich in understanding and in the technical power to express what the mind of the artist has thought and the heart of the artist has felt. Nothing else matters. Everything else is just skating about on the surface of life and of art alike.

Review of Stuart Davis Exhibition at The Museum of Modern Art (1945)

Ad Reinhardt

There's little to add to the deserving tributes paid this month to Stuart Davis, one of our "first" American moderns, now one of our accepted "foremost" painters, who is currently having an impressive retrospective at the Museum of Modern Art. Stuart Davis has always known that his painting was a matter of order, structure, relationships. Once he was merely included in American group "cross-section" exhibitions to "round out" and "liberalize" them, usually all by himself. When a work was needed to represent "modern," "unacademic" or "left" painting in America, a Stuart Davis was invariably selected. And for over a decade he's looked bright and fresh and unique in the company he's kept.

Davis calls himself a "realist," and he's an abstract painter, and abstractionists are "realistic" (when you think about the term). His work is not "naturalistic," though, and his paintings are not "pictures" or "window frames," but rather organizations of lines, colors, spaces (American organizations, if you want). I'm sorry that it seemed necessary for him to bring in the lamp-post, radio-tube and light-bulb business in his later and more abstract paintings, as if to give them "extra" meaning and "ease" their communication. For these representational references make some people try to reduce the paintings to "figure-out-what-it's-supposed-to-be" games (and who's got the goat in those cases?).

Abstract art or non-pictorial art is as old as this century and though more specialized than previous art, is clearer and more complete, and like all modern thought and knowledge, more demanding in its grasp of relations, forms, structures. When abstract artists are asked what "means" their work, they're apt to turn on the questioner and indicate the necessary and intellectual and emotional conditions for the appreciation of their work. Though Davis' paintings don't exactly ask the spectator "What do you represent?" they do demand more participation, more awareness on the part of the onlooker (who isn't helped by titles either).

Our contemporary "art world" forces painters to exploit their individuality and peculiarity, and unfortunately one is always "on one's own." Davis has always known the value of group activity, though, and was once conspicuous in the organized combating of Fascism, bigotry, narrow political and aesthetic ideas. His present political inactivity and his lack of relation to the artists' groups is regrettable for a painter of his integrity and stature.

From *New Masses* (November 27, 1945).

Stuart Davis: True to Life
The Consistent
Invention of America's Pioneer
Abstractionist Is Seen in His Retrospective
at Minneapolis (1957)   *Elaine de Kooning*

Today, when hectic, automatist techniques so often and so surprisingly result in ingratiating, decorative and vaguely naturalistic imagery, a painting by Stuart Davis, with its plain, strong, "ready-made" colors and sharply cut-out shapes, has somewhat the effect of a good sock on the jaw, sudden, emphatic and not completely pleasant.

Davis, now sixty-three, apparently always knew, as few painters have, what he wanted and who he was. The character of his work does not change through the years. The present show (at the Walker Art Center, Minneapolis, and coming to the Whitney Museum in the fall), covering the years 1925–56, is as scrupulously extrovert, conscious and uncompromising as was his retrospective exhibition at the Museum of Modern Art twelve years ago, which included some scenes painted as early as 1912. Comparing the two shows, one is struck again with the singularly impersonal, almost disembodied nature of his art. One does not feel a contact with its inception (as with Abstract Expressionist work) or recognize in it the sensuality of an individual effort. It seems to be there all at once—the product of an aggregate impulse and perception, like slang.

Fiercely independent, but not an eccentric, Davis reacts against the momentum of a current style with a reflex of self-insulation. He has successfully resisted the devouring intellectual camaraderie (or is it anxiety?) that keeps most avant-garde artists breathing down each other's necks and that makes group shows look like the game of Musical Chairs as artists grab each other's styles, subjects and mannerisms before the paint is dry. His style, developed between two continents and two wars, is as insistently remote from the Synthetic Cubism that was his starting point as it is from the American Action-Painting that surrounds him today.

He achieves his separated position by an act of will or rather, by an operation of logic: he chooses to be *à rebours*. His paintings made of, in or through Paris are swept clean of the gentle, expansive and complex intimacies that envelope Parisian art. When he began working in the Cubist manner, he immediately dispensed with their subtle tones, their discreet scale, their paraphernalia of private property and locale. His street scenes of that period, rendered in an over-simplified, almost

From *Art News* (April, 1957).

cartoon-strip style, have a kind of breezy, open, New England quaintness; his still-lifes are about as cozy as factories on Houston Street on Sunday. Cubism, after all, is an indoor art, full of nice, comfortable, old furniture and friends of the family. But, although for Davis a pack of Lucky Strikes could be unobtrusively substituted for a guitar, you really can't have Whitman's Open Road run through the parlor without changing the look of things.

Davis' palette has always been, in spirit at least, strictly red, white and blue. His subject has always been America—not America as seen in American art but as seen on a walk down Broadway or a drive past a harbor in a fishing village. He resists art by being true to life. More intensely than any painter in our history, he offers a specific, objective national experience. It is the experience not of our natural landscape but of America as man-made. The brittle animation of his art relates to jazz, to movie marquees, to the streamlined decor and brutal colors of gasoline stations, to the glare of neon lights, to the flamboyant sweep of three-level parkways, to the fool-proof shine of stainless-steel diners, to the big, bright words that are shouted at us from bill-boards from one end of the country to the other. In our common public existence (which is the only existence Davis, as a painter, is interested in), this is the land of layout and lettering, of engineering and industrial design, of big cities and long roads that Somebody built. Obviously Davis feels a profound sympathy for the grand and broad expression of *Abstract Artists Anonymous*. What are the names of the men who designed the words ESSO or REM or Coca-Cola? Who designed the viaduct at Sixty-first Street and the East River? Or certain juke-boxes? Like this company, he expresses in his work the concept that one glance should be enough to see what you're looking at, since the chances are you're going someplace else fast. And so, although his pictures are not big (as big pictures go nowadays), their expression is. If one were slapped against a building like a bill-board, it would hold its own. In fact, Davis is one of the few abstract painters in the country whose work authentically relates to modern architecture.

Like modern architecture, his art has a distinctly argumentative character. Nothing is suggested or implied. Everything is stated flatly. Here are no evasive tones or ambiguous colors, no vague distances or irresponsible implications of scale, no meandering sentiments. There is in his paint-stroke no description, no point of view; it delivers the unprimed fact to you. Every proportion is measurable, every effect predetermined. Detail is massive. The remnants of stylized representation —the roads, clouds, waves, smoke, chimneys, shingles, ladders, wagonwheels, windows, barrels that still crop up in his work, super-imposed in rigid patterns over the large paper-flat planes—are related with a cheerful, bold and heavy hand to the whole. The taciturn impastoes, the

Stuart Davis

highly deliberate patterns, the inflexible scissor-sharp edges all seem to indicate an insistence on "the last word." And he has it. In the Protestant economy of Davis' art, nothing is superficial and everything is necessary.

His is an art of solid certainties. He never seems to have been involved with those rather bitter changes of heart which beset so many artists and which result in their working consecutively (or what is even more painful, simultaneously) in contradictory styles in their search for an identity. He is aware that his approach is in conflict with the approach of most abstract painters around him and he is somewhat contemptuous of their condition, which might be termed "the anguish of possibility," to use Harold Rosenberg's phrase.

"I think of Abstract Art," Davis wrote in 1951, "in the same way I think of all Art, Past and Present. . . . I see it as divided into two Major categories, Objective and Subjective. Objective Art is Absolute Art. . . . [It] sees the Percept of the Real World as an Immediate Given Event. . . . Subjective art is Illustration, or communication by Symbols, Replicas and Oblique Emotional Passes . . . Its Universal Principle has the character of a Universal Bellyache . . . It has a Perverse Passion for the Detour."

Clearly then, the various possibilities Davis sees, as an Objective artist, are in the realm of solutions, not problems. If, as some critics have pointed out, its solutions always seem to fall more or less in the same territory, there is no sense of self-indulgence, of relaxation of the spirit in the fact that he has never substantially deviated from the style he defined for himself so early in his career. On the contrary, one might get the impression of an iron stubbornness in his cleaving to certain principles of clarity now largely abandoned by painters (although commercial artists and architects are of course still involved with them). His paintings have the "look" of another decade, specifically, the 'thirties—not the provincial but the International "look." But Davis, like Léger and Mondrian, with whom he shares a passion for conscious, objective art, has made his particular "look" timeless. Convictions that ardent keep their immediacy.

In the sense that he starts with the idea that the canvas is a limited area to be divided, to be designed, he is following a European tradition. It is the opposite of the concept of the image which unfolds and spreads out, as in the panoramas of the Hudson River School or the panoramas of American Action-Painting where the edges of the canvas are the last facts to be considered, not the first. Many abstract painters today, for instance, work on unstretched canvas tacked to the wall, and decide on the size and proportions of the painting after it is finished. This would be as unworkable an approach for Davis as it would for Mondrian or Léger, since the exercise of will and consciousness can only be accomplished within a fixed space. For artists who insist on complete control, the world must be square; there must be boundaries to act *against*.

In the face of this framework of calculation, one of the paradoxes of his work is in its extraordinary animation—an element we usually associate with spontaneity. But even here he is deliberate, aspiring to what he has called the "Consciousness of Motion" in art. This he achieves mainly in his use of color, and here he is a craftsman second to none. His colors, although strong and opaque, are oddly without physical presence. They do not create surfaces but rather, sheets or flashes of light. This spurting electric quality of his color has less to do with the choice of pigments—they could be interchangeable, one feels—than with the spacing, proportioning and repetition of the areas into which the colors are so carefully placed. The light doesn't act in but between the colors. The larger areas are pulled and twisted into different dimensions by the contradictory presence of the smaller. He uses the "scale" of different colors—their various propensities for expansion and contraction—to achieve the fantastic, mechanized activity of his compositions.

Stuart Davis

Bibliography

I. Writings by Stuart Davis

(In chronological order)

"Shadow." *Harper's Bazaar,* XLVI (May, 1912), 226–28.

"A Painter of City Streets: An Analysis of the Work of Glenn Coleman." *Shadowland,* VIII, No. 6 (August, 1923), 11, 75.

Letter to Henry McBride on French influence in Davis's paintings. *Creative Art,* VI (February, 1930), supp. 34–35.

"Davis Translates His Art into Words." *Art Digest,* V (April 15, 1931), 8, illus.

"Self-Interview." *Creative Art,* IX (September, 1931), 208–11, illus.

"From Our Friends—Stuart Davis." *Art Front,* I, No. 1 (November, 1934), 2.

Letter on Municipal Art Center. *New York Sun* (January 14, 1935), p. 22.

"Paintings by Salvador Dali, Julien Levy Gallery." *Art Front,* I, No. 2 (January, 1935), 7.

"The New York American Scene in Art." *Art Front,* I, No. 3 (February, 1935), 6. Reprinted in part and with comment in *Art Digest,* IX (March 1, 1935), 4, 21. Thomas Benton replies in *Art Digest,* IX (March 15, 1935), 20–21, 25; reprinted in *Art Front,* I, No. 4 (April, 1935), 4, 8.

"Davis' Rejoinder to Thomas Benton." *Art Digest,* IX (April 1, 1935), 12–13, 26.

Introduction, *Abstract Painting in America,* New York: Whitney Museum of American Art, 1935, pp. 3–5. Exhibition catalogue. Reprinted in *Art of Today,* VI, No. 3 (April, 1935), 9–10. Reprinted in part in HOMER SAINT-GAUDENS, *The American Artist and His Times.* New York, Dodd, Mead, 1941, pp. 224–25.

"A Medium of Two Dimensions," *Art Front,* I, No. 5 (May, 1935), 6.

"American Artists and the 'American Scene.' " *New York World-Telegram,* May 4, 1935, p. 14.

"The Artist Today: The Standpoint of the Artists' Union," *American Magazine of Art,* XXVIII (August, 1935), 476–78, 506.

"Some Chance!" *Art Front,* I, No. 7 (November, 1935), 4, 7.

"The American Artists' Congress." *Art Front,* II, No. 8 (December, 1935), 8.

"American Artists' Congress." *Art Digest,* X (March 15, 1936), 25.

Letter objecting to Mr. Edward Alden Jewell's criticism of Federal Art Project exhibition at The Museum of Modern Art. *The New York Times,* September 27, 1936, sec. 10, p. 9.

"Why an Artists' Congress?" *First American Artists' Congress,* New York, 1936, pp. 3–6.

"The Artists' Congress and American Art." *American Artists' Congress,* second annual membership exhibition, New York, 1938, pp. 2–5.

"Show is Model of Organization of Big Displays." *The New York Post,* April 29, 1939, p. 4WF.

"Art at the Fair." *The Nation,* CXLIX (July 22, 1939), 112.

"Abstraction." *The New York Times,* August 20, 1939, sec. 9, p. 7.

"Art and the Masses." *Art Digest,* XIV (October 1, 1939), 13, 14.

Foreword to *Hananiah Harari.* New York, Mercury Galleries, 1939. Exhibition catalogue.

"Is There a Revolution in the Arts?" *Bulletin of America's Town Meeting of the Air*, V, No. 19 (February 19, 1940), 11–14.

"Davis Explains His Resignation from Artists' Congress." *The New York Times*, April 14, 1940, sec. 9, p. 9.

"Davis Asks a Free Art." *The New York Times*, July 7, 1940, sec. 9, p. 12. Further remarks, *The New York Times*, August 18, 1940, sec. 9, p. 7.

"Stuart Davis." *Parnassus*, XII (December, 1940), 6, illus.

"The Abstract in Mural Art." *United Scenic Artists' Association Almanac* (1940–41), p. 20.

"Abstract Art in the American Scene." *Parnassus*, XIII (March, 1941), 100–103.

"The American Artist Now." *Now*, I, No. 1 (August, 1941), 7–11.

Response to "Bombshell" communication of Mr. Samuel Kootz, *The New York Times*, October 12, 1941, sec. 9, p. 9.

Foreword to leaflet published by *The Pinacotheca*, New York, December 1941.

"Art in Painting." *Marsden Hartley and Stuart Davis*. Cincinnati Modern Art Society, 1941, pp. 7–8. Exhibition catalogue.

Letter to Mr. Edward Alden Jewell denying abstraction of painting *Arboretum by Flash-Bulb*. *The New York Times*, September 27, 1942, sec. 8, p. 5.

"Art of the City." *Masters of Abstract Art*. New York, Helena Rubinstein's New Art Center, 1942, pp. 12–13.

"The Cube Root," *Art News*, XII (February 1, 1943), 22–23, 33–35, illus.

"What About Modern Art and Democracy?" *Harper's Magazine*, CLXXXVIII (December, 1943), 16–23.

"The 'Modern Trend' in Painting." *Think*, XI, No. 1 (January, 1945), 19–20, 36, illus.

Personal Statement: Painting Prophecy 1950. Washington, D.C., David Porter Gallery, 1945. Pamphlet issued in conjunction with exhibition, February, 1945.

Stuart Davis. New York, American Artists Group, 1945, illus. American Artists Group Monographs.

Devree, Howard. "Why They Paint the Way They Do." *The New York Times Magazine*, February 17, 1946, pp. 20–21.

"Contrasts: Paintings by Lucioni and Davis." *American Artist*, X (April, 1946), 34–35, illus.

Letter to the editor, *Life*, XXII (March 31, 1947), 9, 10.

Statement on George Wetling exhibition at the Norlyst Gallery, New York, November 23–December 6, 1947. Brochure, 1947.

Symposium on *Guernica*. Museum of Modern Art, New York, November 25, 1947, unpublished, pp. 58–63.

Louchheim, Aline B. "Six Abstractionists Defend Their Art." *The New York Times*, January 21, 1951, sec. 6, pp. 16–17, illus.

Statement by the artist. *Look*, XV (January 30, 1951), 68–69.

"Arshile Gorky: A Personal Recollection." *Magazine of Art*, LXIV (February, 1951), pp. 56–58.

"What Abstract Art Means to Me." *Museum of Modern Art Bulletin*, XVIII, No. 3 (Spring, 1951), 14–15, illus.

40 American Painters, 1940–1950. Minneapolis, University Gallery, University of Minnesota, 1951, pp. 18–19, illus. Exhibition catalogue.

Contemporary American Painting. Urbana, University of Illinois, 1952, pp. 183–84. Exhibition catalogue.

"Symposium: The Creative Process." *Art Digest,* XXVIII (January 15, 1954), 16, 34, illus.

"Place of Painting in Contemporary Culture." *Art News,* LVI (June, 1957), 29–30.

"Handmaiden of Misery." *Saturday Review,* XL (December 28, 1957), 16–17.

"Is Today's Artist with or Against the Past?" *Art News,* LVII, No. 4 (June, 1958), 43, illus.

"Artists on Art and Reality, on Their Work and on Values." *Daedalus,* LXXXIX (1960), 118–20, illus.

"Memo on Mondrian," *Arts Magazine Yearbook,* No. 4 (1961), 66–67.

Writings About Stuart Davis

(*In chronological order*)

DuBois, Guy Pène. "Stuart Davis." *New York American,* October 31, 1910, p. 11.

Bowdoin, W. G. "Modern Work of Stuart Davis at Village Show." *New York Evening World,* December 13, 1917.

"Critics Laud Young Artist." *Newark Morning Ledger,* June 1, 1918, p. 3.

"Cross Word Puzzle Motif in Art Expressed on Canvas at Museum." *Newark Evening News,* February 9, 1925, sup. sec., p. 11.

Mannes, Marya. "Gallery Notes." *Creative Art,* II (January, 1928), XI.

Jewell, Edward Alden. "Davis Tames a Shrew." *The New York Times,* April 19, 1928, sec. 10, p. 18.

Paul, Elliot. "Stuart Davis, American Painter." *Transition,* XIV (1928), 146–48, illus.

Burnett, Whit. " 'Egg Beater' Painter Led American Interpretive Art." *New York Herald* (Paris), July 7, 1929, illus.

Cary, Elizabeth Luther. "American Abroad." *The New York Times,* October 13, 1929, sec. 9, p. 12.

Harris, Ruth Green. "Stuart Davis." *The New York Times,* January 26, 1930, sec. 8, p. 13.

Goodrich, Lloyd. "In the Galleries." *The Arts,* XVI (February, 1930), 432, illus.

"Stuart Davis . . . at the Downtown Gallery." *Art Digest,* IV (February 1, 1930), 17.

McBride, Henry. "Stuart Davis Comes to Town." *New York Sun,* April 4, 1931, p. 12.

Knowlton, W. "Exhibition: Downtown Gallery." *Creative Art,* VIII (May, 1931), 375.

Gorky, Arshile. "Stuart Davis." *Creative Art,* IX (September, 1931), 212–17, illus.

Jewell, Edward Alden. "Stuart Davis Offers a Penetrating Survey of the American Scene." *The New York Times,* March 10, 1932, p. 19.

"Stuart Davis, Downtown Gallery." *Art News,* XXX (March 12, 1932), 10.

"Davis, 'American Scene.' " *Art Digest,* VI (March 15, 1932), 6.

McBride, Henry. "Stuart Davis . . . Downtown Gallery." *New York Sun,* March 21, 1932, p. 6.

DuBois, Guy Pène. "Stuart Davis." *Arts Weekly,* I, No. 3 (March 26, 1932), 48.

"Stuart Davis, the Difficult." *Art Digest,* VI (April 1, 1932), 2.

SHELLEY, MELVIN GEER. "Around the Galleries." *Creative Art,* X (April, 1932), 302.

"New York by Stuart Davis." *New York Sun,* April 16, 1934, p. 16.

E., L. "Stuart Davis." *Art News,* XXXII (April 28, 1934), 9.

"Stuart Davis and Abstraction." *Art Digest,* VIII (May 15, 1934), 14.

". . . Stuart Davis . . . Whitney Studio Club Galleries." *New York World,* December 13, 1936, p. 12.

KLEIN, JEROME. "Stuart Davis Criticizes Critic of Abstract Art." *The New York Post,* February 26, 1938, p. 24.

"Impression of the New York World's Fair Painted for Harper's Bazaar by Stuart Davis," *Harper's Bazaar,* LXXII (February, 1939), 60–61, illus.

JEWELL, EDWARD ALDEN. "Abstraction and Music: Newly Installed WPA Murals at Station WNYC Raise Anew Some Old Questions," *The New York Times,* August 6, 1939, sec. 9, p. 7.

GILBERT, MORRIS. "Eggbeater Artist Defends Credit to France for Help Given American Painters," *New York World-Telegram,* February 21, 1940, p. 13, illus., por.

SACARTOFF, ELIZABETH. "Rockport, Mass., Looks This Way to Stuart Davis," *PM,* August 4, 1940, p. 46, illus., por.

"Hot Still-Scapes for Six Colors—7th Ave. Style." *Parnassus,* XII (December, 1940), 6, illus.

Current Biography . . . 1940. New York, H. W. Wilson, pp. 228–29, por.

JOHNSON, D. RHODES. "Stuart Davis' Paintings Refute the Silly Notion that All Modern Art Is 'Foreign.' " *Jersey Journal* (July 7, 1941), p. 6.

RILEY, MAUDE. "Stuart Davis Exhibits His Abstracted Views." *Art Digest,* XVII (February 1, 1943), 7, illus.

BURROWS, CARLYLE, "Stuart Davis . . . Downtown Gallery." *New York Herald Tribune,* February 7, 1943, sec. 6, p. 5.

COATES, ROBERT M. "Davis, Hartley, and the River Seine." *The New Yorker,* XVIII (February 13, 1943), 58.

BOSWELL, PEYTON. "Painted Jazz." *Art Digest,* XVII (February 15, 1943), 3.

BARR, ALFRED H., JR. *What Is Modern Painting?* New York, Museum of Modern Art, 1943, pp. 4–5, illus.

PEARSON, RALPH M. *Experiencing American Pictures.* New York and London, Harper, 1943, pp. 36–38, illus.

O'CONNOR, JOHN, JR. "Stuart Davis . . . Awarded Third Honorable Mention." *Carnegie Magazine,* XVIII, No. 5 (October, 1944), 149–50, illus.

JANIS, SIDNEY. *Abstract and Surrealistic Art in America.* New York, Reynal & Hitchcock, 1944, pp. 50, 53, illus.

"Esquire's Art Institute II." *Esquire,* XXIV, No. 3 (September, 1945), 68–69, illus.

CAHILL, HOLGER. "In Retrospect 1945–1910." *Art News,* XLIV (October 15, 1945), 24–25, 32, illus.

GENAUER, EMILY. "Stuart Davis Paintings Shown at Modern Museum." *New York World-Telegram,* October 20, 1945, p. 8.

JEWELL, EDWARD ALDEN. "Mr. Davis, Ralph Earl and Others." *The New York Times,* October 21, 1945, sec. 2, p. 7.

"Stuart Davis Retrospective." *New York Herald Tribune,* October 21, 1945, sec. 5, p. 7.

COATES, ROBERT M. "Retrospective of Paintings: Modern Museum," *The New Yorker,* XXI (October 27, 1945), 52.

"Yankee Doodle and Jive." *Newsweek,* XXVI (October 29, 1945), 108–9, illus.

WOLF, BEN. "Stuart Davis: 30 Years of Evolution." *Art Digest,* XX (November 1, 1945), 10, 34, illus.

"Growth of an Abstractionist." *Time,* XLVI (November 5, 1945), 57–58.

GREENBERG, CLEMENT. Review of Stuart Davis exhibition. *The Nation,* CLXI (November 17, 1945), 533–34.

REINHARDT, AD. Review of Stuart Davis Exhibition, *New Masses,* November 27, 1945.

SWEENEY, JAMES JOHNSON. *Stuart Davis.* New York, Museum of Modern Art, 1945, illus. Exhibition catalogue.

WOLF, BEN. "The Digest Interviews: Stuart Davis." *Art Digest,* XX (December 15, 1945), 21; see also *Art Digest,* XXXLIV (January 1, 1946), 23.

"Exhibition, Downtown Gallery." *Art News,* XLIV (January 15, 1946), 23.

AGER, CECELIA. "Stuart Davis." *Vogue,* III (January 15, 1946), 80–81, 126, illus.

GIBBS, JO. "Stuart Davis Paints a Better Eggbeater." *Art Digest,* XX (February 1, 1946), 9, illus.

"Exhibition, Members Room for Modern Art," *Baltimore Museum News,* VIII (March, 1946), 2.

"Contrasts: Paintings by Lucioni and Davis." *American Artist,* X (April, 1946), 34–35, illus.

"Stuart Davis, by J. J. Sweeney." *American Artist,* X (April, 1946), 47.

SARGEANT, WINTHROP. "Why Artists Are Going Abstract: The Case of Stuart Davis." *Life,* XX (February 17, 1947), 78–81, 83, illus., por.

GUGLIELMI, O. LOUIS. Letter to the editor. *Life,* XX (March 31, 1947), 9–10.

LARDNER, R. "Rhythm." *Art News,* XLVI, sec. 2 (November, 1947), 107–10, 144. Illustrated by Stuart Davis.

"Modern Art in Chaos." *Cue* (June 19, 1948), p. 17, illus., por.

GENAUER, EMILY. *Best of Art.* Garden City, N.Y., Doubleday & Company, Inc., 1948, pp. 81–82, illus.

WIGHT, FREDERICK S. *Milestones of American Painting in Our Century.* New York, Chanticleer Press, 1949, p. 64, illus.

"Virginia Museum Picks Its Winners in 1950 Biennial." *Art Digest,* XXIV (May 15, 1950), 17.

"Winner of Seventh Biennial Exhibition at the Virginia Museum." *Art News,* XLIX (June, 1950), 9.

LOUCHHEIM, ALINE B. "Six Abstractionists Defend Their Art." *The New York Times,* January 21, 1951, sec. 6, pp. 16–17, illus.

"La Peinture aux Etats-Unis." *Art d'Aujourd'hui,* II, No. 6 (June, 1951), pp. 22–23, illus.

"Very Free Association; Critics Battle over Davis' 'Little Giant Still-Life' at the Virginia Museum of Fine Arts." *Art Digest,* XXVI (March 15, 1952), 5.

"Biennale 1952." *Du* (September, 1952), 8–9, illus.

"Paintings from the 1952 Venice Biennale Being Shown by Downtown Gallery." *Art Digest,* XXVII (December 15, 1952), 16.

LOUCHHEIM, ALINE B. "Artist Takes a Turn at Music." *The New York Times,* January 4, 1953, sec. 2, p. 9, illus.

"Paintings Sent to the Biennale in Venice Shown at Downtown Gallery." *Art News,* LI (January, 1953), 45.

WIGHT, FREDERICK S. "Stuart Davis." *Art Digest,* XXVII (May 15, 1953), 13, 23, illus.

SECKLER, DOROTHY GEES. "Stuart Davis Paints a Picture." *Art News,* LII (Summer, 1953), 30–33, 73–74, illus.

VOLLMER, HANS. *Allgemeines Lexikon der Bildenden Künstler.* Leipzig, 1953, vol. A-D, p. 525. Biographical entry containing bibliography. See also *Who's Who in American Art* and other biographical dictionaries.

FEINSTEIN, SAM. "Stuart Davis: Always Jazz Music." *Art Digest,* XXVIII (March 1, 1954), 14–15, 24, ilus.

DEVREE, HOWARD. "Stuart Davis on Display Here." *The New York Times,* March 2, 1954, p. 23, illus.

GENAUER, EMILY. "Reality vs. Realism Theme of Shows." *New York Herald Tribune,* March 7, 1954, sec. 4, p. 8.

"The All American." *Time,* LXIII (March 15, 1954), 84, illus.

COATES, ROBERT M. "Exhibition at Downtown Gallery." *The New Yorker,* XXX (March 20, 1954), 81–82.

"The Jazzy Formalism of Stuart Davis." *Art News,* LIII (March, 1954), 19, 59, illus.

BUCKLEY, CHARLES E. "New Painting by Stuart Davis: *Midi.*" *Wadsworth Atheneum Bulletin,* ser. 2, No. 48 (April, 1954), 1.

"Early Paintings Dating from 1916–23 at Little Studio." *Art Digest,* XXVIII (April 15, 1954), 22; see also *Art Digest,* XXVIII (May 15, 1954), 3.

KRICKE, NORBERT. "An Exhibition of Contemporary American Art." Translated by Stowell Rounds. *Art In America,* XLII (December, 1954), 302–6, illus.

BARR, ALFRED H., JR. *Masters of Modern Art.* New York, Museum of Modern Art, 1954, p. 117.

BAUR, JOHN I. H. *Revolution and Tradition in Modern American Art.* Cambridge, Mass., Harvard University Press, 1954, pp. 25, 48, 64, 65, 69–70, 71, 133, 141, 152, 153.

GENAUR, EMILY. In "This Week Magazine," *New York Herald Tribune,* January 9, 1955, p. 12, illus.

SAARINEN, ALINE B. "Our Arts Salute France," *The New York Times,* April 3, 1955 sec. 2, p. 10.

MYERS, BERNARD S., ed. *Encyclopedia of Painting.* New York, Crown Publishers, Inc., 1955, p. 143.

PRESTON, STUART. Review of exhibition at the Philadelphia Academy. *The New York Times,* January 29, 1956, sec. 2, p. 14, illus.

"The Age of Experiment." *Time,* LXVII (February 13, 1956), 62–67, illus., por.

"American Artists Paint the City." *Arts,* XXX (June, 1956), 26–29, illus.

GENAUER, EMILY. "A Stuart Davis Solo." *New York Herald Tribune,* November 11, 1956, sec. 6, p. 14.

PRESTON, STUART. "Highly Diverse One-Man Shows." *The New York Times,* November 11, 1956, sec. 2, p. 16, illus.

COATES, ROBERT M. "The Art Galleries: MacIver, Davis and Corot," *The New Yorker,* XXXII (November 17, 1956), 229–32.

KRAMER, HILTON. "Month in Review." *Arts,* XXXI (November, 1956), 52–55, illus.

SYLVESTER, DAVID. "Expressionism, German and American." *Arts,* XXXI (November, 1956), 52–55. illus.

T., P. "Stuart Davis." *Arts News,* LV (November, 1956), 6.

BLESH, RUDI. *Modern Art, U.S.A.* New York, Alfred A. Knopf, 1956, pp. 17, 48, 51, 57, 96, 107, 127, 133, 178, 179, 183, 258.

RICHARDSON, E. P. *Painting in America.* New York, Thomas Y. Crowell 1956, pp. 388, 390.

MORRIS, MARGARET. "Tempo of a City Fascinates Artist." *Minneapolis Star,* March 20, 1957, p. 1B, illus., por. p. 10B.

Stuart Davis. Minneapolis, Walker Art Center, 1957, illus. Catalogue of exhibition organized by the Walker Art Center in collaboration with the Des Moines Art Center, San Francisco Museum of Art, and the Whitney Museum of American Art, New York.

SHERMAN, JOHN K. "Davis Paintings Carry the American Flavor." *Minneapolis Star,* April 11, 1957, sec. A, p. 8.

DE KOONING, ELAINE. "Stuart Davis: True to Life." *Art News,* LVI (April, 1957), 40–42, 54–55.

GETLEIN, FRANK. "Painted Jazz in Stuart Davis Seen at Walker Art Center." *Milwaukee Journal,* April 21, 1957, sec. 5, p. 6.

GETLEIN, FRANK. "Big Band Jazz of Stuart Davis." *New Republic,* CXXXVI (May 6, 1957), 22.

SHANE, GEORGE. "Stuart Davis Collection at Art Center." *Des Moines Register,* June 9, 1957, sec. L, p. 5, illus.

FRANKENSTEIN, ALFRED. "A Davis Retrospective and the Dutch Moderns." *San Francisco Chronicle,* August 18, 1957, pp. 23–25.

POLLEY, E. M. "Stuart Davis Retrospective at San Francisco Museum of Art." *Vallejo* (Calif.) *Times Herald,* September 1, 1957.

LUCAS, JOHN. "Fine Art Jive of Stuart Davis." *Arts,* XXXI, No. 10 (September, 1957), pp. 32–37, illus.

WOODRUFF, HALE A. "Stuart Davis, American Modern." *School Arts.* LVII (October, 1957), pp. 36–37, illus.

COATES, ROBERT M. "Art Galleries: Exhibitions at the Whitney." *The New Yorker,* XXXIII (October, 1957), 123.

"East of Fifth." *Art Students League News,* X, No. 9 (October, 1957).

DEVREE, HOWARD. "Three in Surveys: Work by Stuart Davis, Mary Callery and Manolo in Retrospectives." *The New York Times,* October 13, 1957, p. 20.

SCHIFF, BENNETT. "In the Art Galleries." *The New York Post,* October 13, 1957, sec. M, p. 12.

GENAUER, EMILY. "Look Back in Levity at Art Tiffs." *New York Herald Tribune,* October 13, 1957, sec. 6, p. 14.

SOBY, JAMES THRALL. "Stuart Davis." *Saturday Review,* XL (November 9, 1957), 32–33, illus.

"Will This Art Endure?" *The New York Times Magazine,* December 1, 1957, pp. 48, 49.

"Painting for Preserves," *Time,* LXXI (May 19, 1958), 80–81, illus.

PRESTON, STUART. "Then and Now: Watercolors by Davis and Demuth—New Directions for Contemporaries." *The New York Times,* May 25, 1958, sec. 2, p. 10.

"Exhibition at Delacorte," *Arts,* XXXII (June, 1958), 59.

"Exhibition at Delacorte," *Art News,* LVII (June, 1958), 14.

ADLOW, DOROTHY. "The Home Forum." *Christian Science Monitor,* December 3, 1958, p. 12, illus.

GOOSSEN, E. C. *Stuart Davis.* New York, George Braziller, Inc., 1959.

HAMILTON, GEORGE HEARD. In *Art News,* LVIII, No. 6 (October, 1959), 43, 56–57.

KRAMER, HILTON. "Critic of American Painting: The First Six Volumes of the Great American Artists Series" (a review of E. C. GOOSSEN's book). *Arts,* XXXIV (October, 1959), 29, illus.

"Four Masters of Modern Art Select New Talents." *Look,* XXXIII (November 24, 1959), 60–61, illus., por.

Contemporary Painting and Sculpture, Urbana, University of Illinois, 1959, p. 209, illus. Exhibition catalogue.

BLESH, RUDI. *Stuart Davis.* New York, Grove Press, 1960.

GENAUER, EMILY. "Stuart Davis." *New York Herald Tribune,* May 15, 1960, sec. 4, p. 7.

TILLIM, SIDNEY. "Exhibition at Downtown Gallery." *Arts,* XXXIV, No. 9 (June, 1960), 48–49, illus.

BURROWS, CARLYLE. "Davis, on TV, Links Painting with Jazz." *New York Herald Tribune,* July 17, 1960, sec. 4, p. 6.

"Exhibition at Downtown Gallery." *Art News,* LIX (Summer, 1960), 14.

MUNRO, ELEANOR C. "Stuart Davis." *Art News,* LIX (Summer, 1960), 14.

FOLDS, THOMAS M. "Stuart Davis by E. C. Goossen." *Art Journal,* XX, No. 1 (Fall, 1960), 52, 54, 56. A review.

ELLIOTT, JAMES. "Premiere." *Los Angeles Museum Art Bulletin,* XIV, No. 3 (1962), 1–15

KUH, KATHERINE. *The Artist's Voice.* New York, Harper & Row, 1962.

VON ECKHARDT, WOLF. "Turn off the Sound." *American Institute of Architects Journal,* XXXVII (March, 1962), 118, illus.

M., E. In *New York Herald Tribune,* April 29, 1962, sec. 4, p. 7.

SANDLER, IRVING. "In the Art Galleries." *New York Post Magazine,* April 29, 1962, p. 12.

O'DOHERTY, BRIAN. "Art: Paintings of the Honk and Jingle." *The New York Times,* May 1, 1962, p. 34.

"Blaring Harmony." *Time,* LXXIX (May 18, 1962), 62, 67, por.

"Exhibition at Downtown Gallery." *Art News,* LXI (September, 1962), 16, illus.

JUDD, DONALD, and RAYNOR, VIVIEN. "In the Galleries." *Arts,* XXXVI, No. 10 (September, 1962), 44, illus.

MICHELSON, ANNETTE. "L'Abstraction géométrique en Amerique." *XXe Siècle,* ns. 24 (1962), illus.

New York Herald Tribune, June 26, 1964, p. 6. Obituary.

The New York Times, June 26, 1964, p. 27, illus., por. Obituary.

New York World-Telegram and Sun, June 26, 1964, p. 23. Obituary.

"Stuart Davis," *New York Journal-American,* June 26, 1964, p. 23. Obituary.

"Epitaph in Jazz." *Time,* LXXXIV (July 3, 1964), 59, por.

"Born to Paint." *Newsweek,* LXXXIV (July 6, 1964), 75, illus., por.

LYNTON, NORBERT. "Painter of the American Scene." *The Times* (London), July 21, 1964, p. 7.

SMITH, MILES A. *Birmingham News,* July 26, 1964, sec. C, p. 14, illus.

SURO, DARIO. "Homenaje a Stuart Davis 1894–1964." *Ahora!,* III, No. 69 (August 10, 1964), 31–32.

O'DOHERTY, BRIAN. "Stuart Davis." *Famous Artists Magazine,* XIII, No. 1 (Autumn, 1964), 12–13.

LIDMAN, DAVID. "The World of Stamps." *The New York Times,* September 20, 1964, sec. 10, p. 27.

SHUSTER, ALVIN. "Stamps for Art's Sake." *The New York Times Magazine* (September 20, 1964), 30.

HOMER, WILLIAM INNESS. "Stuart Davis, 1894–1964: Last Interview." *Art News,* LXIII (September, 1964), 43, 56, por.

Brown, J. Carter. "The Post Office Goes Abstract." *The Washington Post,* November 8, 1964, sec. G, p. 6.

Henning, E. B. "Language of Art." *Cleveland Museum Bulletin* (November, 1964), pp. 224–25, illus.

Star (Washington), December 2, 1965, sec. D, p. 7.

The New York Times, December 3, 1964, sec. L, p. 24, illus.

McBee, Susanna. "Feelings Run High Around Nation About that Abstract Art Stamp." *The Washington Post,* December 15, 1964, sec. A, p. 3.

"New U.S. Stamp." *American Artist,* XXVIII (December, 1964), 8, illus.

Suro, Dario. "Stuart Davis 1894–1964." *Americas,* XVII, No. 1 (January, 1965), 30–31.

Goodrich, Lloyd. "Rebirth of a National Collection." *Art in America* (June 1965), p. 89.

"Poverty, Politics and Artists 1930–1945." *Art in America* (August 1965), p. 105, illus.

Arnason, H. H. *Stuart Davis Memorial Exhibition,* Washington, National Collection of Fine Arts, Smithsonian Institution, 1965, illus. Catalogue of exhibition circulated by the Smithsonian Institution in collaboration with the Art Institute of Chicago, Whitney Museum of American Art, and the Art Galleries, University of California at Los Angeles.

Rose, Barbara. *American Art Since 1900.* New York, Praeger Publishers, 1968, pp. 137–43.

Geldzahler, Henry. *New York Painting: 1940–1970.* New York, Metropolitan Museum of Art, 1969, illus. Exhibition catalogue, pp. 18, 36, 37, 43, 360, 432, 457–58.

Novak, Barbara. *American Painting of the Nineteenth Century.* New York, Praeger Publishers, 1969, pp. 123–24, 276–77.

index